HEAVEN'S GATE

Heaven's Gate

America's UFO Religion

Benjamin E. Zeller

Foreword by Robert W. Balch

NEW YORK UNIVERSITY PRESS

New York and London

NEW YORK UNIVERSITY PRESS
New York and London
www.nyupress.org

References to Internet websites (URLs) were accurate at the time of writing.
Neither the author nor New York University Press is responsible for URLs that
may have expired or changed since the manuscript was prepared.

LIBRARY OF CONGRESS CATALOGING-IN-PUBLICATION DATA

Zeller, Benjamin E.
Heaven's gate : America's UFO religion / Benjamin E. Zeller ; foreword by Robert W. Balch.
 pages cm
Includes bibliographical references and index.
ISBN 978-1-4798-0381-1 (cl : alk. paper)
ISBN 978-1-4798-8106-2 (pb : alk. paper)
1. Heaven's Gate (Organization) 2. Cults—United States. 3. United States—Religion. I.
Title.
BP605.H36Z45 2014
299'.93—dc23
2014020797

New York University Press books are printed on acid-free paper,
and their binding materials are chosen for strength and durability.
We strive to use environmentally responsible suppliers and materials
to the greatest extent possible in publishing our books.

Manufactured in the United States of America

10 9 8 7 6 5 4 3 2 1

Also available as an ebook

For Emily, without whose support this book would not have been written

CONTENTS

LIST OF ILLUSTRATIONS AND TABLES

Illustrations

Tables

FOREWORD

ROBERT W. BALCH

The subject of this book—the UFO religion Heaven's Gate—has fascinated me since my first encounter with it in 1975. The group, then named Human Individual Metamorphosis (HIM), had been in the news for weeks because dozens of people had suddenly disappeared after hearing its message. Yet almost nothing was known about life inside the group or the identities of its founders. About the only thing anyone knew for sure was that at least one hundred people had given up everything they had in hopes of boarding a spacecraft that would take them to a better world.

Late in 1975, David Taylor and I infiltrated HIM to find out for ourselves what was really happening "behind the scenes." Suffice it to say, instead of a dangerous cult, we found a group so lacking in leadership and structure it appeared to be falling apart. Shortly after we finished our fieldwork, the group stopped recruiting and disappeared from public view, but by then we were hooked. Taylor and I kept track of new developments by interviewing defectors whenever we could find them, and we soon became the acknowledged experts on this obscure cult, if only because we were the only ones who had ever studied it.

Then, in 1997, "our" cult, now calling itself Heaven's Gate, decided to commit mass suicide, and suddenly scholars of every stripe swarmed the carcass. Of course, Taylor and I were among them, but I confess to viewing most of the others as interlopers who either misunderstood the group or didn't have much to add to what we had already written. However, I make an exception for Ben Zeller. Not only has he uncovered intriguing new information about the group's final years, but he approaches Heaven's Gate from a refreshingly different perspective. Perhaps because he is a religious studies scholar and not a sociologist, Zeller examines Heaven's Gate through the lens of belief—both the package of beliefs that made Heaven's Gate a true religion, and belief in the message by individual members.

When I lived with the group in 1975, I was so absorbed by the minutia of everyday life that I didn't think much about its beliefs. They were simply a given. Although I recognized that the belief system shaped and constrained members' actions, I, like other sociologists, was more concerned with the actions themselves than with the beliefs on which they were based. But, as Zeller explains, Heaven's Gate was a true religion with a coherent system of beliefs that explained the order of the universe, gave meaning to human existence, and offered a plan of salvation.

Sociologists haven't neglected this belief system entirely, but they have focused narrowly on how one particular change contributed to the suicide. In 1975, a core belief was that humans did *not* have to die to enter heaven; rather, possession of a living, physical body was required to board the spacecraft. But, by 1997, this belief had undergone a dramatic change. Now, the only way members could get to heaven was by leaving their bodies, or, as they put it, "exiting" their human "vehicles."

Zeller examines this change in detail, but more importantly, he gives close attention to continuities in the belief system, most of which have been ignored or overlooked by others. From my perspective, the most important of these is the theme of separation from all things human. From the beginning, the group was based on the idea of cutting ties with the past, overcoming human attachments, and ultimately leaving Earth altogether. Eventually, suicide came to be seen as nothing more than the final act of separation, the last step on a path members had been following all along.

As Zeller explains, the belief system was the foundation for almost every action in Heaven's Gate, starting with the decision to join. One might think this would be obvious—Heaven's Gate was a religion, after all—but some social scientists view belief as a product of membership rather than a reason for membership. They argue that people join new religions for friendship and community, and that belief develops only after immersion in the group. However, Zeller rightly takes members at their word when they claim that they joined because the message rang true.

As Taylor and I discovered in 1975, the group's method of recruiting maximized the importance of belief as a reason for joining, while minimizing the importance of social bonds. Typically, the first time anyone heard the message was during a short, public presentation. Those who wanted to learn more were called later that night and told the location of a follow-up meeting the next day. After the second meeting, people had to decide. If they chose to join, they had only a few days to settle their affairs, say their goodbyes, and catch up with the group, because the members would already be gone, often hundreds of miles away.

Clearly nobody joined Heaven's Gate because they had made friends with members. There simply wasn't time for that. Rather, they joined because the belief system clicked. For some, it was eminently logical; for others it just felt right. This is not to say that new members became instant converts, but they at least found the message plausible enough to bet everything they had on the hope that it was true.

Upon joining, new members entered a world in which belief infused every aspect of daily life. In most new religions there is a close link between belief and action, but as the reader will discover in these pages, the connection was especially tight in Heaven's Gate. In 1975, the group already was largely sealed off from the outside world, and within a year the leaders restructured it into a kind of boot camp designed to instill discipline and test members' determination to continue. The extent to which the belief system permeated everyday life was reflected in a banner that later hung in one of their houses reminding members that they were "in a classroom twenty-four hours a day." Of course, being in class isn't the same as learning the lesson, but Heaven's Gate also displayed a tight fit between the ideal and the reality.

Does this mean that members committed suicide because they were "brainwashed"? Zeller doesn't think so, and neither do I. Based on his evidence, as well as my own, I propose an alternative explanation: People joined Heaven's Gate because they found its message believable, and they complied with its demands for the same reason. Those who still had doubts eventually defected, and any who remained out of step with the program were expelled, leaving only the true believers to carry on. The process was not much different from becoming a Marine or a monk.

Yet, we rarely give the same credibility to cult members as we do to Marines or monks. Perhaps what I like most about Ben Zeller's analysis is the respect it shows for the members of Heaven's Gate. Living with the group taught me an important lesson: To understand members' actions, we need to look at the world through their eyes instead of our own. It isn't easy to do, especially without the opportunity to interact directly with members, but Zeller has accomplished this feat remarkably well. My experience in Heaven's Gate also made me a bit protective of the group. Once I got to know the people, I realized that they were not just members of some exotic cult, but ordinary people struggling to find meaning in their lives. Overall, they weren't much different from me or many of my friends. At a personal level, I want to see their story told with the empathy it deserves, and this book does the best job of any that I have read.

ACKNOWLEDGMENTS

This book would not have been possible without the guidance, support, advice, and feedback I received from dozens of colleagues, mentors, and friends over the past 17 years. I have benefited immensely from correspondence and conversation with my colleagues in the study of Heaven's Gate, most notably Robert W. Balch and George D. Chryssides, both of whom offered extensive comments on earlier versions of this book. Rob and George are the epitome of collegial, offering generously of their knowledge and advice. My colleague Eugene V. Gallagher read and commented on the entire manuscript, and provided valuable feedback. Emily R. Mace did the same. My mentor and friend Yaakov Ariel read and responded to most of my previous work on Heaven's Gate, and without his advice earlier in my career, this book would not exist.

I have presented many of the ideas found in this book in multiple venues, and I owe thanks to the many individuals who gave me feedback at the annual meetings of the American Academy of Religion and Society for the Scientific Study of Religion, where I presented several papers including the inchoate ideas developed herein. Anonymous reviewers of my previous publications on Heaven's Gate and the feedback from editors at *Nova Religio: The Journal of Alternative and Emergent Religions*, most notably Catherine Wessinger, Douglas E. Cowan, and Rebecca Moore, all benefited me immensely. So too the comments from students at the University of North Carolina, University of Tromsø (Norway), and Hogskolan Dalarna (Sweden) where I have presented lectures on Heaven's Gate. Eons ago (it seems), in the immediate aftermath of the Heaven's Gate suicides, William Scott Green, Anne Merideth, and Douglas R. Brooks all provided feedback and encouragement as I first began to study this movement, and I am very grateful they did so.

Librarians at the University of Rochester, University of North Carolina (Chapel Hill), Duke University, Temple University, Brevard College, and Lake Forest College all assisted me in researching this book, as have special collections librarians and archivists at the Graduate Theological Union and University of California, Santa Barbara. Although it has been years since I left that institution, Temple University Religion Subject Librarian Fred Rowland continues to be a valuable resource. Technology Specialist David Levinson at Lake Forest College's Donnelley and Lee Library assisted me with preparing the illustrations.

Several former members of Heaven's Gate have corresponded with me and have read and commented on my work. Those who permitted me to publicly thank them are Mrcody, Srfody, Neoody, and Sawyer. I thank and respect them for their openness in talking with me about their experiences and knowledge about their time in the Class. I recognize that they may not always agree with what I've written, and it is a credit to their openness that they were still willing to share their thoughts.

Finally, much of the actual writing of this book occurred during my sabbatical semester at Åbo Akademi, in Turku (Åbo), Finland. I am grateful to my kind and generous hosts at Åbo Akademi for accommodating me: Peter Nynäs, Måns Broo, Jan Svanberg, and Sofia Sjö. Funding for my sabbatical was provided through the Fulbright program and the bilateral U.S-Finland Fulbright Commission, which I also thank for their support. Additionally, colleagues at Temple University, Brevard College, and Lake Forest College have been conversation partners during my many years of studying Heaven's Gate. In the final weeks of manuscript preparation, colleague Susan Long made me aware of the UK band Django Django's musical homage to Heaven's Gate. I also wish to acknowledge the Hotchkiss Fund at Lake Forest College, which provided financial assistance for the final stages of manuscript preparation. Finally, the most important acknowledgment is the last: to my spouse, colleague, and partner, Dr. Emily R. Mace, without whose support and guidance this book would not exist. This book is dedicated to her.

Introduction

Black uniforms. Matching "Away Team" patches. New Nike shoes, the "Just Do It" swooshes still vibrant white. Purple shrouds. Rolls of quarters and five-dollar bills in their pockets, duffle bags at their sides. Circumscribing themselves with these elements, in March 1997, 39 people in Rancho Santa Fe, California, ritually terminated their lives. They did so in waves, with each wave cleaning and tidying after the previous, until all 39, including their founder and leader, lay dead in a multimillion-dollar mansion in a posh San Diego suburb. Days after the suicides began, a former member, tipped off by his compatriots as to their intentions, stumbled into and then quickly out of the house. The rest is history: Heaven's Gate.

To outsiders, it was a mass suicide. For insiders, it was a graduation. This act was the culmination of more than two decades of religious and social development of the group, a movement that took several names over its years. It began as a loose collective formed by two self-proclaimed witnesses, Marshall Herff Applewhite and Bonnie Lu Nettles, and ended as Heaven's Gate, the monastic religious movement still led by Applewhite. Along the way the group developed a complicated theology fusing Christian, New Age, and American cultural elements, and a set of religious practices likewise drawing from multiple religions, science fiction, and pop culture. The group ended on its own terms, but not without outside influence. Rumors of an unidentified flying object (UFO) or spacecraft trailing the Hale-Bopp comet precipitated the timings of the suicides, as did years of dwindling success in attracting converts or even serious media interest.

This book answers the question of why the members of Heaven's Gate committed their ritual suicides. But it also asks and answers another set of questions. How did Heaven's Gate originate, and why did it evolve the way it did? What was its draw, and why did people join this group? What did members believe, and how did they develop practices within their religious worldview? How did all of this reflect the American society in which Heaven's Gate developed? I arrive at a variety of answers, which are developed in the pages that follow. The group originated from two individuals and their spiritual quests, but it also emerged out of Evangelical Christianity, the New Age movement, interest in science fiction and UFOs, and conspiracy theories. It evolved in keeping with those influences. People joined because they found in Heaven's Gate something that they felt was lacking in their previous lives. Heaven's Gate offered a chance to feel special and to identify with being an otherworldly spiritual being, a sort of angelic extraterrestrial. It never appealed to many people, but several hundred did join and leave over its history. Members believed, as many other Americans do, in a heavenly Father, the centrality of the soul rather than the body, a battle between good and evil, and heavenly salvation, but they reframed all these beliefs as referring to the literal heavens and extraterrestrial beings. They developed religious practices involving bodily control, prayer, and means of dwelling in this world while simultaneously trying to escape it. People stayed for different reasons, but once a member it would have been very difficult to choose to leave, since adherents believed outsiders lived worthless vegetative lives and would not achieve any form of eternal salvation. (That being said, the majority of people who joined did leave eventually.) The movement reflects American society by revealing some of the same forces at play in bigger, more recognizable, more publicly accepted religions. Heaven's Gate was American culture writ small.

The basic argument of this book is that Heaven's Gate reflected, responded to, and sewed together various strands of American religious thought and practice. I want to admit at the very beginning of the book a methodological bias in my approach. It is somewhat reductionist, by which I mean that I interpret the religious revelations of the leaders and members of Heaven's Gate as manifestations of something else: culture. Rather than assume the position of the leaders of Heaven's Gate that their religious doctrines and positions are the result of direct communication with what they called the Next Level—effectively what most other religious people would call Heaven—I root their religious developments in history and culture. This is not to say that I deny their religious claims, merely that I proceed under the assumptions that such claims—like those of all religious groups—are beyond the realm of empirical observation and therefore cannot be assessed by outside observers. Scholars who take this approach are certainly within the mainstream when we look at new religious movements, but we must admit that the approach is somewhat offensive to the religious believer. For example, many Christians would be offended at the contention by some scholars that the early Church leaders stitched together various doctrines and approaches of Jewish, Roman, Greek, Persian, and Egyptian religion and constructed what we call Christianity. Christians prefer to think of their religion as derived from revelation and a divine plan. Some adherents of Heaven's Gate might react the same way to this book.

It is, however, the best approach. Setting aside whether the claims of the founders of Heaven's Gate or any other religion really derive from supernatural sources—claims that cannot be proven one way or another—it is hard to deny that the culture and society in which a religion develops shape its ultimate form, worldview, practices, and even beliefs. Scholars have proven this beyond doubt for the major religions of the world, all of which were once new religions. In the often-studied examples of Christianity and Judaism, historian of ancient religions Alan Segal has persuasively demonstrated the manner in which a mixing of ancient Near Eastern cultural forces shaped formative Rabbinic Judaism and Early Christianity as they emerged in late antiquity. For Segal, "their social, economic, and political context," or "the real social matrix in which religious thought existed" fundamentally shaped how these two major religions developed.[1] Esteemed and recognized scholars of Judaism and Christianity such as Jacob Neusner, Daniel Boyarin, and Bart D. Ehrman have all made similar arguments and claims about these two religions, and represent the academic consensus.[2] Religions emerge out of cultural environments and social conditions, and must be understood with reference to those conditions, not as *sui generis* entities.

So too for new religious movements (NRMs), the study of which led to the emergence of a new field of scholarship in the mid- to late twentieth century. The first wave of scholarship on NRMs paid extensive attention to how social forces and conditions impacted their development. Some of the earliest and most foundational studies considered issues of social transformations such as new trends in college education, population shifts, and delayed adolescence in the formation of the NRMs that seemed to sweep through Western society in the 1960s and 1970s.[3] Scholars also paid attention to how culture shaped these emergent religions, with special attention to the counterculture and its elements of free love, drug use, spiritual exploration, and utopian communal experiments.[4] All of these cultural and social developments influenced the NRMs that emerged out of them in the 1960s and 1970s. This remains true for new religious movements such as Heaven's Gate that emerged and developed into their final form in the late 1970s into the 1980s.

Why Study Heaven's Gate?

When people learn that I've been writing a book on Heaven's Gate they usually want to know why. Wasn't this a small group, just under forty people, which killed itself off in a far corner of America's West Coast? Since the group is now long gone, why bother studying them now? I have some sympathy for these sorts of questions, since there seem to be so many important contemporary trends in American religion that merit serious attention, trends upon which scholars like me perhaps should focus instead of studying a small group of dead people. Why not consider the rising number of Americans who consider themselves "none of the above" when asked about their religious affiliation (the "nones"), a group that represents up to a fifth of the U.S. population according to one recent study?[5] Why not study the rise of Evangelicalism, Fundamentalism, and the various forms of conservative American religiosity that have had such a powerful impact on American politics and society? What of the fusion of religion and popular culture, of individuals who find spiritual satisfaction in bookstores, movies, science, and other individually focused activities?

These are good questions, and good research topics. And, in fact, this study of Heaven's Gate is just another way of answering the same questions and considering similar themes, since it uncovers the religious transformations and developments that occurred during the 1970s, 1980s, and 1990s that led to these new characteristics within American religion. The religious "nones," for example, reject the forms of institutionalized, denominationalized, professionalized religion that members of Heaven's Gate did as well, and they engage in the same sort of search for alternatives as did the movement's adherents. Likewise, the same forces that helped Evangelicalism rise and become so prominent also helped Heaven's Gate, just as some of the same theologies of being set apart and looking toward heavenly rewards shaped these two very different movements. And members of Heaven's Gate certainly reflected— and pre-dated—the recent turn toward various forms of popular culture and individual spiritual quests as sources of religious truths. All this is to say that, although the group was small and is now defunct, the study of Heaven's Gate reveals some very important facets of American religious culture.

But beyond that, I have found that nearly everyone with whom I have spoken regarding this group and my research has agreed that Heaven's Gate is intriguing and merits a detailed analysis. People find it so fascinating and interesting because it is the sort of transgressive religious movement that seems so utterly foreign and strange that it defies explanation, yet makes the same sort of trite claims of offering salvation, eternal life, and heavenly rewards that bombard Americans every day on the airwaves, public squares, billboards, and streets. Heaven's Gate's basic message of offering heavenly salvation and leaving behind a broken life on Earth is not that far removed from the message offered by most forms of American Christianity, yet its specific form of salvation and the means of achieving it transgress the basic assumptions of most Americans. One simply does not wait for the arrival of flying saucers to escape the Earth's atmosphere, and one does not commit suicide to force the issue. This mixture of religious banality and religious transgression marks Heaven's Gate as innately interesting to many people. Put another way: the study of a group offering eternal heavenly rewards is not particularly new or noteworthy, nor does it attract much outside interest. The study of a group making seemingly bizarre claims about space aliens and suicide is noteworthy but also foreign and strange. Yet when one combines the two, one discovers a group that is simultaneously foreign and familiar, exotic and ordinary.

Finally, there is another reason that I have written about Heaven's Gate. Members of the movement sought above all else to transcend their humanity. They tried to dehumanize themselves and become extraterrestrial heavenly beings. Ironically, after their death the media and broader public sentiment did the same thing: dehumanized them. Journalists, comedians, media commentators, and religious leaders engaged in rhetorical attacks on the Heaven's Gate dead, dismissing them as crazy, delusional, and better off dead. Yet these were thirty-nine human beings who died in Rancho Santa Fe, and they had histories, feelings, and religious beliefs and practices. In other words, they had a story. This book tells their story.

But Weren't Members of Heaven's Gate Brainwashed?

This book's method of study focuses on unpacking the worldview, beliefs, and practices of members of Heaven's Gate. Yet many in the media and public consider this group a cult, filled with brainwashed victims rather than real religious adherents. One might raise an obvious objection about studying the group in the way I do: weren't members simply brainwashed into believing and practicing what they did, and therefore the specifics are somewhat irrelevant? Would they not have believed and done anything? In a word: no. In somewhat more words: members of Heaven's Gate chose to join a group that significantly curtailed their freedoms and ultimately asked of them their lives, but they did so because they felt that they were making the best choice they could. To quote Nichelle Nichols, the actress who played Uhura in the *Star Trek* series much beloved by members of Heaven's Gate, and the sister of one of the adherents who had committed suicide, "[m]y brother was highly intelligent and a beautifully gentle man. He made his choices and we respect those choices."[6] While one does not need to accept the decisions made by members of the group, one must still accept them as decisions.

The contemporary academic theories of conversion, socialization, and what one might call "brainwashing" (though few scholars call it that any more) admit that the process works better to keep people engaged within a religious system they have already accepted than it does to explain why they joined in the first place, though one should be clear that most scholars in fact reject the very notion of brainwashing as pseudoscientific.[7] As we will see, the idea of brainwashing originated in the Cold War era as an explanation for why some captive American soldiers had defected to North Korea, and at its base it is a theory that assumes its victims are prisoners of war subjected to torture, confinement, sensory and nutritional deprivation, and a single-minded attempt to manipulate them. This model does not work very well outside of the prisoner-of-war scenario, as numerous sociologists of religion have noted.[8] Members of Heaven's Gate were not physically confined, nor were they tortured or forcibly imprisoned.[9] During the formative stage of the group's history, its members seldom even saw their leaders. The traditional model does not work.

This is not to say that members of Heaven's Gate were not influenced by their leaders, nor that one can so easily dismiss various theories of psychological persuasion. Clearly the leaders of Heaven's Gate engaged in acts of religious persuasion. They used adherents' emotions, preexisting convictions, hopes, and fears to attract them to join the movement and stay within it, though it must be noted that they also encouraged members who seemed to be waffling to leave. This is of course basic advertising, and one finds the same process at work in most religious movements. Heaven's Gate represents an extreme example because the group's leaders demanded so much from their followers and offered far more in return. According to the rational choice model of religious social dynamics, this sort of trade-off of high demands and high rewards functions to attract a niche of serious spiritual seekers, just as very costly commercial goods (expensive cars or foods) also attract niche consumers.[10] This also helps explain why Heaven's Gate remained so small. Members joined not because of some sort of magical psychological or spiritual trick that the leaders conjured, but because they were looking for something and believed that they found it in Heaven's Gate.

Yet members did report that the leaders of the group were special, and this specialness can help explain why individuals stayed in the group even though so much was asked of them. The founders and leaders of Heaven's Gate, Marshall Herff Applewhite and Bonnie Lu

Nettles, exerted a powerful influence and control over their followers that scholars of religion call charisma. In Max Weber's formulation, charisma is "a certain quality of an individual personality by virtue of which he is set apart from ordinary men and treated as endowed with supernatural, superhuman, or at least specifically exceptional powers or qualities. These are not accessible to the ordinary person, but are regarded as of divine origin or as exemplary, and on the basis of them the individual concerned is treated as a leader."[11] While much of this definition and approach relies upon highly subjective observation and interpretation, first-hand accounts of Applewhite's and Nettles' leadership indicated that the two exerted profound charismatic authority and leadership over their followers. While this does not support the idea of brainwashing, it does indicate why some people joined the movement. It also helps explain why some people stayed, since those who left would immediately lose access to the powerful charisma of the movement's leaders and the ensuing feeling of connection to the "superhuman," in Weber's words. Yet others who joined did so without ever having met Nettles or Applewhite, so one can hardly argue that charisma alone accounts for the rise of Heaven's Gate.

Still, while the two leaders' charisma functioned to solidify their authority, it was the content of their religious teachings—namely beliefs and practices—that adherents used to structure their lives and seek transcendence. It is those aspects of the religious system of Heaven's Gate that are considered here. At its heart, this book presents two basic arguments. First, there is a reason that Heaven's Gate began, developed, and ended the way it did. The movement's history and the story of its religious evolution must be understood as integral to understanding why the members of Heaven's Gate ended their earthly lives the way they did. A lack of attention to the lives and history of the movement's members before the suicides leads to a failure to understand why people joined, stayed, and died as they did, and why many more stayed for a while but then left. Second, I argue that Heaven's Gate was not a complete aberration. It reflected many of the same currents at work in American culture and society. Culture and society shaped the movement, and only with reference to them can we understand it. The afterword of this book extends and flips this argument, showing that the study of Heaven's Gate also reveals certain aspects of American culture and society.

The first chapter, "The Cultural and Religious Origins of Heaven's Gate," considers the manner in which the movement that eventually took the name of Heaven's Gate arose and developed. It is the only strictly chronological chapter in the book, and looks to how the two co-founders of the movement developed a new religious synthesis and social movement based on their individual spiritual pursuits. I argue in this chapter that Heaven's Gate reflected not only the idiosyncratic perspectives and experiences of its founders but also the cultural context of its time. Specifically I look to the religious context within which both founders moved and operated, including the theosophical tradition, New Age spiritual seeking, and an apocalyptic-oriented Christianity. I trace the development of the movement from its two co-founders to its eventual fruition into an inchoate social movement that grew, shrunk, then coalesced into a roving monastic community. This initial chapter ends roughly with the summer of 1976, when the movement went "off the grid" and ended its active engagement with the outside world. The only other generally chronologically organized chapter in this book, the final one, likewise considers only the end of the movement.

Sandwiched between these historically oriented chapters are four thematic considerations of Heaven's Gate. The first of these, "The Spiritual Quest and Self-Transformation: Why People Joined Heaven's Gate," looks to why and how individuals converted into the Heaven's Gate movement. In following the original sociological scholarship that Robert W. Balch and David Taylor produced in the first year of the movement, I argue that members joined because they were spiritual seekers on quests for religious truth. Heaven's Gate offered an opportunity to embrace that quest, but it also offered a certainty and finality that allowed adherents to end their spiritual quests and commit to a single religious path. Looking to the movement's converts from the 1990s I find the same pattern. Finally, this chapter considers the approach of Janja Lalich and her model of bounded choice, which offers some perspective on why members stayed within the movement but is of only limited value in considering their trajectories into the group.

The third chapter looks to what scholars of religion call the world-view of Heaven's Gate. Heaven's Gate emerged out of two theological worlds: Evangelical Christianity and the New Age movement, particularly the sub-movement within the New Age tradition concerned with alien visitations and extraterrestrial contact. Heaven's Gate's leaders and members drew from a broad array of influences, including secular ufology (the subculture of people interested in UFOs), science fiction, and conspiracy theories, in addition to their religious influences. I argue in this chapter that such bricolage or pastiche reflects contemporary post-modern culture, but I disagree with scholars who envision the movement's bricolage as an end in and of itself. Rather, underlying Heaven's Gate's postmodern pastiche of ufology, Christianity, the New Age, science and technology, and science fiction was a single ideal of what I call an *extraterrestrial biblical hermeneutic*. The adherents of Heaven's Gate read the Christian Bible (primarily the New Testament) through a fundamental set of assumptions shaped by their various influences, but framed by Christian assumptions. My approach in this chapter resolves a scholarly debate over the nature of the Heaven's Gate movement as either fundamentally Christian or New Age.

Chapter 4 turns to the specific beliefs that adherents of Heaven's Gate upheld. Members created a system of beliefs that contained all the usual hallmarks of a religious theology, namely beliefs about salvation (soteriology), the order of the universe (cosmology), and the end of things (eschatology). As a Christian group, they also developed an understanding of the nature of Jesus (Christology). From the perspective of Heaven's Gate members, their beliefs provided them with meaning, identity, and a sense of their place in the universe. This chapter pays special attention to the development of the movement's millennialism, specifically the way in which the group adopted and adapted a form of Protestant Christian apocalypticism called premillennial dispensationalism. It also traces how Applewhite and Nettles successfully transformed their movement's theology at several points when their apocalyptic predictions failed to materialize, and how after Nettles's death Applewhite was able to fundamentally transform Heaven's Gate's vision of the nature of the human self and the form that salvation would take. This more than any other shift permitted the eventual adoption of a theology of suicide and propelled members to believe that their beliefs demanded of them that they lay down their lives if they truly desired eternal salvation.

While beliefs are important, so too are religious practices. Chapter 5 considers the development of the religious practices within Heaven's Gate, particularly the manner in which adherents used these practices to structure their terrestrial lives with reference to the extraterrestrial salvation that they sought. I make use of historian and cultural theorist Thomas A. Tweed's theorization of religion as a constellation of practices related to crossing and dwelling, showing how members both dwelt in religiously created homes and sought to cross to an idealized home in the heavens. Since self-transformation lay at the heart of Heaven's Gate's religious message from its very first days until the end of the movement's history, unsurprisingly, practices aimed at self-transformation lay at the heart of the group's religious practices. Self-transformative practices of dwelling included building communal homes, members rhetorically transforming their homes into spacecraft, and recreating the individual as a monastic member of a crew. Self-control and self-purging also served central roles in the lives of members of Heaven's Gate and in their daily religious practices as they sought to cross out of this world into that of the eternal salvation of the Next Level. This included techniques such as prayer, fasting, meditation, and astrology.

The final core chapter, "Why Suicide?: Closing Heaven's Gate," focuses on why the group's members were led by their convictions to embrace a theology of suicide as the best option for securing eternal salvation. I trace the development of a metaphysically and culturally dualistic worldview within the movement and an increase in pessimism toward the outside world and its value. This relates to transformations within the group's apocalyptic thought and its context, as well as the advent of conspiratorial thinking within Heaven's Gate and the broader social context of such thought, especially as Michael Barkun has recently traced in American society. I therefore conclude that dualistic thinking about the self and the world, a pessimistic outlook and the experience of rejection by outsiders, failed expectations about a potential government raid on the group, and the mass public attention to the Hale-Bopp comet and an alleged UFO trailing the comet all led to the eventual suicides.

The book concludes with an afterword that positions Heaven's Gate as representative of many of the same forces shaping the broader American religious environment and religions in the United States. I argue that Heaven's Gate was American religion wrought small, a social barometer that revealed the religious climate at the turn of twenty-first-century America. This includes aspects such as the centrality of biblical interpretation, Christian primitivism, spiritual seeking, and alternative spiritual practices, appeals to science and scientific legitimacy, and apocalyptic thinking.

* * *

When considering the overall argument and thrust of this book, a related set of ideas should emerge as most pertinent. First, Heaven's Gate must be studied within the context of its emergence, growth, and death. Biographers take the same approach when studying their subjects, indicating how individuals reflect their cultural, historical, and social contexts, but also reveal those same contexts through crystallizing such forces into a single life. I see Heaven's Gate as doing something analogous, and this book aims for the same sort of contextualization that one finds in a biography. Heaven's Gate both reflects the context of its environment—Christian apocalypticism, New Age spiritual practices, the religious quests of baby boomers, new religions of the counterculture, the narcissistic pessimism of the 1990s—as well as reveals how those forces interacted in the form of a single religious body.

Second, this book should make clear that we need to take seriously the religious beliefs, practices, worldviews, and life choices of adherents of alternative, belittled, and discredited religious movements. It is far too easy to dismiss the members of Heaven's Gate as either insane or victimized, and in both cases we fall into the same sort of trap of demonization that colors the dehumanizing political discourse of the twenty-first century.

Third, this book has a historiographic point as well. The study of new religious movements has long been ghettoized within the academic study of religion. Scholars of NRMs—such as myself—have formed our own academic groups, journals, and associations. While these are appropriate processes for any subfield within the study of religion, it has unfortunately meant that the study of individual new religious groups tends to become linked only to the study of other NRMs. We not only assume that the context of our study includes other new religions, but we tend to reify the concept of "new religious movement" as a sort of distinct type of religion that sets it—and us, as scholars of the phenomenon—apart from other religions and their study.

This book is not about new religious movements, though Heaven's Gate is of course one such group. Rather, this book is about a group, its religious history, and its religious environment. I do not see Heaven's Gate as representative of a reified category of NRM, but as an indicator of American culture and society. The implicit argument of this book is that scholars must study new religions as parts of broader religious environments and not as stand-alone movements. Heaven's Gate has more in common with other religious movements of the 1970s, 1980s, and 1990s in the United States—Christian Evangelicals and yoga practitioners, for example—than it does new religious movements of other times and places.

Finally, a note on sources, and another on language: one reason that scholars have written comparatively little on Heaven's Gate—as opposed to groups such as the Branch Davidians or Peoples Temple—is the relative paucity of sources. No proper Heaven's Gate archives exist, and few publicly assessable collections hold materials produced by the group. I have made use of the few available archival materials, held in the Special Collections at the University of California Santa Barbara's American Religions Collection. Several published interviews also exist, as well as various news stories produced by reporters over the years. The articles written by sociologists Robert W. Balch and David Taylor based on their ethnographic fieldwork in the group in the 1970s are most helpful. Several journalists and non-academic historians have produced histories and assessments of the movement, notable Rodney Perkins and Forrest Jackson's *Cosmic Suicide: The Tragedy and Transcendence of Heaven's Gate* (1997) and Bill Hoffmann and Cathy Burke's *Heaven's Gate: Cult Suicide in San Diego* (1997). Since neither book is properly peer reviewed, and both are rather sensationalistic, I have not used these books themselves, but rather mined them for the primary sources that the authors themselves had uncovered. In all cases, I have verified any materials that I first encountered from these books or other media sources.

But most of the materials I have used in writing this book come directly from the movement itself: its 1997 self-published anthology and the videos that the movement produced in its final half decade, including a twelve-part series in 1992 and two hour-long instructional videos produced in the last year of Heaven's Gate's existence, audio tapes from 1982 to 1985, and interviews and statements made by ex-members. Some of the most useful of the sources are the "Exit Videos," the videotaped messages left by members just before their suicides. Some have called these video suicide notes, but I prefer to think of them as videotaped epistles. Like letters, they are exhortative and pedagogical, offering instruction and advice to those left behind after the members have left the Earth. For a short window of time, adherents believed, heaven's gate remained open. These intensely heartfelt Exit Videos called for family, friends, and the general public to follow members through that gate. I have also spoken with, interviewed, and exchanged emails with numerous former members, all of whom have provided details into the history and development of this religious group.

Those exchanges made it very clear to me that my use of religious studies language differs greatly from the language within the group. What I call a ritual, members called an exercise. What I call prayer, they called focusing. What I call a religious movement, they called a class, and what I call members, they called students. I have continued to use the language most familiar to scholars of religion, but I do wish to note from the onset that the members of Heaven's Gate—or students in the Class, to use their terminology—would not have used the same words. Ex-members have nevertheless recognized the same phenomenon behind the different labels. Even Applewhite himself admitted that such labels were appropriate, remarking on how the group did not refer to itself as a religion, but that it certainly fit the definition.[12]

The most notable case of a fundamental difference in language, and one that reflects a basic difference between the worldview of members of Heaven's Gate and the majority of those outside, involves the suicides themselves, which members and ex-members refer to as "exits." For members, the true self transcended the body, and death of the body seemed almost inconsequential. I do not support suicide, religious or otherwise, but in listening to the voices of the adherents of Heaven's Gate I have taken seriously their religious claims. While keeping in mind the tragic end of this new religious movement, this book focuses equally on its beginning and middle. In doing so one discovers how much Heaven's Gate reflected American culture, and how its development represents a story of the birth, life, and death of an American new religion. Heaven's Gate is not just a suicide cult, as it is often called. Heaven's Gate is America's UFO religion.

1

The Cultural and Religious Origins of Heaven's Gate

One problem that scholars have had in studying Heaven's Gate is that the movement changed radically over its twenty-five-year history. For example, the group that we call Heaven's Gate only used that name to refer to itself in its final days on Earth. For much of its history, the group members called themselves Human Individual Metamorphosis, Total Overcomers Anonymous, and often simply "the Class." Today we know this new religious movement as Heaven's Gate—and I will continue to call it that—but its name often changed. (While admittedly anachronistic to refer to the movement throughout its history using the moniker of Heaven's Gate, I continue to do so because it is simpler for both author and reader.)

The group's organizational structure changed too. At first, Heaven's Gate existed as merely two people: its founders Marshall Herff Applewhite (1932–1997) and Bonnie Lu Nettles (1927–1985), who used names like Guinea and Pig, Bo and Peep, and eventually Ti and Do, as well as "the Two."[1] (I will refer to them by their birth names, or as "the Two" when they acted in concert to lead the movement.) As they attracted followers and adherents, something odd happened: the group became even less organized. Researchers and journalists who studied the group in its first months discovered that its leaders often did not attend recruitment meetings, seldom traveled with the group, and exerted only minimal control over the organization of this inchoate religious movement. All this changed in 1976, when the Two instituted a rigid hierarchal social structure predicated on their absolute control over the social and religious lives of their adherents. That style of organization characterized Heaven's Gate until its end in 1997, though Nettles had died in 1985, leaving Applewhite as the sole leader.

In terms of the movement's religious practices, equally substantial changes occurred. The shifts paralleled the organizational changes. At first, Applewhite and Nettles exerted little control over the religious practices of their followers, though they did provide guidelines and some requirements. Yet followers often skirted these requirements and invented their own ways of following the guidelines. Later, the Two put into place more stringent requirements and instituted a monastic style of living that adherents used to rigidly control their lives. Again, that later pattern of practices lasted until the end of the movement.

Religious beliefs also changed. Most fundamentally, in the early days of Heaven's Gate the Two taught that followers would journey to outer space (what they called the "Next Level") on UFOs while still alive, bringing their physical bodies with them through a process akin to metamorphosis. They emphasized biological, chemical, and metabolic changes that would enable this process. After the death of Nettles in 1985—which followers understood to represent only the death of her physical body and the release of her true self to return to outer space— Applewhite taught that adherents may have to die in order to journey on to the Next Level. By the end of the movement's history, physical death had become a necessity rather than a mere possibility.

These many changes make Heaven's Gate more difficult to characterize and study, but they actually reveal something very important: Heaven's Gate functioned as a living, changing religion whose leaders and members adapted to unexpected developments through institutional, practical, and theological modifications. The group demonstrated flexibility. As it changed, it reflected the changing society around it. In this chapter I develop an overall picture of how Heaven's Gate evolved in its formative years, before Nettles's death. The overarching theme that emerges shows two extremely creative religious innovators who founded a new religious movement predicated on multiple strands of religious thought.

The Early History: The UFO Two

Bonnie Lu Nettles had not been particularly religious growing up, nor was she a rigorous proponent of any one spiritual path, though she had dabbled in astrology and theosophy. Marshall Herff Applewhite had been raised by a preacher and even attended seminary, but his real love was music and, as a closeted bisexual in 1970s Texas, the church would not have seemed a natural home regardless. It is odd, then, that these two individuals, one a part-time astrologer and the other a former seminarian, would found one of the world's most famous UFO religions. But they did. The early history of Heaven's Gate is the history of the meeting and spiritual partnership of Bonnie Lu Nettles and Marshall Herff Applewhite.

Neither Nettles nor Applewhite had particularly noteworthy backgrounds before meeting and creating the new religious movement that would become known as Heaven's Gate. A native of Houston, Nettles was a registered nurse, mother of four children, and partner in a failing marriage. She had been raised Baptist, but she was not particularly fervent in her Christian faith. A high school friend described Nettles's church attendance as primarily social, attending "just because the gang [of friends] did."[2] As an adult she was biblically literate and interested in religion, but not devout. By the time she met Applewhite, her religious interests had taken a far less conventional turn.

Astrology and the occult fascinated Nettles. A lapsed member of the Houston branch of the Theosophical Society in America—an eclectic religious body emphasizing a variety of spiritual practices—and an amateur astrologer, Nettles inhabited a New Age subculture of disincarnated spirits, ascended masters, telepathic powers, and hidden and revealed gnosis.[3] She channeled spirits, including a nineteenth-century Franciscan monk named Brother Francis, held a séance group in her living room, and was interested in UFOs. She also authored an astrology column in a local newspaper.[4] Such unconventional religious practices were even more important to her than her interpersonal relationships: Nettles's husband did not approve of her spiritual activities, and the couple's relationship had begun to disintegrate even before Nettles found a new spiritual partner in Applewhite. They divorced in 1972.[5]

Though Nettles and Applewhite would later discount the value of Nettles's theosophy, her involvement in the Theosophical Society indicates one of the formative religious influences in her life, one that clearly influenced her later religious thought. Even after Nettles and Applewhite met and began formulating their new religious understanding, they sold theosophical material in their short-lived New Age bookstore, The Christian Arts Center.[6] Theosophy is the product of the late nineteenth century and another famous pair of religious innovators, Helena Petrovna Blavatsky (1831–1891), Henry Steel Olcott (1832–1907), and their circle of friends and associates. Scholar of theosophy Robert Ellwood traces the movement to multiple sources: nineteenth-century romanticism, the Victorian debates over the relationship between science and religion, and the Western discovery and fascination with the East, especially India.[7] Theosophy's founders combined an earnest commitment to progressivism with all of these religious influences, forming a new religious movement that promulgated a philosophy drawing on Buddhism, Hinduism, Christianity, and the Western Occult tradition. Its most important features include the evolution of the human soul through multiple incarnations, and access to and learning from a series of spiritual masters inhabiting distant physical or spiritual places or planes. Theosophy also idolized science. All of these elements later became central doctrines of Heaven's Gate, though in modified forms.[8]

Nettles's Theosophical Society in America had been shaped by other religious innovators before it reached her. Theosophists Annie Besant, Charles Webster Leadbeater, Jiddu Krishnamurti, William Q. Judge, and Katherine Tingley all formed and reformed theosophical sub-movements that evolved from Blavatsky and Olcott's teachings and materials. Mid-twentieth-century theosophical popularizers Guy Ballard (1878–1939) and Edna Ballard (1886–1971) emphasized the notion of the "Ascended Masters," transcendental beings who served as spiritual masters to members of the Ballards' "I AM" movement. This movement became very popular in American theosophical and later New Age circles, and left an obvious mark on Heaven's Gate. The Ballards extended Blavatsky and Olcott's notion of Mahatma masters—who originally included living masters, spiritual beings, and extraterrestrial Venusians—and focused on the latter two categories. I AM's Ascended Masters generally existed in spiritual or extraterrestrial realms, and offered religious teachings through channeling and other spiritual means of communication. Importantly, the Ascended Masters were embodied, having "ascended" from Earth to the higher realms that they now inhabited. This approach—and especially the idea of embodied masters—became an important part of Heaven's Gate's thought. Channeling certainly found a home in the new religion that Nettles founded with Applewhite. Nettles's séance group channeled not only deceased human beings such as Brother Francis, and in one case Marilyn Monroe, but also extraterrestrials from planet Venus.[9] While the Two borrowed the idea of extraterrestrial beings offering religious truth and knowledge, they repudiated other aspects of the theosophical worldview, notably the plurality of spiritual teachers, its liberal acceptance of a multiplicity of truths, and most of its religious practices.

As compared to Nettles, Applewhite possessed a more convention-ally Christian background. A Texan by birth, he was the son of a popu-lar and successful Presbyterian preacher, Marshall Herff Applewhite, Sr. Called widely by his middle name, Herff, the younger Applewhite attended Austin College in Sherman, Texas, where he was remembered as an extrovert with a magnetic personality that "he put to only positive uses," in the words of a former college roommate.[10] He served as a cam-pus leader in the a cappella group, judiciary council, and association of prospective Presbyterian ministers, and graduated with a degree in phi-losophy. College acquaintances remember him as a budding musician as well as interested in religious ministry.[11]

After graduating from college in 1952, Applewhite enrolled at Vir-ginia's Union Theological Seminary, a Presbyterian divinity school, but left after two years to study music.[12] Following a brief stint in the Army Signal Corps, he earned a Masters degree in music and voice from the University of Colorado, though he never strayed far from a reli-giously oriented vocation.[13] A talented vocalist and charismatic instruc-tor, Applewhite directed the chorus at Houston's St. Mark's Episcopal Church and the fine arts program at the University of St. Thomas, as well as working at a string of churches and even a synagogue.[14] He mar-ried fellow Texan Anne Pearce shortly after graduating, and had two children, but the couple separated in the mid-1960s and divorced in 1968.[15] He remained estranged from his ex-wife and children until the end of his life. Applewhite bounced between various jobs, teaching and conducting music, until he met Nettles eight years later. Yet Applewhite also dabbled in astrology, and he clearly was somewhat of a religious seeker. A friend reported that Applewhite had become interested in UFOs, science fiction, and ancient mysticism shortly before meeting Nettles.[16]

His religious life would change forever when he met Bonnie Lu Nettles in the Houston hospital where she worked in 1972. Numerous accounts exist of why Applewhite was in the hospital, but all agree that Applewhite was at a moment of life change and even crisis. His sister indicated that he had suffered a "near death experience" and was hospitalized because of a serious heart blockage.[17] Robert W. Balch, a sociologist who produced the first notable studies of Heaven's Gate, indicated that the encounter was "chance" and that Applewhite had been visiting a friend who was recovering from an operation, a position that Applewhite also took. (Balch also noted that Applewhite's life was in a state of confusion and flux at the time.)[18] Evan Thomas, a reporter who investigated the group following the Heaven's Gate suicides, claims that Applewhite was a mental patient who had suffered a serious mental collapse, though he provides no evidence of that claim; neither does he indicate from where he derived that rather late interpretation.[19]

While the exact reasons for Nettles's and Applewhite's meeting will never be fully known, clearly both were in the midst of significant life changes. Nettles was separated and in the process of divorcing. Her husband did not support her spiritual pursuits, and she felt called to something more than her current situation. Her daughter remembers going outside with Nettles to look at the sky, with both talking about how they hoped that a flying saucer would land and take them away.[20] Applewhite's situation was even more muddled. He was a bisexual, yet neither his relationships with women nor men had brought him any long-term happiness. In addition to his divorce, he had suffered a broken engagement and a series of homosexual relationships about which he felt deeply ambivalent. He admitted to a friend that he felt his relationships were "all failures" and that "any kind of relationship is stifling and short lived." He considered giving up intimate relationships entirely, but also admitted that he longed for a partner.[21] He had recently been fired from a well-paying job and found himself isolated from both former friends and family, as well as struggling financially. Regardless of whether he was a patient at the hospital where he met Nettles, he had suffered from various health ailments including frequent headaches and anxiety.

Some scholars and journalists have argued that the two's life circumstances, especially Applewhite's sexual and relationship problems, directly led them to create the religious worldview of Heaven's Gate, with its emphasis on celibacy and control.[22] Scholar of communications Robert Glenn Howard posited that Applewhite's "apparently obsessive beliefs" about "human psychic problems of identity formation," in combination with either his sexual confusion or a mystical experience, led to the specific form that Heaven's Gate took.[23] For Howard, total rejection of the body, gendered social norms, and sexual identity led directly to the eventual suicides.[24] Sociologist Susan Raine goes even further, rooting the theological development of Heaven's Gate in Applewhite's "lifelong struggles with his own sexuality, coupled with his mental health problems."[25] The actual evidence of Applewhite's madness is slim. He did seem crazy to some people, especially those who met him and Nettles during their initial "awakening" period, but apparently he did not present any such behavior after 1975.[26] While Raine is sometimes careful to admit that Applewhite's mental health problems were merely "alleged," she nevertheless presents an image of Applewhite as both schizophrenic and delusional, and argues that these conditions led to the creation of Heaven's Gate's belief system.[27]

Such approaches are overly reductionist and not very helpful. Many psychological, social, and cultural factors were at play and influenced Applewhite and Nettles as they created Heaven's Gate. While it is easy to dismiss someone who believes in unconventional religions as ipso facto delusional or schizophrenic—as Raine does—there is no clinical reason to assume that a person who believes in UFOs and extraterrestrial communication is any more insane than a person who believes in angels and prayer. Such arguments are inherently circular, since the primary evidence for Applewhite's apparent madness is his founding of an alternative new religion, and that is precisely what such arguments also attempt to explain. These explanations also fail to consider the role that Nettles played in the creation of Heaven's Gate. Her theosophical and ufological background were at least as important as the religious or psychological experiences that Applewhite brought to the movement, and she contributed as much to the theological content of the system as did he. Arguments that discount her relevance therefore fail on basic empirical grounds.

Rather than reduce Heaven's Gate to the result of Applewhite's alleged psychological state, one must consider the cultural and social dimensions of their past histories and shared experiences, and the development of the group itself. For example, representations of space aliens and UFOs in popular culture and the ufology subculture, Nettles and Applewhite's past studies of Asian religions, theosophy, and Christianity, and the social dynamics of the counterculture of the late 1960s and 1970s all provided equal muses as the two constructed their religious worldview. That being said, rejection of sexual relationships, settled jobs, and middle-class life did become hallmarks of Heaven's Gate. All of these American cultural norms had failed the group's founders as well. Yet this is merely one aspect of a highly complex religious ideology and practice.

Becoming the Two

In the months after Nettles and Applewhite met in the Houston hospital, they forged a lasting spiritual bond that became the center of Heaven's Gate, even after Nettles died in 1985. On a psychological level, the two provided each other the supportive relationship that each desperately needed, and on a religious level the two brought their disparate experiences and perspectives together to form a nexus of theosophy, Protestantism, the New Age, and ufology.

Whereas the accounts at the end of Heaven's Gate tended to focus almost exclusively on how Applewhite shaped the ensuing movement, it was Nettles whose worldview primarily influenced the development of the two's spiritual journey, and former members recount that it was she who served as the real leader of the movement.[28] Applewhite had undergone several mystical experiences in the previous months, but seemed unable to find the words or framework for explaining them. According to one account recollected by a friend and collected by Balch, Applewhite had had a visionary experience and needed help processing and interpreting. "He said a presence had given him all the knowledge of where the human race had come from and where it was going. It made you laugh to hear it, but Herff was serious. And he didn't seem crazy."[29] Elsewhere, Balch reports that Applewhite had experienced "strange voices, and later bizarre dreams and out-of-body experiences."[30]

Yet Applewhite's limited dabbling in astrology and readings about ancient mysticism failed to provide him a convincing interpretive schema with which to understand and frame his experiences.

Nettles provided that. In a 1976 interview, Applewhite explained that the moment they met was life-changing, but that he had also been looking for just such a moment. "I felt I had known her forever. I had wanted someone to do an astrological chart on me, so when I met her, I ran right out to my car and got my birth certificate."[31] As Applewhite indicated, he had wanted someone like Nettles to help him process his experiences. In particular, he hoped that person would use an astrological chart to do so.

For believers in astrology, charts function as a religious technology that aids in revealing the intrinsic contours of personality, identity, and destiny of the individual. A chart determines and locates the position of planets and stars during the precise moment of the individual's birth— hence Applewhite's need to retrieve his birth certificate. A trained astrologer not only creates a chart but also interprets it, explaining how the stars and planets have led to specific influences in the subject's life. Depending on the astrological system that the subject and astrologer utilize, the chart may also reveal secrets about the subject's past lives and future fate.

Nettles did Applewhite's chart. They determined that they had known each other in a previous life and that they had an important mission to perform together in their new incarnations.[32] They used this new realization to explain not only Applewhite's recent mystical experiences, but all the relationship ills and other interpersonal dramas that had plagued the two of them over the previous years. As they later explained in another 1976 interview, "it was as if we were being guided by forces greater than ourselves. We were snatched from our previous lives. We went through a very confusing period of transition."[33] Importantly, the astrological framework that Nettles offered Applewhite helped both of them to understand and interpret their experiences, to give meaning to the (admittedly pedestrian) suffering that the two had undergone. Like all religions, the inchoate kernel of Heaven's Gate offered meaning and solace. It provided sanction for them to reject the most painful parts of their lives—broken relationships—and forge a new (platonic) partnership together based on mutual spiritual development.

The two decided to found a joint venture that they named the Christian Arts Center. At the center they sold books and offered classes on a variety of New Age topics, including astrology, meditation, mysticism, theosophy, healing, metaphysics, comparative religions, arts, and music.[34] Despite the name of the center, the two had moved rather firmly away from the Christianity of Nettles's Baptist upbringing and Applewhite's Presbyterianism, and into the realm of the New Age movement. The New Age is notoriously difficult to define, since it functions as a loose movement of individuals and groups. New Age practitioners focus on means of self-transformation through spiritual technologies and practices such as astrology, channeling, body work (yoga, breath meditation, etc.), and diet. Scholar of new religions J. Gordon Melton argues that such goals of self-transformation and planetary transformation are the hallmark of the New Age, and that all New Age practices orient toward these goals.[35] James R. Lewis cautions that even this generalization may not sufficiently define such a diffuse movement, and instead argues for a set of defining traits such as healing, syncretism, transformation, and appeals to psychic powers.[36] Scholars identify theosophy, astrology, Western esotericism, channeling, alternative healing, Christian mysticism, and ufology as parcels and influences in the contemporary New Age movement.[37] Regardless of how one defines the New Age, Applewhite and Nettles had clearly positioned themselves and their new entity as part of this phenomenon.

The Christian Arts Center failed after only a few months, so the two moved "out into the country" to found a retreat center that they named Know Place, a name that capitalized on both the sense of "knowing thyself" and the homonym of a "no-place," that is a liminal utopia wherein one finds oneself. There they taught classes on New Age topics such as astrology, theosophy, and mysticism, and met individually with students. They also focused more on their own spiritual development. They delved into theosophical material, including Blavatsky's *The Secret Doctrine*, and many other New Age, Christian, and theosophical texts.[38] They also consulted with a Filipino occultist with interests in Hindu mysticism, who concurred with them that they had a special mission to accomplish.[39] The mystic renamed Nettles as Shakti Devi (meaning "Powerful Goddess") and Applewhite as Shri Pranavah (roughly translating to "Auspicious Mantra"), providing an important symbol of their rebirth. The names did not last, though the effect did. The two were no longer just two individuals. They were on the road to becoming—as they would soon refer to themselves—The Two.

The Revelation of Self-Discovery

Had Applewhite and Nettles continued their semi-solitary musings at Know Place it is unlikely that they would have formed a new religious movement. Instead, they left the isolation and safety of the Houston environ and began a multiyear process of religious searching and proselytizing that eventually resulted in the formation of a small religious community. This community would grow from its two founders in 1973 to one more person in May 1974 to several dozen a year later in May 1975, and finally to several hundred in late 1975 and early 1976.

Nettles and Applewhite understood themselves as seekers, and after closing Know Place in January 1973, they spent more than a year wandering throughout North America on a religious quest for self-identity. They read a variety of New Age, theosophical, science fiction, Christian, and Asian religious materials. As Applewhite later described it, "[w]e studied everything we could get our hands on that had to do with any sort of awareness—spiritual awareness, scientific awareness, religious awareness. Our thirst was absolutely unquenchable."[40] The Two had become religious seekers, trying out new beliefs and identities as they sought a new means of understanding themselves and their relationship to each other and the world.

In adopting the mantle of seekers, Nettles and Applewhite were not aberrations, and while their method of dropping all familial and social connections to wander may seem extreme, it in fact represented a far broader religious milieu. The 1950s had witnessed Jack Kerouac and the beatniks engaging in a similar phenomenon, and in the 1960s of course waves of countercultural youth had wandered the nation's cities and byways and become known as the hippies. The late 1960s and early 1970s were a decade of seekers. Sociologist of religion Wade Clark Roof surveyed the baby boomer generation that came of age during this era and found that seeking functioned as a major theme of their religious experience. While neither Nettles nor Applewhite were boomers—they were born too early—their experiences nevertheless captured the gestalt of the time. In assessing his survey findings, Roof defined the religious world of this time as focused on a "turning inward." He explains that a "common theme in this turning inward is the emphasis on exploring religious and spiritual traditions. Exploration gets elevated to the level of a spiritual exercise in an age that is aware of the great diversity of religions."[41] Roof found that 60 percent of boomers preferred to explore differing religious teachings and learn from them. This seeking undoubtedly had an impact. By 1988, when Roof performed his survey, a quarter of boomers accepted astrology and reincarnation.[42] By 2008, a quarter of all Americans did as well.[43] Spiritual seeking has tremendous impact in American religious culture.

Nettles and Applewhite's period of seeking ended when they came to a more definitive view of themselves and their new identities. While camping in July 1973 along the Oregon coast near the Rogue River, the Two—as they now almost always called themselves—came upon a firm realization of their identities and mission. They were the two witnesses described in the Christian New Testament's Book of Revelation, destined to be martyred and resurrected before an unbelieving world, which they dubbed "the demonstration." They based this belief on a passage in Revelation 11, one that they explicitly cited in later sources, which indicates two witnesses being slayed by a "a beast that ascendeth out of the bottomless pit" and after being resurrected, "ascend[ing] up to heaven in a cloud" (Rev. 11:3–12, King James Version).

In pinning their religious identities and missions on this passage in Revelation, the Two had veered from their initial New Age forays into the apocalyptic millennialism that characterized the conservative Evangelical Protestantism of the time. In fact, they came to promote a variant of dispensational premillennialism, a type of apocalypticism that focuses on deciphering the clues in Revelation and the Hebrew Bible's Book of Daniel to develop a precise time line of the end-times, with reference to great "dispensations" of time. Crucially, dispensationalism also posits a "rapture of the faithful" wherein the elect meet Christ in midair and journey to Heaven. The Two would later transform this system and these beliefs within their own religious worldview.

All of this represented a radical departure from astrology, theosophical teachings, and New Age spiritual seeking. An obvious question is why. While both Nettles and Applewhite had been raised Christians, Nettles admitted to its lack of influence in her adult life. She always believed more strongly in the Eastern religions, as she had explained previously.[44] Meanwhile the Presbyterianism of Applewhite's youth and college years generally eschews apocalypticism, with the leaders of Applewhite's own regional Presbyterian association—of which his father was a member—having declared dispensationalist pre-millennialism a heresy.[45] Since it did not emerge from either's cradle tradition, the Two must have picked up their millennial ideas either from their religious explorations or broader culture. The former is far more likely, given their self-descriptions of religious seeking and reading. Fellow Texan Hal Lindsey had published his best-selling book *The Late Great Planet Earth* in 1970, and it had quickly swept through Christian circles. In the book Lindsey interprets Revelation and other prophetic texts with reference to contemporary culture, and develops predictions for the end-times that place the apocalyptic scenario in the immediate future. Nettles and Applewhite had an identical project of deciphering the biblical text, though they came to differing conclusions. Lindsey's book sold more than fifteen million copies during its first twelve years in print, indicating the tremendous cultural sway of millennialism. Nettles and Applewhite responded to such millennialism in creating their own religious identities, and used such interests in their eventual proselytizing.[46] They may have even read Lindsey and been directly influenced by his dispensationalist approach, though this is conjecture. Regardless, they came to similar conclusions that the end-time was near, and adopted a similar view of the dispensations and the coming rapture.

Yet the Two had not abandoned their New Age perspectives, but rather merely combined them with Christian millennialism. The New Age movement itself assumes a millennial perspective, albeit one less destructive in outlook, and looks to the dawning of the eponymous new age when human potential shall finally be achieved. This form of millennialism—"progressive millennialism," as historian Catherine Wessinger has called it—envisions a radical disruption to the world as it currently exists, but without the violence and upheaval popularly associated with apocalyptic scenarios. Apocalypticism as envisioned in the popular consciousness—emphasizing portends of doom, natural disasters, and wars—follows a more common Christian form of eschatology technically called "premillennialism," or more helpfully "catastrophic millennialism" in Wessinger's typology.[47] Regardless, Nettles and Applewhite seemed to blur the boundaries between them.

Figure 1.1. Marshall Herff Applewhite and Bonnie Lu Nettles in a picture taken October 16, 1975, in Harlingen, Texas. Image © Bettmann/CORBIS.

Nettles and Applewhite declared that, following their predicted martyrdom and resurrection, a UFO would descend in a technological enactment of the rapture wherein it would hover midair to pick up the Two and anyone else who believed them and accepted their message. The UFO would then return to outer space, delivering its passengers to a heavenly utopia. The bodies of the Two and their followers would transform through biological and chemical processes into perfected extraterrestrial beings, and they would live indefinitely in the "Next Level" or "Evolutionary Level Above Human," as the Two later called it, in a state of near-perfection. While similar to the Christian idea of Heaven, the Two's ufological vision also bears similarity to theosophy's visions of the higher planes, especially as the I AM variant of theosophy proclaimed. Its emphasis on bodily self-transformation and perfection similarly echoes New Age themes, and of course the presence of beliefs in extraterrestrials and UFOs marks their beliefs as part of a specific segment of the ufological-oriented New Age movement.

In May 1974, the Two decided to return to Houston to proclaim their new gospel, and they first approached a former client named Sharon, whom they knew from their days of running the Christian Arts Center and Know Place. Like Nettles's and Applewhite's experiences before meeting, this former student was in the midst of a bad relationship and was seeking a higher truth to buttress and reaffirm her identity. Sharon decided after six days of meeting with the Two to accept their religious message, and like them she chose to abandon her family and become a religious wanderer. Leaving her wedding ring and notes for her family, Sharon began traveling and preaching the gospel of the Two. Like a latter-day John the Baptist, she hurried ahead of the Two, advertised their impending arrival, and sought to arrange for audiences to hear them.[48].

The Two and Sharon canvassed the country, seeking to spread the word of the Two's religious discoveries. These attempts failed. In one notable exchange in June 1974, Nettles and Applewhite evangelized to a Boise State University anthropology professor, and later to a Boise-area professional psychic. The professor, Max Pavesic, recounted that the Two "walked into my office and asked me to drop everything and leave with them. They were very sincere and intense but they had weird eyes." The Two indicated that they would be "publically crucified" as a "demonstration" to the world of their truth, and that only a small sub-set of people who had agreed to walk away from their lives would be able to join them on the UFOs and journey on to the higher realms of outer space, a highest level of evolution . . . a metaphysical state where the mind is evolved out of the body into infinity."[49] Both Pavesic and the psychic—who reported a nearly identical offer—declined, and the Two departed. Throughout their time with Sharon the same pattern repeated. The three of them failed to make a single convert during their stop in Boise or anywhere else they went.

Like most of the Two's converts, Sharon eventually left the fold. Though ambivalent about whether she still accepted their religious mes-sage, her guilt over abandoning her family—including a two-year-old daughter—eventually led her to return home. Four months after joining the Two, her husband and daughters confronted her, and Sharon opted to return to a more conventional life. Like many former members of new religious movements, Sharon was ambivalent about her departure. She worried that "she had disappointed God and forfeited her place" onboard the UFO, she later told a reporter.[50] Yet many other converts would eventually take her place.

Trial, Prison, and Growth

Sharon's departure had an immediate impact on the Two, and not just in terms of their self-confidence. Sharon's husband had charged Nettles and Applewhite with credit card fraud for their use of Sharon's credit card during her time as their follower. While Sharon later admitted to permitting them to use the card, the accusation resulted in the Two's arrests. Police declined to charge Applewhite and Nettles with the credit card fraud, but their arrests led to the discovery of another warrant against Applewhite for theft of a rental car.[51] Applewhite was arraigned and transferred to Missouri, where he was imprisoned for six months awaiting trial. Nettles returned to working as a nurse during this time.

The theft of the rental car hints at an important element in the Two's developing theology, what scholars call antinomianism. From the Greek word "opposed to the law," antinomianism in Christian theology means that moral or religious laws no longer hold for those who have been saved. Martin Luther (1483–1546) coined the term during a dispute with fellow reformer Johannes Agricola (1494–1566), who championed a view that the laws of Moses (such as Sabbath observance) no longer held for Christians. For Agricola, God's grace overrode the laws of the Old Testament. In all cases, individuals and groups possessing an antinomian outlook believe that their religious convictions permit them to violate laws that other people or groups follow. In the case of Heaven's Gate, Applewhite and Nettles believed that their status as the two witnesses and the importance of their spiritual mission permitted them to violate human laws. The police and courts begged to differ.

Applewhite's trial was brief, and he was sentenced to time served. He was released in March 1975, and Nettles rejoined him immediately thereafter. Yet his imprisonment offered somewhat of a silver lining for Applewhite. The "isolation," as he later called it, led to "significant growth," during which he came to realize that he and Nettles were in fact not human at all, but extraterrestrials merely inhabiting human bodies.[52] He gave two different explanations for this over the following years—either that they had incarnated into these bodies during their lifetimes or during their natal development, or that they had entered into bodies specially prepared for them by the Next Level. This bears some similarity to the concept of "walk-ins," a New Age concept that became popular several years later which supposes that beneficial spirits—sometimes extraterrestrial ones—can enter into human beings to accomplish certain tasks to assist humanity.

During his imprisonment Applewhite composed a statement of his and Nettles's beliefs, summarizing their position that they were visitors from an extraterrestrial realm who offered human beings a chance to overcome their limitations and evolve into perfected extraterrestrial creatures. This is the same basic message that Heaven's Gate continued to offer two decades later, after Nettles had died. Applewhite's statement also described Jesus as an earlier extraterrestrial visitor, and noted the prophetic role that he and Nettles were to play in the near future. Again, the fundamental positions remained the same even twenty-two years later.[53] Applewhite and Nettles edited the statement together and mailed it later that month from a retreat in Ojai, California, a bucolic town near the coast between Santa Barbara and Los Angeles. They targeted groups and individuals associated with new and alternative religions and holistic living in their mailing.

The evening of April 9, 1975, marked a turning point for the Two, and the creation of the movement that would eventually be called Heaven's Gate. Introducing themselves as "Guinea" and "Pig" (though they would soon thereafter adopt the monikers of "Bo" and "Peep"), the Two met with a Los Angeles area metaphysical group led by Clarence Klug and meeting in the house of psychic Joan Culpepper. Details on this meeting vary among the Two's own recounting, that of attendees, and outside investigators. Yet all agree that it was momentous, and that the Two presented themselves as charismatic leaders bearing an important new spiritual message. Between forty-one and eighty people attended.[54] Between twenty-three and twenty-seven individuals decided to join them, depending on which sources one accepts as accurate.[55]

Klug's group centered on what he called "Self-Initiation," an alchemical process whereby his followers could transcend their human limitations and evolve into beings of light. He rooted this process in his interpretations of the Christian book of Revelation, which he read as an allegory for ancient alchemical secrets. Klug's interpretive approach drew heavily from Hindu mystical traditions, especially the Hindu view of the chakras, centers of energy in the spine. Klug also incorporated Hindu Tantra in his theology. Tantra promises mystical experience and spiritual development through controlled sexual activities, especially control of sexual orgasm. Klug offered such Tantric secret teachings to the inner circle of his followers.[56] Klug's movement seemed as eclectic as the teachings of the Two, and Klug's followers clearly already demonstrated comfort with religious bricolage and emphasis on seeking transcendence through bodily salvation. Importantly, this predisposed them to at least listen to Nettles and Applewhite's teachings.

As sociologist Robert Balch indicated in his study of the early history of Heaven's Gate, Klug's group was "at the crossroads" when Nettles and Applewhite arrived. A social collapse among his followers had resulted in a precipitous membership decline, and a failed attempt to self-publish his teachings had led to financial ruin for some members of his group. Members reported various social tensions, destructive gossip, and relational ills as well.[57] A rampant sense of fear also characterized the group: fear that Klug had been wrong, fear that someone else— Nettles and Applewhite, for example—was right, fear that they might miss their chance for spiritual advancement.[58]

Though their host Culpepper later became a critic of the Two, apparently her initial reactions were positive. She described Applewhite and Nettles as masters of creating a spiritual connection with their audience. "[T]hey had a charisma and gave off an aura of love and understanding. The man, especially, had hypnotic eyes, although I can't explain the thing by hypnosis. It went deeper than that. . . . They gave off this love thing, which had to be mentally controlled, as later they came on as two of the most negative people I'd ever met."[59] Culpepper's later dismissal of their motivations to the contrary, the Two's ability to attract the attention, respect, and eventually adherence of a significant portion of this audience points to a special interpersonal quality that observers such as Culpepper routinely noted: charisma.

The most influential definition of charisma derives from sociologist of religion Max Weber. As already noted in this book's introduction, Weber defined charisma as a special superhuman quality that sets a leader apart from others.[60] According to this classic approach to defining and delineating charisma, it is a characteristic innate to a person that allows him or her to effectively lead on the basis of what followers believe is the leader's special abilities, nature, or features. The prophet functions as a classic example in the biblical literature, since he or she (usually he) claims a special ability to speak for God, and those who accept the prophet base their acceptance on that supposed ability. In the Hindu tradition, a guru offers another example. Gurus possess special spiritual gifts developed through yogic practices, inborn characteristics, or gifts of grace from the deities. Those who become their disciples predicate their devotion on the gurus' gifts, and the gurus base their leadership and teaching authority on those gifts as well. Many of Heaven's Gate's members—and some detractors—identified the root of Nettles's and Applewhite's leadership abilities in this notion of charisma.

Despite Weber's assessment of charisma—which has shaped much of subsequent religious studies scholarship—charisma is very much in the eye of the beholder. Recall that until this April 1975 meeting, the Two had failed in every attempt but one to attract converts. Even Sharon, the one adherent that they convinced to join them, eventually left. Many of the people in attendance at the Klug/Culpepper gathering also did not accept the message or become followers of the Two. Charisma is not magic, nor is it particularly effective when judged against the numerous failures of the Two to attract converts. In fact, rather than understand charisma as an inborn state or quality of personality, it is better to look at it as a mutual construction of the leader and followers. As sociologist Roy Wallis argued in his study of the Children of God—a new religion founded in the decade before Heaven's Gate—"charisma is essentially a relationship born out of interaction between a leader and his followers."[61] A "system of exchanges" marks the creation and nego-tiation of charisma, Wallis found, and the leader and followers in that new religion continually engage in a process of recreating charisma.[62] The leader invests in the self-esteem and religious worth of certain indi-viduals, who then invest in the religious leadership and charisma of the leader. By cultivating these relationships, the leader establishes his or her charisma and authority of leadership.

Based on Wallis's findings—and those of other sociologists[63]—rather than envision Nettles and Applewhite as possessing some sort of mag-ical or unusual charismatic ability, it is better to understand them as developing a sense of charisma and leadership authority through skill-ful relationship-building with their followers. That being said, certainly Applewhite possessed a powerful personality and highly practiced vocal abilities, and both Applewhite and Nettles projected religious authority based on their extensive studies and religious practice. The two used these qualities to build a sense of charisma and leadership. Charisma is therefore more of a rhetorical concept—a useful idea for those who did decide to join the Two, who employed the idea of "charisma" in order to understand their experiences and beliefs that the Two were somehow special. For those who were repulsed by the Two, and especially those who joined and then left, charisma also explained the apparent ability of Nettles and Applewhite to convince evidently sane people to merely walk out of their lives. It helped them process why they had made deci-sions that in retrospect they regretted. For ex-members like Culpepper who shared a New Age worldview with the Two, the notion of charisma possessed additional features of being rooted in various beliefs about hypnosis, psychic control, and mesmerism.

Approximately two dozen people at the Culpepper/Klug gathering decided to join the Two by walking out on their lives. The Two directed them to meet at a campground in Gold Beach, Oregon on May 5, 1975. Though all but three of the several dozen members who joined the group would eventually leave, this formative gathering in Los Angeles propelled the Two from lone spiritual gurus to founders of a movement.[64] Within months, they would also make national headlines and even the national television nightly news. Heaven's Gate was about to receive its first big publicity.

Waldport and Beyond

On October 7, 1975, the religious group led by Nettles and Applewhite made national news. "20 Missing in Oregon After Talking of Higher Life," trumpeted a *New York Times* headline, granted one buried on a back page.[65] The article described Nettles's and Applewhite's biggest meeting to date, a massive affair at the Waldport Inn in Waldport, Oregon held on September 14, 1975. More than two hundred and fifty people attended according to this article, though other journalists reported a smaller number closer to one hundred.[66] Of the attendees, between twenty and thirty-three people decided to accept the teachings of the Two, give up all their possessions, and walk out on their lives.[67]

The content of the Waldport meeting matched the Two's earlier teachings. One attendee described it as "vaguely Biblical . . . I guess the implication was that you might leave in a U.F.O."[68] Other attendees reported more specificity. One man who joined the group explained that those who followed the Two would "leave for a better life on another planet" after completing their training under the Two's guidance. The Two indicated to their audience that they were from that other planet, and that the Bible described extraterrestrial visitors such as Jesus, Ezekiel, and Elijah who had brought similar messages to Earth in earlier eras.[69] Other attendees used more explicitly Christian language. "It's the Second Coming," one new member wrote to a friend, apparently grasping the Two's allusions to the Book of Revelation.[70]

A limited transcript of the meeting provides more details on the content of the Two's teachings in Waldport. Having booked their hotel and meeting room under the name of "UFO and the Kingdom," Nettles and Applewhite focused on those two concepts: the kingdom of God and UFOs.[71] This "kingdom," which the Two generally referred to as the "Next Level" in this meeting, represented both the Heaven of the Bible and the heavens of science. "A kingdom nestles life that is real, that can be reached among those who attain to it. . . . a next level [and] a level that you refer to as the Kingdom of God."[72] The Two explicitly argued that the Next Level of which they spoke was a physical, corporeal place, and not an ethereal plane of existence. One reached it through physical travel aboard a UFO and one needed to bring one's physical body in order to do so. They offered to teach a process that they called "Human Individual Metamorphosis"—which became the first name for the group—to help individuals transform their bodies and prepare themselves to leave the planet. Importantly, at this stage in the group's existence there was no mention of suicide. The Two explicitly taught that the process required transforming the living human body and physically leaving onboard a UFO.[73] When journalists at the meeting asked one of the Two's followers from the Los Angeles group whether you had to die to get into the Two's version of heaven, the response was clear: "Absolutely not."[74]

The Two stressed the need to abandon the comfortable trappings of one's human life in order to join them and engage in Human Individual Metamorphosis. "You would have to literally overcome every human indulgence and human need . . . it is the most difficult task that there is . . . you have to lose everything. You will sever every attachment with that world that you have."[75] They specified that those who followed them had to give up their belongings, relationships, and attachments. They were to leave behind everything they owned and loved. Elsewhere, they specified that only adults could join them, and that parents either had to abandon their children or not join them at all.[76] The process was demanding and the Two insisted that giving up one's human attachments represented the first step to overcoming humanity and literally becoming a perfected extraterrestrial creature. Newspaper accounts show that those who took them up on that offer abandoned property, houses, cars, personal possessions, spouses and significant others, and even children.[77]

The converts from Waldport and some of those who had earlier converted in Los Angeles rendezvoused a few weeks later near Fruita, Colorado, a small town along the western slopes of the Rocky Mountains famous for its orchards, recreational activities, and campgrounds.[78] There the Two set up a camp where followers could begin the process of severing their human attachments and—they believed—begin transforming their bodies chemically and biologically into new extraterrestrial bodies. Converts who wrote letters to family members and friends remarked on a lack of firm plans for the immediate future of the group, but did not seem particularly alarmed by this prospect. One wrote: "It's real. It's the Second Coming. We don't know yet what's next. The mountains are nice. We are all going home."[79] The combination of trite observation and profound religious statement characterized much of the statements of early members of the group that was now calling itself Human Individual Metamorphosis. Nettles and Applewhite had also fully adopted new names for themselves by this time, settling on Bo (Applewhite) and Peep (Nettles).

Bo and Peep did not keep their new followers together for long. Just after their first successful mass conversion in Los Angeles after meeting with Clarence Klug's group, the Two had decided to split the growing movement into groups of two. They partnered each individual with another who was to serve as a "check partner" and help the other overcome their human attachments. Since Bo and Peep taught that sex, drugs, and recreation were forms of human attachments and hence forbidden, the Two charged the partners with keeping each other from engaging in these actions. They paired together heterosexual women and men, and gay men and women in single-sex pairings, so as to force the partners to confront their sexual attractions and overcome them. Citing the words of the Two, a journalist who had feigned interest in the group in order to see its inner workings described it as an attempt to "produce a kind of 'catalytic conflict' relationship to promote the process of 'overcoming' in each individual."[80] Partners traveled the country trying to overcome their human attachments and seeking converts along the way, rendezvousing occasionally with the group throughout the summer and fall of 1975 in campgrounds across the Western United States. Some of the partners ended up losing touch with the main group, and evidently Bo and Peep engaged in very little logistical leadership.[81] The image that emerges is one of a well-defined set of beliefs about the need to transcend the human level of existence through monastic self control, but complete disorganization at the level of social functioning and community building.

Becoming a Movement

In the autumn and early winter of 1975, very little about Human Individual Metamorphosis looked like what we normally consider a new religious movement, or especially the stereotypical image of a cult. The leaders preached an admittedly stringent gospel with strict rules of conduct, and insisted that adherents sever their connections with the world outside the movement, but they did not actually enforce these rules. Because the group seldom gathered as a whole, and even then the Two did not generally focus on day-to-day issues, many members described a nebulous process of trying to figure out *how* to engage in human individual metamorphosis. Some partners dropped out of the group, and others became lost and disconnected. A former member named Danny, one of the Two's first converts to leave the group and share his story with the media, described membership as a "rather dull routine" of daily living and proslytzing.[82] He also noted that the partnerships functioned as intended, but that the increased sexual tension was too much for him. "Nobody was having sex, and everyone was talking about it," he recounted.[83] Many of the adherents at this point had formerly belonged to Klug's Tantric sex-oriented group in Los Angeles, perhaps explaining these conversations. Regardless, Danny left after using marijuana that a fellow member had smuggled into the camp. "I tried all this but I didn't find any communications with the higher beings," he told the *San Francisco Chronicle*.[84]

When Nettles and Applewhite were interviewed by a journalist in February 1976, they did not know how many members of the group they had attracted, nor did they know about the recruitment efforts of the various partners. They estimated between three hundred and one thousand members of their group, a rather significant range. At times the reporter seemed to know more about their followers than did the Two.[85] In a retrospective history of this formative era of the group written more than a decade later, in 1988, Applewhite recalls that they eventually realized that they had to "become more organized in their groups and more systematic with their communication between cities [i.e., when not hosting large recruitment events]."[86]

As an example of the clear level of social dysfunction, two of the group's adherents resorted to giving a newspaper interview in order to try to find their way back to the group. This partnership, formed by converts from the Los Angeles meeting, became separated when they were three days late to a group gathering in Colorado, and since that time had lost the ability to communicate with the movement's leaders.

They described a system of communicating utilizing a series of postal general deliveries and short-term post office boxes.[87] Clearly this system possessed a serious flaw: missing a single community gathering meant that members could not track down the group afterwards. As Balch summarized, based on his empirical study of the group, "the dispersion of groups all over the country also contributed to disorganization. Each group went wherever its members felt led to go, and they rarely had contact with each other while they traveled."[88] Because they gave their interview using assumed names, one cannot know if these two converts ever made it back to the group, but, judging from statements made during their interview, neither seemed to think that possibility likely.

Human Individual Metamorphosis had become truly dysfunctional. Balch described a movement whose founders had abandoned the members to live in seclusion without appointing new leaders or installing a clear leadership structure. Adherents relied on their own senses of right and wrong, spiritual development, and occasionally democratic decision-making to make their choices. Boundaries between members and non-members had collapsed, with adherents coming and going to visit friends, chat with strangers, and engage in alternative forms of spiritual growth. Balch noted that almost half the group defected during this time.[89]

Had things continued in this vein the movement would have collapsed. Nettles and Applewhite therefore decided that the group had to cease its frenetic wandering and come together for a longer period. They also decided to stop recruiting and focus on creating a better functioning group among those individuals who had already joined. On April 21, 1976, Nettles declared that "the harvest is closed—there will be no more meetings."[90] A few months later, the Two gathered their flock in the isolated and geographically remote Medicine Bow National Forest in Wyoming in order to create a single community within the Human Individual Metamorphosis movement. Eighty-eight individuals arrived to do so.[91] The leaders instated a far more rigid set of behavioral guidelines and made it clear that adherents needed to follow these rules. They also solidified all religious and temporal authority as seated within themselves. Nettles and Applewhite transformed themselves from messengers and guides to the centers of the group from which all teachings and direction emerged.[92] Later that year they expelled nineteen members who—depending on who is recounting the story—either were weaker in belief or practice, waffled in their dedication, or failed to respect the authority of the leaders.[93]

The Two's transformations had the desired effect. The defection rate decreased, and the group reestablished a firm boundary between its members and the outside world. The movement became far more sectarian in the classic sense of drawing a firm line between members and non-members, with clear norms and expectations of adherents. Later that year, when the movement ran out of funds, members had to take outside jobs to provide financial support. Rather than result in more departures from the group, adherents remained committed. The founders of Human Individual Metamorphosis had managed to navigate from a loosely organized social group to a centralized religious movement comparable to a roving monastery.

Heaven's Gate began as two individuals, blossomed into a socially diffuse collective of spiritual seekers, and finally coalesced into a distinct religious movement. Just as this chapter has looked to the origin of Heaven's Gate, the last chapter of this book considers the end of the movement. But one important development occurred in 1985 that reshaped everything that came in between: the death of Bonnie Lu Nettles, considered in depth in chapter 4 since it so powerfully reshaped the beliefs of the adherents of Heaven's Gate. In the formative years of Heaven's Gate until 1985, Applewhite and Nettles taught that members of their movement would achieve salvation through bodily transformation and physical departure onboard UFOs. They indicated that if an adherent suffered an accidental death that Next Level technology could repair damaged bodies or even create new ones as replacements, an extension of their earlier treatment of their martyrdom and resurrection, i.e. "the demonstration." After Nettles's death this possibility became more and more central, as Applewhite shifted the theology of the group to focus on escape from Earth, corrupt human society, and eventually the human body itself. Nettles's death in 1985 opened the door that led to the suicides in 1997. It also forced Applewhite to take sole control of the movement and enabled him to shift the beliefs and practices as he saw fit. The remaining chapters of this book look at how that process unfolded.

2

The Spiritual Quest and Self-Transformation

Why People Joined Heaven's Gate

Who Joined Heaven's Gate?

In the first academic study of Heaven's Gate, Robert W. Balch and David Taylor's *Salvation in a UFO* (1976), the authors asked who joined the movement that they were studying, then called simply "the UFO group" or alternatively Human Individual Metamorphosis, the name its founders used for the group at that time. Based on their fieldwork, Balch and Taylor summarized that "nearly all were long-time seekers of truth" who had joined and left numerous other new religious groups, and would leave the UFO group as well.[1] A year later in a different study, the two sociologists provided an even more complete assessment of the religious background of the members. Members were "metaphysical seekers" shaped by the cultic milieu and metaphysical subculture. "Before joining [Heaven's Gate], members of the UFO cult had organized their lives around the quest for truth. Most defined themselves as spiritual seekers."[2]

Balch and Taylor lean on Colin Campbell's notion of the cultic milieu. Campbell defined the cultic milieu as "the cultural underground of society . . . it includes all deviant belief-systems and their associated practices. Unorthodox science, alien and heretical religions, deviant medicine, all comprise elements of such an underground."[3] Today scholars identify multiple religious strands within Campbell's cultic milieu, and in fact religious innovators have developed so many different new religious movements that fall within that milieu that finding commonalities is rather difficult. The cultic milieu from which members of Heaven's Gate emerged includes what many scholars would today call

Western esotericism, the New Age, alternative lifestyles, holistic healing, and nature-oriented spirituality. Though some scholars have in fact
developed interpretive schema to separate and analyze these strands
within the cultic milieu, since so many of the Heaven's Gate members
combined elements of these different alternative religious and quasi-
religious beliefs and practices, it is easiest to consider the cultic milieu
holistically.[4] Individuals living within this religious paradigm look to
alternative religious, scientific, educational, social, and cultural systems
to provide them meaning, practices, beliefs, and ways of living in the
world. These range from amalgamations of various non-Christian spiritual practices to alternative health care to vegetarian eating to alternative sacred geographies indicating sacred places within the landscape.

Journalists' reports and interviews during the early days of Heaven's
Gate support Balch and Taylor's contentions. Oregon State Trooper
Melvin Gibson was one of the first law enforcement officers to investigate the sudden disappearance of several dozen people in Waldport,
Oregon who had joined Heaven's Gate. "Most of these people were hip-
pie types, I guess you'd call them," he summarized, by which he later
explained that he meant they had never put down roots where they
lived.[5] They also demonstrated a high level of spiritual searching. One
of the first journalists to interview members of the group described its
members as "people already into metaphysical and spiritual studies—a
sort of spiritual underground."[6] As a spouse of a newly converted Heav-
en's Gate member indicated, "Judy has been really into religion lately.
She got baptized three times. She was a Catholic when we got mar-
ried but recently had been going to several different churches."[7] Other
adherents of the new religion told similar stories. One explained, "I'm
of Jewish background, but I used to sort of have my own religion, which
was sort of a conglomeration of everything. I was into yoga, meditation,
and I read different things, I studied metaphysics, I just tried to be, you
know, nice in my own way."[8]

This woman's self-description bears remarkable similarity to a famous
account described by Robert Bellah and his co-authors in *Habits of the
Heart* (1985), a groundbreaking study of Americans' approaches to civic
society and their view of community. Bellah and colleagues found that
Americans during the 1970s and 1980s took remarkably idiosyncratic
and incongruous approaches to understanding individualism and

THE SPIRITUAL QUEST AND SELF-TRANSFORMATION   >>   45

community, combining intensely individualistic views with longing for genuine community. In terms of spirituality, Bellah and his co-authors discovered a propensity for religious syncretism alongside a tendency toward spiritual seeking. Scholars have come to call this approach "Sheilaism" based on an interview Bellah conducted with a pseudony-mous woman who viewed her spiritual path as inherently her own. In Bellah's phrasing,

> Sheila Larson is a young nurse who has received a good deal of therapy and describes her faith as "Sheilaism." "I believe in God," Sheila says. "I am not a religious fanatic. I can't remember the last time I went to church. My faith has carried me a long way. It's Sheilaism. Just my own little voice." Sheila's faith has some tenets beyond belief in God, though not many. In defining what she calls "my own Sheilaism," she said: "It's just try to love yourself and be gentle with yourself. You know, I guess, take care of each other. I think He would want us to take care of each other." Like many others, Sheila would be willing to endorse few more specific points.[9]

Both Sheila and the aforementioned Heaven's Gate member created their own religious paths, even calling it their own religion, and stress-ing such qualities of their religion as its faith, flexibility, inward nature, and ethical approach to living. According to Bellah's research, up to 80 percent of Americans echoed similar sentiments during this period, and he later declared that "On the basis of our interviews, and a great deal of other data, I think we can say that many people sitting in the pews of Protestant and even Catholic churches are Sheilaists who feel that religion is essentially a private matter and that there is no particular constraint on them placed by the historic church, or even by the Bible and the tradition."[10] Other demographic studies show similar trends.[11]

Many such Sheilaists joined Heaven's Gate, but of course not all Sheilaists did so. The founders of Heaven's Gate made an ironic reli-gious offer: they appealed to spiritually individualistic seekers, but they also declared that they offered the single best religious system and that one no longer needed to continue one's search. Nettles and Apple-white's system promised definitive spiritual results in exchange for leav-ing behind all other spiritual pursuits and following their approach exclusively. Candidates must "walk out the doors" of their lives, abandoning possessions, families, and attachments. They must abandon even the spiritual quest itself, as Nettles and Applewhite explained, "the 'walking out the door' formula should not be confused with a seeming similar experience that so many have tried, the search for 'self.'"[12] Elsewhere they made similar statements about the apparent similarity of their approaches to other forms of spiritual development, but again stressing that one must leave behind such alternatives and follow their approach alone.[13] This marked the religious system of Heaven's Gate as quite dissimilar to the diffuse spiritual practices and groups of the New Age out of which Applewhite and Nettles emerged, and much more akin to other new religious movements such as the Unification Church, Scientology, or Hare Krishnas who insisted on exclusive religious commitment. It also marked them as akin to the many new forms of Evangelical Christianity emerging at this time that marketed themselves to spiritual seekers but insisted on offering exclusive truths and not mere spiritual options.[14]

Yet Nettles and Applewhite also explicitly invoked the theme of individualism so as to appeal to spiritual seekers. They closed each of their initial three statements—the ones they widely distributed in the early days of the movement to potential converts—with clarion calls aimed at individualistic spiritual seekers. "If this speaks to you—respond— according to your capabilities or needs. For your sake—give this opportunity your best," declared the closing words of the First Statement.[15] "Why not *you*?" asked the Second.[16] The Third Statement blended a sense of fate with free will, one of the hallmarks of the New Age movement that emphasizes the ideas of both destiny and choice:

> If YOU are ready for YOUR "final exam," leaving behind your "nest" and trying your "wings," the "two" here to demonstrate can help prepare you for that "exam." FIND THEM! Take that step NOW. You are probably one of those who is incarnate at this time for that express purpose. Don't miss your chance. Don't waste a moment. Let's work toward *your* Easter now![17]

Such an approach encapsulated the individualistic approach of the spiritual seekers to whom Nettles and Applewhite appealed. It invoked

Table 2.1: Members of Heaven's Gate at the time of the 1997 suicides

Religious Name within Heaven's Gate	Year of Entrance / Initial Membership
Do	(Founder)
Alxody*	1975
Glnody†	1975
Chkody†	1975
Jnnody†	1975
Jwnody†	1975
Lggody†	1975
Lvvody†	1975
Mllody	1975
Nrrody†	1975
Ollody	1975
Prsody	1975
Slvody†	1975
Snnody	1975
Stlody	1975
Stmody†	1975
Wndody	1975
Anlody†	1976
Brnody†	1976
Dymody	1976
Drrody†	1976
Dstody	1976
Jmmody†	1976
Smmody†	1976
Sngody	1976
Srrody	1976
Strody	1976
Tllody	1976

†: contributed to the Heaven's Gate anthology ("Purple Book")
*: did not appear in videotaped Exit Videos

Table 2.1 (Continued)

Religious Name within Heaven's Gate	Year of Entrance / Initial Membership
Trsody	1976
Evnody*	1991
Avnody*	1994
Gldody	1994
Leody*	1994
Qstody†	1994
Tddody†	1994
Wknody†	1994
Yrsody†	1994
Vrnody	1995
Dvvody	1996

†: *contributed to the Heaven's Gate anthology ("Purple Book")*
*: *did not appear in videotaped Exit Videos*

three metaphors—that of the bird leaving its nest, of a student graduating, and of Christ's Easter resurrection. The first two emphasize positive transitions wherein an individual takes charge of its existence and becomes more independent and intentional. The last focuses on a profound transformation and transition in status from worldly existence to an eternal one. Of course, the Two required that converts accept their particular mandate of spiritual practices. Their rhetoric skillfully combined appeals to individualistic spiritual seeking and the sort of exclusivist religious message one expects in a high-demand religious group.

In appealing to the spiritual seeker but offering a product that claimed exclusivity, the founders of Heaven's Gate situated their movement within the American religious marketplace in a place where they could appeal to spiritual seekers looking to escape from a cycle of Sheilaism and devote themselves to a single religious pursuit. Sociologist Wade Clark Roof has written of this pursuit as part of a "quest culture" that developed during the American postwar period. Roof locates this "open, spiritual searching style" among not just spiritual seekers but members of institutionalized religions, "Christian

Evangelicals, Pentecostals, and Charismatics, and in addition, many mainline Protestants, Catholics, and Jews, and others who might not think of themselves immediately in such terms, yet for whom the language of 'journey' and 'walk' and 'growth' are commonplace."[18] While most Americans remained rooted in their quests within single religious traditions—analogous to how most travel by highways on their physical journeys—others looked beyond the mainstream traditions into groups within Campbell's cultic milieu. Roof calls this the "spiritual marketplace" in which numerous spiritual and religious groups compete to offer destinations or excursions to America's spiritual pilgrims.

The individuals who joined Heaven's Gate were all spiritual seekers, but they hailed from a diverse range of locations within the American spiritual marketplace. In journalist James S. Phelan's interviews with members and ex-members, he found a diverse range of individuals. One man joined Heaven's Gate because of a longtime fascination with UFOs, another called herself a lifelong spiritual seeker, a third was raised Catholic, but trekked across the country to find the group and described it as the "first time in my life [that] I have a firm faith that there is something higher."[19] Others included an agnostic who experimented with hallucinogenic drugs and looked for meaning in the stars, and a Jewish seeker from New York who had journeyed to Israel and India to try *kibbutzim* (communes), drugs, and gurus. Phelan summarized his subjects as sharing "one common denominator among almost all the converts. Almost all are seekers . . . They have spent years, in the trite phase, 'trying to find themselves.' Many have tried Scientology, yoga, Zen, offbeat cults, hallucinogens, hypnosis, tarot cards and astrology. Almost all believe in psychic phenomena."[20] Years later, an analysis of the thirty-nine members who committed suicide in 1997 revealed that little had changed. While they hailed from different places, social locales, and generations, the majority of members had long histories of spiritual exploration.[21]

Yet it would be a mistake to assume that all the individuals who joined Heaven's Gate were hippies. Several were quite well-to-do, and comfortably middle class. John Craig (Lggody, as he was called within the group), who joined in summer 1975 and remained with the group until the suicides, was a successful land developer and former Republican candidate for Colorado's House of Representatives. His business colleagues described him as "the last guy in the world you'd think would do a thing like this," "an ideal businessman with no problems," and "having perhaps the finest family in town."[22] In the case of Craig, looks were obviously deceiving. While not demonstrating any of the usual characteristics of a spiritual seeker, Craig clearly was. A family friend introduced him to members of Heaven's Gate and he left to join the group shortly thereafter.[23] Craig remained with the group until the end. A post-suicide tabulation published by the *New York Times* showed that several members, like Craig, came from the upper social strata of America, including the daughter of a judge and a child of a major telephone company executive.[24] As Roof noted, spiritual seekers belonged to all of America's religions, not just the alternative ones or counterculture. Historian James Hudnut-Beumler has traced a rich tradition of subtle resistance against the "religion of the American dream" throughout the 1950s and 1960s, emblemized by individuals such as Kerouac and the other beatniks. While Craig and others joined Heaven's Gate a decade later, Hudnut-Beumler's contention still holds that even white middle-class conservative American Christians longed for meaning in a variety of ways, inside and outside of the conventional churches.[25] Robert S. Ellwood made a similar set of claims in his study of the mainstream American religion of the suburbs, finding an "underground religious economy" of beatniks, UFO enthusiasts, and monastics.[26] No shortage of options for alternative religious questing existed, and Heaven's Gate fit within that cultural world.

Those who joined Heaven's Gate had generally experimented with other new or alternative religions previously. In her study of the Unification Church, another new religious movement from this era, sociologist Eileen Barker found massive defection rates and a revolving door of converts and apostates. A little more than half the members who joined were still members a year later, and more than two-thirds had left within four years. In terms of those who had merely attended a meeting of this new religion and not actually joined, less than half a percent of individuals who visited the Unification Church center Barker studied were affiliated with the group two years later.[27] Evidence from scholars who have studied other NRMs parallels Barker's results, revealing high levels of defection.[28] In many cases, individuals bounce from one group to another, becoming serial converts.[29] Clearly, numerous members of

Heaven's Gate had been involved in other new religious movements, sectarian groups, and alternative living experiments, ranging from communes to alternative food practices to membership in actual new religious movements. The vast majority of people who attended informational meetings hosted by Heaven's Gate and who even joined the group left the movement, but those who stayed found what they had been looking for in their spiritual quest.

Heaven's Gate promised a chance for a way out of the endless revolving doors of spiritual seeking. Certainly the movement's theology did not appeal to everyone. Despite the fact that in its early days the founders exerted little control and made few actual demands, its theology demanded exclusivism, and the religious practices Applewhite and Nettles required were puritanical—avoidance of sex, drugs, alcohol, and recreation. Yet for individuals who sought spiritual answers, enough found Heaven's Gate appealing that they joined. Once they did so, they located themselves in a movement that both assumed and challenged the popular elements of the spiritual quest and the cultic milieu. Heaven's Gate accepted the premise of the spiritual quest and valorized the search for spiritual knowledge, but it also curtailed it and offered a ready-made answer to the questions raised by the quest.

Post-1970s Converts

Heaven's Gate had a relatively unique historical trajectory in terms of proselytizing and membership. While leaders and members of the group actively evangelized in the first formative years of the movement's history, they ceased seeking converts in the spring of 1976 and generally refrained from proselytizing during the group's remaining twenty-year history. They emerged from their self-imposed seclusion only five times during that time: in 1988 when the movement's members produced a booklet that they mailed to various New Age centers; in 1991–92 when they produced a series of satellite television broadcasts; in 1993–94 when the movement placed a national newspaper advertisement and once again began active proselytizing through a series of nationwide meetings; and in 1997 shortly before the mass suicides when the group used the Internet to try to reach potential converts. New members joined during each of these periods with the exception of the 1988 effort (see table 2.1). Because they converted during a social period quite different from the mid-1970s, their individual trajectories into Heaven's Gate deserve additional attention.

Ten of the thirty-nine individuals who belonged to Heaven's Gate at the time of the suicides had joined during these recent periods of the group's evangelization: Of these, all but three of the more recent converts either contributed to the movement's anthology or produced Exit Videos—videotaped farewell notes that all but four members created—to publicly state their views and beliefs about the group. These seven converts who left their own words about having joined in the 1990s—the earliest in 1991 and the latest in 1996, just six months before the suicides—tell tales of religious exploration and increasing frustration with an inability to find religious fulfillment until discovering Heaven's Gate.

Tddody—members of Heaven's Gate took new six-letter names ending on "-ody," as discussed and analyzed in chapter 5[30]—offers an interesting case of an individual who joined the movement in its first years, left, and then rejoined in the 1990s. As to the first experience that drew him into the group, Tddody describes it as a type of fate. "I first came in contact with Ti and Do (my Teachers) in the mid-70s at a meeting in California. At that meeting, things occurred that in no way could be called coincidence. As Do spoke, questions would come to mind, and as I would think the question, Do would say something like, 'Some may wonder about . . . ' and state the question I was thinking. When this occurred, I felt as if I were in a tunnel with Do at one end and me at the other. Although I sat in the back of a packed auditorium, it was is [sic] if no one else were there, but He (Do) and His Older Member (Ti) and myself."[31] Tddody joined and spent three years in the movement before leaving.

Tddody also emphasized fate in telling the story of his reentry into Heaven's Gate. "In October of 1994, I was guided by the grace of the Next Level into a 'chance meeting' with my former classmates, and I expressed my sincere and earnest desire to re-enter the class," he explained.[32] But Tddody also described his disgust at the broader world and a narrative of pain and disillusionment as driving him away from conventional living and toward spiritual seeking. "While in the world, I had tasted success and found it to be very rude, mean, aggressive, and quite abrasive and distasteful—'qualities' I have no wish to enhance or develop. I have seen the world through a thousand pairs of eyes and despised it each and every time—without exception!" Continuing, Tddody indicates that "In the world, I'd been harassed, beat up, lied to, cheated, threatened, robbed, and abused in almost every way thinkable."[33] Clearly Tddody considered his time away from Heaven's Gate at best a learning experience and negative reference, and at worst a sort of hellish nightmare.

Tddody also indicated that he had tried many different spiritual paths in the intervening years since he first met the founders of Heaven's Gate. "I've been down many different paths . . . I've tried it all and nothing worked," he explained in his Exit Video. Tddody intentionally avoided discussing the alternative approaches he tried in the time before returning to the movement, referring to that period as "time wasted . . . walking down paths that were dead ends." This pattern repeated in the narratives of the other recent converts to Heaven's Gate, most of whom described a life of questioning, exploration, and seeking before joining Heaven's Gate, but (intentionally?) omitting the description of what sort of spiritual pursuits they had tried.

Qstody, who takes his religious name within Heaven's Gate from the word "quest" and the idea of being on a spiritual quest, offered nearly the same assessment as Tddody. He offered a bleak assessment of his life before joining the movement, describing a spiritual journey that had resulted in frustration rather than elucidation, and specifically critiqued the various religious options outside the movement as "[l]ike programmed puppets worshipping false myths, rituals, futile belief systems and counterfeit fantasy gods. I felt angry, alienated, hopeless, incomplete and utterly unsatisfied in this world no matter what I tried. Many times I could barely keep from going into a complete coma, trying to stay awake enough to muster a desperate constant prayer, to keep my hope and motivation alive in this space alien HELL."[34] The theme of alienation and living in an alien world emerge most forcefully, and especially ironically, since members of Heaven's Gate sought extraterrestrial salvation. But their belief system emphasized that maleficent space aliens actually controlled human society, and hence Qstody found in Heaven's Gate a worldview that explained his deep sense of alienation as entirely appropriate and proper. In fact, Heaven's Gate reinforced this sense of alienation by offering to Qstody a vision of himself transcending the world and rejecting the human condition.

The spiritual quest emerges as a commonality among most of the converts from the 1990s. Like Tddody, Qstody did not specify what sort of spiritual pursuits he followed before joining Heaven's Gate, though he did describe his efforts generally as "constant asking long before I entered the class [which] was the key . . . the constant begging for the real facts, the real truth."[35] Gldody, a member who had joined only three years before the suicides, similarly explained that he had been "searching for a long time" before Tllody first introduced him to the group through some posters and fliers.[36] Wknody, a 1994 convert, also did not indicate the details of her spiritual quest, but described her previous life as a growth experience preparing her and culminating in her eventual encounter with Heaven's Gate. "I [had] more lessons to learn in order to meet the requirements needed to graduate from this human kingdom to the Next Level," she explained of her life before joining the movement.[37]

Of the recent converts, only Yrsody gives any indication of the sort of spiritual pursuits and religious quests in which she participated before joining Heaven's Gate. While she avoided any mention of such topics in her Exit Video, her written statement made frequent mention of her rejection of "cosmic consciousness," the "new age," "meditation, mantras, and many other [meditation] techniques," and various forms of channeling. Yrsody's familiarity with meditative approaches and the various channeling techniques indicate her likely previous association with such spiritual pursuits. Her explicit description of the manner in which channelers access spirits and her rejection of it as dangerous because such "disincarnate spirits" posed significant spiritual and psychological harm indicate that she was at least highly fluent with New Age religious pursuits, if not an active participant.[38] One can safely infer that Yrsody had explored various New Age spiritual pursuits including channeling and Asian-derived practices before she joined Heaven's Gate.

Although not among the thirty-nine adherents who ended their terrestrial lives in Rancho Santa Fe, a Heaven's Gate member named Gbbody offers another example of the trajectory in—and in his case, out—of the group. Gbbody joined in 1993 after reading one of the group's newspaper advertisements. His sister remembers Gbbody as introverted yet curious, and Gbbody had previously explored topics including Wicca, Gnosticism, ufology, Buddhism, American transcendentalism, and science fiction. He claimed to have seen a UFO as a child.[39] He joined the movement after corresponding with members, flying to Texas to rendezvous with them shortly after Christmas. There he found individuals who shared the same interests and passions, including the same spiritual topics. But more than spiritual connection, Gbbody found a sense of belonging in Heaven's Gate. His sister reflects, "I could hear the increased awareness and communication skills in the words he chose. I also heard the strong feelings for the cult that was his chosen family, and the struggle to find his own life."[40]

Gbbody left the movement because he felt he could not live up to the demands of his fellows in Heaven's Gate. Yet the attraction to the movement and the sense of belonging remained. In Gbbody's own words, written shortly after departing the group in 1995, "But more than anything else they were my family. I loved them dearly. We were a tight group. Leaving was the hardest thing I've ever done. I miss them greatly."[41] Here we see the same combination of forces that drew other converts into the movement: a search for meaning and identity, but in Gbbody's case an even stronger need to find a spiritual community in which he belonged. Two months after the Heaven's Gate suicides Gbbody took his own life, seeking to join his coreligionists in the Next Level.[42]

What then can we say about the individuals who (re-)joined Heaven's Gate almost two decades after it began, nearly all of whom never had an opportunity to meet the movement's co-founder? In terms of their religious journeys into the movement, very little distinguished those individuals from the first wave of converts in the 1970s. All members had engaged in forms of spiritual exploration and the spiritual quest, in at least one case (and probably more) participating in the same sort of New Age spiritual pursuits though separated by two decades. The picture that emerges of converts to Heaven's Gate is that of spiritual seekers who had become frustrated by their many pursuits, rejected the various alternatives within the existing religious marketplace, and in turn had begun to reject the very nature of human earthly society. Heaven's Gate offered a literal escape from this atmosphere.

Brainwashing and Bounded Choice

Just three years after Tddody, Qstody, and Yrsody joined Heaven's Gate, the movement ended in the mass suicides of its members when the adherents and leader of Heaven's Gate abandoned what they considered a corrupted broken Earth to seek salvation in the stars. In the immediate aftermath of the discovery of the bodies in Rancho Santa Fe, the news media characterized Heaven's Gate members as "brainwashed." Perhaps the most explicit description, since it invoked the original cinematic imagery of brainwashing that subsequently flavored all use of the word, came from literature and arts critic Frank Rich. He opined in the otherwise staid *New York Times* that Heaven's Gate members were the victims of "psychological coercion achieved through isolation and sensory deprivation," and likened them to "a brainwashing victim in 'The Manchurian Candidate.'"[43] Rich's *Manchurian Candidate* reference points to a 1959 book and 1962 movie that describes a psychologically conditioned soldier kidnapped and brainwashed by Communists, then released as a sleeper agent to destabilize American society. In popular religious culture, the reference alludes to the image of the brainwashed victim as a passive object of destructive mind control, and was a staple of Cold War stereotypes of American defectors to Communism as well as countercultural youth who had become involved in new religions. This sort of rhetoric discounts the entire notion of religious conversion and why a person would join a group like Heaven's Gate by offering a ready-made answer: they were duped and psychologically manipulated.

Brainwashing offers a simple explanation for why people would engage in religious practices and accept religious beliefs that the majority of Americans consider bizarre or invalid. Looking at other examples of how journalists and members of the public employ the term "brainwashing," it generally functions to distance the subjects of the term from broader society and explain their non-normative behavior. In their study of the phenomenon, sociologists Thomas Robbins, Dick Anthony, and James McCarthy found that the idea of brainwashing was a "social weapon" used by critics of new religious movements, rather than a concept rooted in any empirical evidence.[44] Robbins, Anthony, and McCarthy go so far as to accuse advocates of brainwashing of "legitimating repression" through their bias against new religions.[45] While striking a far less accusatory tone, historian Sean McCloud has noted that descriptions of brainwashing within media sources served as means of exerting social control, labeling which groups ought to be considered legitimate and which illegitimate. McCloud notes that the claim of brainwashing served to mark authentic from unauthentic religion with special reference to race—groups led by Asian leaders that drew white American converts were especially likely to be seen as brainwashing, though by the time of the Jonestown deaths in 1977, the trope of brainwashing had come to extend across the racial divide.[46]

Brainwashing certainly makes it easier for families to understand why their loved ones joined a group like Heaven's Gate, since it makes the members victims instead of adherents. It also provides a rhetorical tool for ex-members who were embarrassed or ashamed of their former membership in such a group, since it abrogates them of any responsibility for their past actions. Research into the rhetoric of brainwashing shows that this is precisely how individuals use the concept—as a means of transferring responsibility from the adherents of a group to the leaders. It functions on a rhetorical level to delegitimize new religions such as Heaven's Gate. James T. Richardson, one of the foremost scholars of new religions and the law, notes that the term functions as a powerful metaphor in precisely this way:

> "Brainwashing" is a metaphor, but has become a powerful social weapon to use against unpopular groups or other entities which are attempting to recruit participants. It is impossible to wash someone's brain, of course, but the term has come to refer to any form of disfavored persuasion. The concept is the antithesis of agency and volition, and assumes that individuals can be tricked or persuaded by some magical psychological techniques to literally change their minds if not their basic personality.[47]

Brainwashing as a rhetorical tool therefore functions as a powerful tool in assuaging public anxieties over the legitimacy of new religions by effectively limiting the need to take them seriously. In the case of Heaven's Gate this need was particularly acute, since religious suicide is deeply threatening to the social order. Brainwashing also functions as a ready-made explanation for family and friends of those who joined the group, excusing their actions on the grounds that they were not really in control of themselves.

Useful as it may be rhetorically, the concept of brainwashing has lost all academic credibility. The clearest refutation of brainwashing derives from Eileen Barker's longitudinal study of the Unification Church, a movement often accused of brainwashing. As already noted, Barker found that the movement she studied failed to successfully recruit the vast majority of individuals with which it came into contact, and that many who did join eventually left. In her interviews with prospective, current, and former members of the Unification Church, Barker found no evidence of brainwashing, but rather a small group of individuals who sought what Barker calls "freedom in a cage," a sense of spiritual fulfillment achieved by joining a strict and insular religious group.[48] The numbers in Heaven's Gate support this perspective. Hundreds joined the group and most left, with all but three of the first group of converts having abandoned the movement. Only thirty-eight (plus Applewhite) remained, with several more having left the movement in the months preceding the suicide itself. Since 1989, the Society for the Scientific Study of Religion, American Sociological Association, and American Psychiatric Association have all officially gone on record rejecting any sort of scientific claims as to the validity of brainwashing. Richardson notes that American courts consider the concept pseudoscientific and that the U.S. legal system has rejected its validity both in criminal cases (*U.S. v. Fishman* [743 F. Supp., N.D. Cal., 1990]) and civil cases (*Green and Ryan v. Maharishi Mahesh Yogi et al.* [US District Court, Washington, DC, 13 March 1991, Case #87-0015 OG]).[49]

In addition to failing on empirical grounds, brainwashing fails on a fundamental level of logic: it is circular. Proponents of this doomed theory have proffered numerous attempts to define brainwashing, yet all attempts to create distinctions between brainwashing and routine religious conversion are entirely subjective and therefore dependent on the perspective of the outside observer. As J. Gordon Melton has indicated, these attempts to define brainwashing lack scientific rigor and are seldom presented in a scholarly peer-reviewed forum. Distilling the various approaches of delineating brainwashing, Melton summarizes the brainwashing paradigm as it is popularly conceived as "that people are put into a hyper-suggestible altered state of consciousness through hypnosis, drugs, debilitation or other means, and then their worldviews are transformed against their wills through conditioning techniques."[50] Yet determining what is or is not against one's will—especially when the 'victim' claims not to be brainwashed and acting within their own free will—is impossible. Nor is there any clear distinction between "hyper-suggestible states" and normal human credulity (some might say gullibility). Fundamentally, one cannot distinguish a victim of brainwashing from any other sort of religious believer without first knowing whether the person was brainwashed! While the vast majority of people—including myself—find the message of Heaven's Gate unconvincing and its final religious acts appalling, our own psychological or even spiritual discomfort does not provide a good enough reason to simply assume that its members were brainwashed.

Bounded Choice and Heaven's Gate

Several proponents of a revived academic theory of brainwashing have offered new formulations of the concept. Such attempts have resulted in a great deal of controversy within the field of the study of new religious movements, and very few scholars within the subfield have entertained such revivals of what specialists consider a flawed and inherently biased concept. Yet one attempt to craft a modified reformulation of brainwashing bears direct relevance for the study of Heaven's Gate. This is Janja Lalich's concept of "bounded choice," a form of psychological entrapment related to the classic idea of brainwashing. Lalich offers her formulation of this concept in an eponymously named book, and in fact she focuses on Heaven's Gate as one of the two case studies supporting her theory. In Lalich's assessment, Heaven's Gate members represent an example of such bounded choice. Its members lived within a "self-sealing" system wherein they experienced only an illusion of choice, and in fact had become entrapped by the charisma, beliefs, and social controls of the movement. As such, their choices had become bound to the group and its charismatic leader, resulting in their inability to make any choice other than suicide in 1997. This is a somewhat darker version of Barker's idea of the freedom of the cage, with the added idea that the cage is actually and not only metaphorically locked.

Lalich's approach does not really consider why members converted. Rather it focuses on why members stayed, which marks her approach as distinct from the older brainwashing approaches. That is, the bounded choice model presupposes membership and adherence within a group before it can explain why individuals acted as they did. Lalich does not claim that members of the movement were duped, deluded, or manipulated into joining the movement, which marks her approach as far more nuanced than earlier brainwashing theories. This approach therefore does not answer the question posed by this chapter of why people joined Heaven's Gate. Yet it does attempt to answer the related question of why they stayed, and therefore merits consideration.

The concept of charismatic commitment functions as the core of the bounded choice concept. According to Lalich, charismatic commitment exists as a state wherein members of a group centered on a charismatic leader or leaders exhibit "a fusion between the ideal of personal freedom (as promised in the stated goal of the group or its ideology) and the demand for self-renunciation (as prescribed by the rules and norms)," with the result that "the believer becomes a 'true believer' at the service of a charismatic leader or ideology."[51] Adherents demonstrating charismatic commitment willingly perform actions that otherwise they would not, and engage in practices and hold beliefs that outsiders would consider irrational or bizarre. Lalich notes as examples beliefs such as claims of raising the dead, polygamy, and terrorism.[52] For members of the movements predicated on charismatic commitment—groups defined by Lalich as cults—the only true choices present are whether to accept and obey the instructions and requirements of their group, or to leave. Yet even departure may be difficult, for Lalich indicates that leaders exert psychological pressure on their followers to stay, and have configured their belief and social systems to discourage defection.

Lalich emphasizes a sort of role-oriented maintenance of beliefs and membership, a set of assumptions and practices by which adherents of groups like Heaven's Gate come to believe that they must follow a strict set of guidelines and cannot deviate from them. As Lalich explains,

> To be a participant in the group means playing by the rules; and in such groups, there is only one set of rules, or rather only one set of rules that matters. Once a person "chooses" to stay in the group, the impermeable, albeit invisible, confines of the structure do not allow for the possibility to "act otherwise" in any significant sense— unless, of course, the person leaves the group.[53]

Within Heaven's Gate, one can find numerous such rules. Most of them appear quite early in the movement's history, and exist in written forms in the documents that Applewhite and Nettles produced in the late 1970s. These include prohibitions against sex, drugs, entertainment, and various other activities associated with the human level rather than the Next Level. As Lalich points out, individuals who chose to join and stay within Heaven's Gate accepted the validity and value of these rules, and saw no possibility of acting outside them. Yet I do not quite understand Lalich's use of scare quotes around "chooses" or "act[ing] otherwise," nor the claim that these various rules were in some way invisible. Those who chose to join Heaven's Gate knew exactly what such rules entailed. The group's 1977 statements that they distributed to potential members *before joining* included instructions to leave behind one's humanity, abandon one's family, give away all of one's possessions, and avoid all human qualities. The third statement explicitly notes that members will not engage in any forms of affection, sex, or vocation.[54] Those who attended the recruitment meetings reported that the founders insisted on a puritanical set of behavioral guidelines. Potential members who joined in the 1980s and 1990s were provided an explicit set of rules that noted restrictions against everything from reliance on one's own mind (rather than the Next Level mind), putting oneself first, or criticizing the other members or leaders of the movement.[55] Members entered a highly regimented system of social control, but they did not only appear to "choose" (as indicated by Lalich's scare quotes), they really did choose.

Lalich argues that these behavioral restrictions resulted in a sense of bounded choice wherein members felt they could not act other than the ways in which their leaders wanted. Members lived within a sort of forced membership within a group predicated on psychological control and manipulation. As Lalich indicates: "it is my contention that the combination of a transcendent belief system, an all-encompassing system of interlocking structural and social controls, and a highly charged charismatic relationship between leader(s) and adherents results in a self-sealing system that exacts a high degree of commitment (as well as expressions of that commitment) from its core members."[56] To put Lalich's approach into simple and direct language as it relates to Heaven's Gate: members believed that one cannot achieve salvation apart from the religious system that Nettles and Applewhite taught, and that the only means by which they could achieve their goals of transcending human existence were to follow the strictures set forth by the Heaven's Gate religious system. They accepted their leaders as offering a form of charismatic leadership that one could not challenge, and that only through Applewhite and Nettles could one achieve communion with the Next Level. They therefore followed them unconditionally.

Lalich's approach of bounded choice offers some guidance in understanding why members of Heaven's Gate remained within a group that made strong demands on them, and in fact eventually demanded their suicides. Her approach has merit because it does help indicate how members would have conceived of their own choices as free but also limited, as something akin to Barker's "freedom of the cage." While I think Lalich is wrong to imply that members were somehow duped into this belief, I concur that as a result of their choices, adherents would have considered leaving the movement to be an act of spiritual suicide. Yet we must remember that some members *did* leave the group, and that the movement lost adherents throughout its history. While choices within Heaven's Gate may have been bounded, choices still existed, and individuals such as Neoody, Swyody, Srfody, Mrcody, and Crlody not only chose to leave the group but are still actively discussing and disagreeing with each other about the true nature of Heaven's Gate a decade and a half after the suicides.[57] Each of these individuals not only chose to leave but chose particular strands of beliefs and practices within Heaven's Gate on which to base their religious lives outside of the movement.[58]

Lalich's brush paints a broad stroke. Everyone's choices are bound, and the sort of psychological self-limitation that she describes exists equally within the confines of nearly every religious movement, especially those demanding adherence to a set of ethical or behavioral guidelines. One can equally well apply bounded choice to describe membership in a Catholic monastery or convent, adherence to forms of Protestant fundamentalism requiring obedience to strict moral codes, Orthodox or Ultra-Orthodox Judaism, and a variety of forms of conservative Islam. In each of these cases, members believe in transcendental belief systems, strict social controls, charged relationships with charismatic leaders, and totalistic systems requiring high levels of commitment. As Lalich describes, they even subscribe to beliefs that outsiders consider bizarre. Tellingly, Lalich notes that individuals affected by bounded choice believe such bizarre claims as the raising of the dead, or the legitimacy of polygamy. Yet nearly every form of Christianity accepts the validity of the various stories of Christ's miracles, including his raising of a dead man named Lazarus—not to mention the Resurrection itself! Similarly, proponents of Judaism, Christianity, and Islam have all upheld the validity of polygamy at various points. Such claims and practices are bizarre only from the perspective of those outside the religious communities that hold or perform them. Bounded choice affects all religious believers. While one can certainly adopt Lalich's perspective to explain why members of Heaven's Gate stayed within this strict religious system that ultimately called for the laying down of their terrestrial lives, a much simpler answer is even more evident: they believed it. The rest of this book considers why.

3

The Religious Worldview of Heaven's Gate

In the immediate hours after the discovery of the bodies of Heaven's Gate's adherents in Rancho Santa Fe, the news media began a frenzy of producing copy. The sheer oddness of the suicides—the uniforms, the incongruity of mass death in an exclusive gated community, the media-savvy way that the group had left behind a web page and videotapes—attracted international media attention. The vast majority of the articles that the media quickly spun out attempted to frame or characterize the religious beliefs and practices promulgated by Applewhite and the members of Heaven's Gate. Yet this was no easy task. Even scholars debate the extent to which Heaven's Gate represented a religion predicated on the New Age, Christianity, ufology, or science fiction. Media reports generally conglomerated all these influences together. To consider only one example, that of the major American newsweekly *Newsweek*, its journalists depicted Heaven's Gate as a "strange brew of Christian theology, castration, science fiction, belief in UFOs and mastery of the Internet," "a delusional cocktail of just about every religious tradition and New Age escapist fantasy," and a "farrago of early-Christian heresy and 1970s-era science fiction."[1] The magazine's full-length article on the beliefs of members introduced its subject as "a bit of everything, from the Gospels to science fiction to Eastern mysticism. Inside their twisted theology [was] an odd mixture of Biblical apocalypse, New Age mysticism and science fiction."[2] While journalists associated with more staid outfits such as the *Los Angeles Times* or *New York Times* wrote less sensationalistic descriptions, their inability to pigeonhole the beliefs held by members of Heaven's Gate percolated through their articles. The *Los Angeles Times* characterized the group as possessing a "complex theology and strident beliefs . . . a synthesis of ancient and modern religious themes, mixing space-age images with biblical citations in a quest for salvation," and invoked everything from present-day Christianity to *Star Wars* to ancient Gnosticism to explain the group.[3]

Yet the beliefs and theology of Heaven's Gate did not represent, in *Newsweek's* words, "a bit of everything." Nor did its sources include "just about every religious tradition." (Whether it was delusional is of course a matter of perspective.) Heaven's Gate emerged out of two theological worlds: Evangelical Christianity and the New Age movement, particularly the element of the New Age movement concerned with alien visitations and extraterrestrial contact. The movement's leaders and members certainly drew from a broad array of influences, including secular ufology, science fiction, and conspiracy theories, in addition to their religious influences. Yet ultimately the group's theology was a Christian one, as read through a New Age interpretive lens.

This chapter looks to what scholars of religion call the worldview of Heaven's Gate. A direct translation of the German concept *Weltanschauung*, a worldview encapsulates the basic approaches and assumptions that an individual or group of individuals bring to how they perceive and understand the natural and social cosmos in which they live. Scholars of religion have made extensive use of the concept, with Ninian Smart's treatise on the world's religions as worldviews perhaps the best known example.[4] Scholars have employed the concept of worldviews to consider topics ranging from African Christian communities to Asian Buddhists to postmodern theology.

Religious studies scholar Gregory R. Peterson argues that religious worldviews possess three characteristics: they are fundamental, meaning that those who accept them consider them centrally important and relevant; they are explanatory, giving meaning to the surrounding cosmos; and they are global, meaning they encompass all of existence. Peterson calls these religious worldviews "orienting" and "normative," meaning that they root individuals in their visions of the world and that individuals use them to make judgments and value considerations of that world.[5] The worldview of Heaven's Gate functioned precisely in this way, providing a means by which members understood and interpreted the world around them, rooted themselves in a livable cosmos, and made value judgments about their world. Another way to consider this idea of worldview is through social theorist Pierre Bourdieu's idea of *habitus*, what he calls "a lasting, generalized and transposable disposition to act and think in conformity with the principles of a (quasi) systemic view of the world and human existence."[6] For Bourdieu, habitus is the socially constructed world of meaning, value, and order. Like Peterson's approach, Bourdieu's notion of habitus stresses a set of meanings and values that transcend specific doctrinal belief statements and imbue individuals' ways of looking at the world around them. Both worldview and habitus describe the pre-cognitive assumptions and approaches that characterize how persons try to make the world around themselves livable. As I use it, the concept of worldview envelops that of habitus, since it not only includes the meanings and values of a community but also how they use those values to contextualize, understand, and relate to the world around them.

Postmodern Pastiche

Before considering the elements and influence of the habitus or worldview of members of Heaven's Gate, one must consider its influences, sources, and characteristics. Hugh Urban, in one of the first academic studies produced on Heaven's Gate after the 1997 suicides, argued that this new religious movement represented "the ultimate postmodern pastiche and the idea of spirituality for the age of hypertext."[7] Urban is not a scholar of Heaven's Gate itself, and some of his characterizations of the group are not correct—notably, the group was not a "technological, on-line religion," as Urban states; in fact it came to the Internet very late in its history—yet his overall assessment offers some value to understanding how the leaders and members of Heaven's Gate assembled their religious worldview.[8] According to Urban, Applewhite and Nettles—and presumably the group's adherents—constructed their theology through a process of pastiche (creating a medley of various components), drawing from multiple sources to construct a meaningful theological worldview. These included Protestant Christianity, ufology, contemporary theosophical thinking, science fiction, and New Age mysticism.

Urban is fundamentally correct that the contemporary United States—what he characterizes as the postmodern capitalist world—enables and ennobles the sort of processes of pastiche that defined the theological work and worldview of Heaven's Gate's founders and members. Individualism, consumption, and technology have created a world wherein pastiche defines culture. Personal choice in terms of religion and a capitalist-derived emphasis on consumption combine to permit the sort of religious borrowing that characterizes religious pastiches. Just as consumers purchase jeans at one retailer, shirts at another retailer, and accents drawn from fashion and technology—ranging from purses to iPods—from other retailers, so too do religious consumers draw from multiple sources in the construction of their religious worlds. This is true far outside of the world of new religious movements. Adherents of one of the fastest growing sectors in American religion during the era that Heaven's Gate emerged, Evangelical Christians, borrow theology from different denominations, social patterns from different eras of Christian history, and practices that originate in medieval Christianity, turn-of-the century America, and even other world religions, e.g., "Christian yoga."[9]

In fact, pastiche is not particularly new in religion, though Heaven's Gate may represent a heightened form of it. Throughout religious history such pastiche has defined how new religions create and foster new cultures. To take just one example, early Christian leaders adopted elements from Pagan and Roman winter holidays—generally occurring just before the winter solstice—and fashioned the Christian holiday of Christmas, while simultaneously drawing from Jewish traditions as well.[10] Art historians have linked Christian iconography with Egyptian and Greek traditions, and certainly some early Christian traditions mirror those of Greco-Roman mystery religions.[11] Northern European Yule traditions shaped the eventual cultural practices of Christmas. Analogous examples of pastiche exist for all the other major religions of the world in addition to Christianity, most notably the evangelizing religions of Buddhism and Islam that seek to adopt local practices and adapt them to the spread of the new religion. Pastiche seems a basic fact of religious operation rather than something unique to postmodern American culture.

Urban envisions Heaven's Gate as predicated on such practices of pastiche. "I would suggest Heaven's Gate be regarded as a specially late capitalist or postmodern religion—a religion not simply containing elements of syncretism of religious borrowing, but one essentially founded on the art of pastiche and the free-wheeling appropriation of a remarkably wide diversity of religious and cultural artifacts."[12] In Urban's reading, the founders of Heaven's Gate self-consciously drew from a variety of religious traditions in producing the theology of Heaven's Gate. He sees this process as fundamental to the movement, and wide in scope. While Urban is correct in noting the presence of pastiche, it would be wrong to argue that admixture represented the sole operating principle at work as the leaders and members of Heaven's Gate developed their theology. Pastiche represents the process, not the principle. The principle is that of hermeneutics, or interpretation. As I will argue later in this chapter, Heaven's Gate developed a hermeneutical approach founded on a set of principles drawn from ufology and the New Age, but it applied this interpretive framework to Christian sources. Urban's approach is valuable in that it indicates the place of combinativeness, but one must not read too much into that process. Applewhite and Nettles were quite careful in choosing the sources from which they drew and how they used them. It was not a "free-wheeling appropriation." Rather, the idea that truths existed in multiple sources and that religion exists as a form of pastiche served as one of the assumptions within the Heaven's Gate worldview. It was not so much a principle or intention as it was an assumption.

That being said, something about American culture in the 1970s and 1980s—when Heaven's Gate emerged and grew—made the membership in new religious movements and the production of religious pastiche particularly apt. Postmodernity does provide part of the answer. As George D. Chryssides has argued in his study of Heaven's Gate, the movement possessed several fundamental features of postmodernity. He notes that the movement engaged in an eclectic combinativeness, piecing together elements of various sources without any apparent interest in producing a systematized academic theology. "Consistent with postmodernity, there were no grand theories to explain or legitimate, or inherent connections between the disparate ideas, only fragments blended together."[13] Chryssides is entirely correct that Heaven's

Gate functioned in this manner, and that Applewhite and Nettles some-what spontaneously produced new aspects of their theology predicated on bricolage rather than rigorous empirical or positivist study. Apple-white did not learn Greek so as to better understand the New Testa-ment, for example, and neither did the members study astronomy so as to better understand the physics of space travel.

Postmodern bricolage is in fact a growing aspect of American reli-gious culture, and while Heaven's Gate represented a radical form of such, it was quite representative. In some ways it foreshadowed what was to come in the decade that followed. The Pew Forum's 2009 study of American religious life revealed that Americans combine a variety of Christian, New Age, Asian, and quasi-scientific positions in their self-conceived theologies. For example, 29 percent of Americans (both Christians and non-Christians) believe they have communicated with the dead, 18 percent claim to have seen a ghost, and 15 percent have consulted a psychic. Among self-professing Christians, the numbers are nearly the same, with 17 percent claiming to have seen a ghost and 14 percent having visited a psychic. Clearly, American Christians have no trouble combining elements of Spiritualism in its classic sense—com-municating with the dead and ghosts—with their spiritual practices and activities. When it comes to beliefs, American Christians reveal the same predilection for combinativeness, with 23 percent believing in the presence of spiritual energy in trees, the same percentage believing in astrology, and 17 percent believing in the evil eye. One in five Ameri-can Christians accept reincarnation and believe that yoga can be a spiri-tual practice, showing that in their religious pastiches, such individu-als draw from not only the Western occult tradition but Asian religious traditions as well.[14] In some cases, Americans look to new religions that explicitly combine these disparate beliefs within a single religious tradi-tion, as opposed to creating their own. Demographer Barry Kosmin's 2008 American Religious Identification Survey (ARIS) survey showed a small but growing number of Americans looking to such traditions, with just over 2.8 million Americans identifying with a new religious movement in the most recent 2008 survey, versus 1.3 million in 1990. Such new religions—Kosmin provided a few examples, such as Eckan-kar, Scientology, Druidism, and the Rastafari—follow the same patterns of religious pastiche as Heaven's Gate.[15]

While the Pew Forum and ARIS surveys pointed to religious culture in the decade following the demise of Heaven's Gate, the 1970s and
1980s were no different. During this era religious seekers flocked to new
and alternative religions. Sociologists Charles Y. Glock and Robert N.
Bellah labeled this "the new religious consciousness," and rooted in it
an extension of the counterculture of the 1960s. For Glock and Bellah, this new religious consciousness represented a rejection of mainstream American religion and an embracing of alternatives rooted in
Asian, esoteric, political, or psychological traditions.[16] Fellow sociologists and specialists in the study of new religions Dick Anthony and
Thomas Robbins similarly noted "new patterns of religious pluralism"
born of new and alternative religions. They understood these new religions as emerging from the ferment of American culture. "The growth
of nontraditional new religions and quasi-religious therapies is taking
place in the context of a broader challenge to American society. Various
factors—Vietnam, Watergate, increasing structural differentiation of
the public from the private sector—have undermined traditional civil
religion and created a legitimation crisis for the nation."[17] Within this
context, Heaven's Gate offered one among many possible options for
spiritual seekers. Again, seekerhood served as part of the worldview (or
habitus) of the adherents of Heaven's Gate.

Christian or New Age?

Despite the overall level of pastiche present within Heaven's Gate, a
debate exists among scholars over the nature of the group. Some scholars, notably myself, George D. Chryssides, Christopher Partridge, and
Eugene V. Gallagher, envision Heaven's Gate as a fundamentally Christian movement with some New Age elements. Others, including Robert W. Balch and James R. Lewis, understand Heaven's Gate as a New
Age movement that also drew from Christianity, though Balch cautions
that the movement seemed to vacillate and sometimes drew more from
Christian sources.[18] In fact, one must be careful to not draw too sharp
a distinction: New Age groups often incorporate Christian concepts
such as "Christ consciousness" and angels, and contemporary Christian
groups sometimes draw on New Age themes such as positive thinking
and mind cure. Indeed, all of the scholars noted above indicate that

Heaven's Gate blended influences from both the New Age and Christian sources. The question is how and according to what logic.

I argue here that while Heaven's Gate emerged out of both Christian and New Age milieus—as the previous chapter indicated—Applewhite and Nettles ultimately rooted their theology within Evangelical Protestant Christianity. However, they adopted a particular interpretive schema predicated on ufological ideas drawn from the New Age movement. Heaven's Gate was Christian, but read through a New Age lens. Leaning on the idea of worldview, one can understand this position as meaning that the group's fundamental presuppositions and way of interpreting and giving meaning to the world began with Christian assumptions but read these through New Age approaches.

In his "The Evolution of a New Age Cult: From Total Overcomers Anonymous to Death at Heaven's Gate," written shortly after the 1997 suicides, Robert W. Balch sets out the position that the movement was primarily a New Age one that drew from some Christian material. He roots this position in the group's history and the social origin of its converts. Applewhite and Nettles's first major recruitment success came when they attracted the allegiance of Clarence Klug's followers in the Los Angeles area. Though Klug was certainly also eclectic in his approach, his movement encapsulated many of the aspects of the New Age movement. Klug incorporated Western esotericism, Christian mysticism, and Asian influences, but Balch argues that his movement was overall a New Age one. "Students were drawn to Clarence and his teachings for many reasons. . . . Yet diverse as they were, they all belonged to a subculture that today is known as the *New Age movement*."[19] Balch identifies monism—the belief that everything is God—humanism, spiritual seeking, the pursuit of personal growth, and individualism as some of the hallmarks of the New Age movement and Klug's group. Balch argues that Heaven's Gate inherited and continued some of these New Age characteristics after absorbing Klug's movement.

Balch and his co-author David Taylor's earlier work on Heaven's Gate also championed this view of the group as predicated on the New Age, though they used equivalent terms since that moniker was not yet in popular use. Balch and Taylor identify Heaven's Gate as part of the "cultic milieu," "occult social world," and "metaphysical subculture," in their 1977 study.[20] Specifically these two scholars looked to the "social world of the metaphysical seeker" as one way of understanding who joined the movement and why. "Before they joined, members of the UFO cult shared a metaphysical worldview in which reincarnation, disincarnate spirits, psychic powers, lost continents, flying saucers, and ascended masters are taken for granted."[21] That cultic milieu—what today we would call the New Age—defined the religious lives of potential converts, and they brought those expectations with them as they joined Heaven's Gate. In that regard, Balch and Taylor are correct to root the movement within the New Age, though as they note, that meant drawing from some Christian esoteric traditions as well.

James R. Lewis similarly envisions Heaven's Gate as located within the New Age. Looking to the end of the movement's existence, Lewis's "Legitimating Suicide: Heaven's Gate and the New Age Ideology" identifies the movement as fundamentally New Age. Lewis argues that "though not all aspects of Applewhite's theological synthesis were drawn from New Age thinking, most components of the group's overarching worldview were characteristically New Age."[22] He specifies the theosophically oriented idea of Ascended Masters, metaphysical teachings about UFOs, ancient astronaut theories, the idea of "walk-ins" (extra-worldly beings who take over human bodies), the educational metaphor of personal growth, and the out of body experience as specific examples of New Age beliefs within Heaven's Gate. Lewis argues that "though I do not want to downplay the Christian component of their ideological synthesis, it seems clear that the Christian elements were grafted onto a basically New Age matrix."[23] Lewis also identifies the fact that most of the members were drawn from New Age subcultures as supporting his contention.

Lewis and Balch are correct that Heaven's Gate drew most of its adherents from the New Age movement, or the cultic milieu to use the older terminology. They are also correct to note the presence of many New Age beliefs within Heaven's Gate. Despite this, Heaven's Gate was not fundamentally a New Age movement. Here I concur with Partridge and Chryssides, who envision the movement as a Christian one that adopted some New Age elements. Relying on Peterson's approach to worldview, one can understand that the fundamental ways that members of Heaven's Gate explained their surrounding world, oriented themselves within it, and created a sense of norms and values all derived from Christian sources. Yet adherents crafted individual practices, beliefs, and approaches within this worldview from New Age sources.

Historian of religions George D. Chryssides envisions Heaven's Gate as "remarkably Biblical in [its] teachings."[24] Indeed, the movement's founders and leaders cited the Bible in most of their writings, advertisements, public addresses, lectures, and videos. Though the movement's members and founders had many other influences, Chryssides argues that "Applewhite's ideas can largely be accounted for in terms of his idiosyncratic understanding of the Bible."[25] Though it seems counterintuitive, elements of Heaven's Gate such as alien visitations, salvation through UFOs, celibacy and monastic living, and psychic powers all originated in Nettles's and Applewhite's reading of the Bible. As Chryssides points out, Applewhite applied a particular set of interpretive lenses to the biblical text, resulting in a reading at odds with most other Christians. One can look to the Raelian movement, a more recent Christian UFO group, as engaging in a parallel sort of endeavor.[26]

Christopher Partridge, also an historian of religion and culture, similarly understands Heaven's Gate as a Christian movement, and specifically its apocalyptically oriented Protestant sub-current. Partridge correctly argues that the group's theology emerged from premillennial dispensationalism, a form of Christian millennialism that emphasizes specific timetables for the end of the world and follows a specific interpretation of the biblical book of Revelation as promulgated by C. I. Scofield (1843–1921) and most recently popularized by Hal Lindsey (b. 1929). "While drawing on New Age ideas, science fiction, and the contemporary UFO subculture," Partridge explains, Heaven's Gate "needs to be understood primarily as a vernacular and idiosyncratic form of fundamentalist premillennialism."[27] The movement's millennial timetable, vision of heavenly rapture aboard UFOs, and even its predestinarian theology all originate in various Christian theologies drawn from millennial Evangelical Protestant Christianity. While shaped by the New Age movement, Partridge argues that Heaven's Gate was most essentially predicated on conservative Christian ideas.[28]

I agree with Chryssides and Partridge. Heaven's Gate was fundamentally Christian. Its most important theological positions and texts originated in Christianity. Yet Balch and Lewis are also correct when they argue that the movement appealed primarily to individuals drawn from the New Age, and many of the movement's ideas and practices seemed to outsiders to be influenced by the New Age movement, albeit sometimes aspects of the New Age movement that themselves originate from Christian sources. Heaven's Gate read its Christian theology and texts through the lens of the New Age. Because its adherents came from the New Age subculture, they brought their assumptions, approaches, and worldviews with them and used these assumptions—whether intentionally or not—as lenses through which to interpret Christian ideas. Heaven's Gate was Christian, but Christian as read through the New Age. Again, the notions of worldview or habitus help explain why. But in order to consider how a group of bricoleurs could fuse a basically Christian habitus with various elements drawn from different traditions, one must turn to another theoretical approach within religious studies, that of *hermeneutics*.

Extraterrestrial Biblical Hermeneutics

Hermeneutics is the science of interpreting texts (usually sacred texts), and as scholars use the term, a hermeneutic functions as a set of guiding positions used to read, interpret, and analyze such sacred texts. Myriad forms of hermeneutics exist: just within biblical hermeneutics one finds historicist hermeneutics, feminist hermeneutics, existential hermeneutics, and hermeneutics associated with a variety of religious perspectives, such as Jewish hermeneutics or Evangelical Christian hermeneutics. Various hermeneutical methods highlight certain questions and invoke different lenses in its interpretation of the texts. Readers who employ feminist hermeneutics forefront issues of gender, whereas Jewish hermeneutists highlight connections to the Midrashic and Talmudic literatures. Yet all hermeneutics guide a reader to focus on specific parts of texts, find particular themes within those texts, and provide a framework for understanding the meaning of the texts. Importantly, hermeneutists all read the same texts, but come to radically different conclusions.[29]

Heaven's Gate employed an *extraterrestrial biblical hermeneutics*, reading the Christian Bible (primarily the New Testament) through a fundamental set of assumptions: that life exists on other planets, that such alien life has interacted with Earthlings in the past and will in the future, and that biblical evidence points to such relationships. This hermeneutics draws upon a reservoir of New Age religious thought. However, the hermeneutics utilized by Heaven's Gate is primarily biblical, since it highlights the Bible and places it at the center of its analysis. Unlike many UFO groups, Heaven's Gate never strayed far from the Bible. The founders and members of Heaven's Gate utilized the Bible to explain their beliefs, attract members, defend their religious positions, and ultimately to rationalize leaving their earthly bodies behind.[30] While others, such as Chryssides, understand this combination as "an idiosyncratic interpretation . . . a postmodern tendency to combine sources that are not conventionally or readily juxtaposed," I see Applewhite and Nettles's biblical interpretations as following a rather clear set of hermeneutical guidelines.[31]

The extraterrestrial biblical hermeneutics of Heaven's Gate derived from the group's founders, so it makes sense to start with the Two to consider its origins. As was previously noted, Bonnie Lu Nettles had a history of interest in UFOs and ufology before meeting Applewhite, whereas Applewhite brought with him a background in the Bible from his childhood as a preacher's son and his short time at a Presbyterian seminary. This nexus of Christianity and theosophically inspired ufology served as the origin for the emergence of the Heaven's Gate belief system.

Nettles's interests in UFOs must be situated within the history of both esotericism and ufology. While the nineteenth-century founders of Theosophy proper had alluded to Venusian extraterrestrials who aided humans' spiritual practices, and the I AM offshoot tradition had elevated such extraterrestrial masters' importance, Nettles received both of these traditions filtered through the lens of Western esotericism, sometimes also called the occult. Esotericism includes a number of substrands, including astrology, alchemy, magic, spiritualism, and theosophy. Scholar of Western esotericism Arthur Versluis explains that esotericists claim to possess "inner or hidden knowledge" hidden throughout history and known by only a select few. With such knowledge, Versluis indicates, "aspirants seek direct spiritual insight into the hidden nature of the cosmos and of themselves."[32] The esoteric nature of reading the stars (astrology), journeying to them (astral travel), and communicating with extraterrestrials (channeling) all fit within the esoteric worldview. Nettles inherited this worldview from her involvement in the Houston Theosophical Society, and both Nettles and Applewhite explored this esoteric world through their readings. It served as one of the influences to their later extraterrestrial biblical hermeneutics, though crucially they rejected esotericism's foundational assumption that esoteric knowledge must remain secret. Like good Protestants, they claimed that the evidence of the Truth was evident in the biblical text, and that everyone can and should recognize it.

The other source of the extraterrestrial component of their extraterrestrial biblical hermeneutics derived from the subculture known as ufology. Ufology emerged in the United States in the 1950s in the wake of pilot Kenneth Arnold's sightings of what came to be called "flying saucers" in the Pacific Northwest and the crash of an unidentified flying object (UFO)—the nature of which is still in dispute—near an Army Air Base outside of Roswell, New Mexico, both in the summer of 1947. By the early 1950s, Americans had reported numerous sightings of UFOs, attracting the interest of scientists, government officials, and military analysis. Cold War fears, the dawning of the space race, the emergence of nuclear science, and the conspiracy-oriented culture of the era all contributed to a subculture of ufology wherein individuals traded knowledge and experiences about their encounters with UFOs and attempts to study them.

Historian of religions Brenda Denzler has found that the ufology subculture had clear antecedents in religion and clear connections to religious belief and practice. Individuals described encounters with UFOs using religious language to characterize their numinous encounters, and those who claimed contact with extraterrestrials generally offered narratives in keeping with either demonology or revelation. Early "contactees"—those who claimed to communicate with extraterrestrials—"had their roots not in UFO experience and investigation, but in esoteric groups," Denzler found.[33] In Denzler's assessment, other members of the ufological subculture had created a form of Christ-less Christianity wherein UFOs offered otherworldly illumination, meaning, explanation, and salvation without referent to God, but paralleling Christian theology in their emphasis on heavenly salvation from human corruption.[34]

Ufology's specific influence on Nettles's and Applewhite's hermeneutic lay in what has come to be called "ancient astronaut theory."

Proponents of this approach claim that in prehistoric or ancient times, extraterrestrials visited planet Earth, interacted with its inhabitants, and subsequently led Earthlings to record these visits using the limited linguistic and scientific abilities of the day. Epics such as *Gilgamesh*, Homer's *Odyssey*, the Hebrew Bible, the Vedas, and *Mahabharata* all contain coded evidence of this history, supporters claim. Devotees of this theory also claim that archeological sites indicate records of ancient astronauts, often in the forms of carved images of figures wearing helmets or flying on strange contraptions.[35] Denzler has located dozens of major texts and proponents associated with the ancient astronaut approach, any one of which Nettles and Applewhite might have encountered in their avowed explorations of spirituality and ufology.[36] The most likely is Erich von Däniken's (b. 1935) *Chariots of the Gods?* (1968), a best-selling book wherein the author claimed that everything from the Bible to Mesoamerican architecture evidenced the interaction of ancient extraterrestrials with premodern human beings. Von Däniken went further than most other ancient astronaut theorists in claiming that most human religions originated in these alien encounters, a position he amplified in *Gods from Outer Space* (1970). Von Däniken proposed that the sacred texts of the world's ancient religions, including both the Hebrew Bible (Old Testament) and Hebrew Apocrypha, describe alien visitation (Gen. 1:6, Gen. 6:1–2, Ex. 25:40, Ez. 12; 1 Enoch), utilizing language appropriate to their own time and place. Space ships became chariots and clouds, since the biblical authors could only understand extraterrestrial technology with reference to nature or primitive vehicles. Anthropologists Anne Cross and Pia Andersson have found wide evidence of the spread of ancient astronaut theory throughout the ufology subculture, both among religious and secular proponents of alien visitation.[37] Applewhite later cited as recommended readings several videos and books that prominently featured ancient astronaut theory.

The belief that the Bible contains a record of ancient extraterrestrials interacting with human beings, and the corollary perspective that the Western biblical religious tradition is therefore one centered on extraterrestrial contact, served as the center of the hermeneutic that Nettles and Applewhite developed. All hermeneutics require assumptions. The Heaven's Gate approach had the following assumptions: that intelligent extraterrestrial life exists, that such beings have and will interact with human beings, and that the Bible records this interaction. As an explicitly Christian approach, the extraterrestrial biblical hermeneutics of Heaven's Gate builds upon von Däniken style biblical ancient astronaut theory. It assumes ancient astronaut theory's materialistic model of envisioning supposed miracles or hierophanies as merely extraterrestrial technology or visits. In the Heaven's Gate belief systems, all such religious events as recorded in the Bible actually represent extraterrestrial encounters mediated by alien technology. Prophetic calling was merely extraterrestrial communication, healings just medicine, angels just aliens in disguise, and visions of heavenly chariots or clouds that bear prophets or messiahs simply extraterrestrial UFOs misunderstood and recorded with what limited comprehension the ancients possessed. As Nettles and Applewhite developed their perspective, even Christ himself became an extraterrestrial, and salvation became not rebirth into Heaven, but into the literal heavens.

This approach highlights one of the central features of extraterrestrial biblical hermeneutics, that of philosophical materialism. Christopher Partridge calls the same phenomenon physicalism, but I prefer the technical term drawn from the study of philosophy of religion, which is materialism. As philosophers define it, materialism is a philosophy that roots fundamental existence within the physical reality around us that can be perceived through empirical means, understood in a rational manner, and interacted with through ordinary means. Materialists hold that life is purely a physical phenomenon, and reject claims to supernaturalism, spiritual existence, or forms of philosophical dualism that root human existence within a mind or soul apart from the body.[38] For Heaven's Gate's founders and members, materialism functioned as one of their fundamental assumptions. They therefore read the Bible through that lens, interpreting stories of miracles, visions, and supernatural beings as purely material happenings misunderstood by ancient people as somehow non-material.

Heaven's Gate's extraterrestrial biblical hermeneutics provided for its founders and members a way of interpreting the biblical text and deriving meaning from it. They used this approach to search the text for evidence of extraterrestrial contact with humans, and to try to understand the extraterrestrials' teachings and instructions. As Heaven's Gate grew and its founders further developed their theologies, they modified their earlier assessments of the meanings of the text. Most crucially, they shifted their self-understandings and views of their missions. Yet throughout their history they used the same hermeneutical approach.

Science and Technology in the Worldview of Heaven's Gate

Though the main scholarly debate over the nature of the Heaven's Gate worldview has focused on whether the group predicated itself on Christian or New Age themes, several other major influences and elements also characterize the movement's worldview. Like many other groups in the modern world, Heaven's Gate elevated issues of science and technology within its theology and ideology. The founders and members of new religious movements of the mid- and late-twentieth century have tended to make extensive use of ideas about science and technology, owing partially to the tremendous rise in the public place of science, and partially to the advent of the contemporary age that makes science and technology central parts of popular culture.[39] Religious historian Steven M. Tipton writes of this new scientific age as rooted in the basic facts of modernity: "[i]ts growing influence over American life derives in part from the compatibility of utilitarian individualism with the conditions of modernity: technological economic production, bureaucratic social organization, and empirical science," he explains.[40] Science and technology have infused contemporary social structures, and therefore culture as well.

Within Heaven's Gate, science played a central role as a rhetorical tool used to understand the movement, its identity, and its relationship with outsiders. As a UFO religion, this is hardly surprising. Historian of new religions John Saliba has postulated, "UFO phenomena are a new type of religion that attempts to formulate a worldview that is more consistent with the culture and technology of the twenty-first century."[41] Both I and Christopher Partridge have made similar arguments that attraction to technology and science serve as hallmarks of UFO religions, and Carl Jung's famous declaration that UFOs function as "technological angels" offers perhaps the most standard view of how religious groups predicated on belief in UFOs and space aliens have used ideas drawn from science and technology in place of those traditionally ascribed to religion.[42]

The founders and members of Heaven's Gate spoke extensively about how scientific their movement was, and how science supported their beliefs. Most directly, Applewhite declared of his religious beliefs in a 1997 video, "This is as scientific—this is as true as true could be."[43] The equation of truth with science goes to the heart of what Tipton and others note as the manner in which science has achieved a sort of cultural preeminence. Elsewhere, Applewhite and others invoked biology, chemistry, and physics to support their religious positions. Their transition into perfected Next Level beings was an "evolution," they wrote, and was accomplished through "biological and chemical" means.[44] Members invoked technological references as well, often computer-based ones. The self existed on a "hard drive," the body as a form of "hardware," and the true self in the form of "software," wrote several of the members.[45] The movement's website even linked to a (now defunct, and sadly un-archived[46]) web page, "Science Without Bounds," that Heaven's Gate webmaster, probably a member named Glnody, described as "A Synthesis of Science, Religion, and Mysticism."[47]

One must partially read the use of science as a rhetorical tool to differentiate the group from other religions, and particularly from the forms of Christianity that actually shared the most in common with Heaven's Gate on a theological level. For example, as opposed to the "superstitious" Christian concepts of Heaven that members of Heaven's Gate deplored, adherents of the group believed their heaven to be empirically verifiable, and therefore scientifically proven to be real. Of course, it would be extremely difficult to actually disprove the existence of the Next Level, requiring advanced feats of astronomy. High and distant, it is unlikely that any human would be able to marshal proof enough to discount the Next Level's existence. However, like the medieval image of Heaven hovering above the clouds, their heaven was as real as a rock or a tree. One could fly a spaceship to it. One didn't need to be dead to physically encounter it (at least as members initially believed). In the minds of the members of Heaven's Gate, any person with sense enough to believe in the existence of the Earth had no recourse but to believe in the Next Level. It required no leap of faith, only the recognition that our telescopes had not yet pierced the farthest reaches of the sky.

This physicalism extended to the movement members' beliefs that biological Next Level entities were in fact what religious people mistakenly believe to be supernatural beings. In an early interview Nettles and Applewhite explained that the figure Christians call Lucifer or Satan actually was an extraterrestrial, a living biological being who had "displeased the Chief by getting into his own ego trip" with the consequence of Lucifer's banishment to planet Earth and the nearby cosmos.[48] Members continued to hold this belief until the end of the movement. By the end of the group's terrestrial existence, adherents described the Christian concept of grace as an implanted chip, prayer as a type of radio transmission, and the miracles described in the Bible as technological wizardry. As Heaven's Gate member Jwnody—a prolific spokesperson for the group who authored much of the materials that the movement's leader Do did not— wrote in a statement published in the group's anthology, "*Urgent Warning*: The lawless, the criminals, the major corrupters of the inhabitants of this world, from the Kingdom of God's point of view, are human-equivalent *space aliens* who have been deliberately deceiving—victimizing—your most prominent religious leaders. These technologically advanced alien species have succeeded in having these leaders look to them as 'Almighty God.'"[49] Using their technological devices that humans mistake as miracles, the Luciferian extraterrestrials answer prayers of unwitting religious people, situating themselves as the Lords of the planet.

The belief that Heaven's Gate's worldview was somehow "scientific" and that religious people lacked this bona-fide legitimate rational sense of perspective undergirded Jwnody's writing. "Just who are the real occultists? Where are there more meaningless rituals performed than in the church, e.g., baptism, burial ceremonies, marriage ceremonies, genuflection, crossing oneself, kissing the Father's ring, . . . ? And who, in reality, are the number one promoters of idolatry?"[50] Christians, she answers. Worst of all, under the yoke of Christianity, "you are encouraged to pray to some 'god' or mythical concept of Jesus."[51] Jwnody's scare quotes and her vitriol indicate the degree to which she believed her own beliefs modern, scientific, and rational, and unlike those held by members of other religions. Lest Asian religions escape unscathed from the group's rhetoric, in his lament for the "victims" of world religions, Jwnody's co-religionist Stmody laments that Buddhism is no better than Christianity, a religion predicated on "ritual and myth," which he equates to superstition. Echoing Karl Marx, perhaps unconsciously, Stmody accuses Buddhism of dulling the mind of the masses. "But Buddha's message . . . is mainly ritual and myth that keeps people sidetracked, hooked on the 'drug' of spiri-tuality."[52] Stmody, Jwnody, and other members of Heaven's Gate connote religion with the belief in myths, a suspect epistemology to self-professed "cynical, skeptical" spiritual seekers. They contrast this with what they considered the rational and scientific beliefs that they held.[53]

Finally, the adherents of Heaven's Gate's embraced science only partially, circumscribing it within their clearly religious worldview. Heaven's Gate members critiqued science on the same grounds on which they critiqued religion: the movement's adherents saw both as epistemologically questionable worldviews. Ultimately, science itself functioned as an alternative religion, the "cult of Science" or "temple of science," as two members of Heaven's Gate labeled it.[54] Heaven's Gate criticized science as relying upon dubious naturalist assumptions, just as religion relies upon dubious supernaturalist assumptions. A move-ment that claimed the existence of disincarnate spirits, extra-sensory perception, and the evolution of souls, Heaven's Gate was as leery of purely naturalistic explanations of reality as it was repulsed by what it considered superstitious religiosity. Members rejected what philoso-pher of science Mikael Stenmark calls epistemic scientism, "[t]he view that the only reality that we can know anything about is the one science has access to."[55] Applewhite therefore contrasted faith with scientific proof, arguing that faith leads to true knowledge, whereas science does not. Setting the word within quotes, Applewhite revealed his suspicion that scientific "proofs" do not prove anything. "[N]o 'proof' that would ever satisfy the scientific community was offered (no spacecraft landed in our backyard). But, through the nurturing of faith, we came to know the reality of the Next Level and that Ti and Do are our Older Mem-bers," he wrote of himself and his movement.[56] Adherents of a religious ideology, the members of Heaven's Gate self-consciously understood their epistemology as deductive rather than inductive: it required faith, not empiricism. While members embraced science, they implicitly real-ized its limits within the confines of their religious system.

Science Fiction, Invented Religions, and Religions of Fiction

While science certainly served a central role in how members of Heav-en's Gate thought about themselves and their movement, so did science fiction, which served as one of the most important ways in which the group's members synthesized the various components of their religious bricolage as they assembled a meaningful worldview. Beginning with the first media coverage of the group after the 1997 suicides, journalists have fixated on this aspect of Heaven's Gate. Magazines and newspapers—ranging from the sober *New York Times* to the popular *TIME* and *Newsweek* to the sensationalistic *National Inquirer*—all called Heaven's Gate a "science fiction cult" and covered aspects of its "science fiction theology." To take just one example: The *Los Angeles Times*, which because of its geographic proximity to Rancho Santa Fe became the newspaper of record for the coverage of Heaven's Gate, framed Heaven's Gate as a product of science fiction. The April 2, 1997 edition of the *Los Angeles Times* referenced a popular science fiction television series in the subtitle of its front-page article on the group. "'I Want to Believe' is the mantra not just for TV's 'X-Files' but also for many Americans who look to science or sci-fi—or what lies in between—to explain life's mysteries." The article that followed focused on how Heaven's Gate was part of "an increasingly popular culture in which the search for meaning has turned to a fuzzy fusion of science and science fiction."[57] Another article in the *Los Angeles Times*, this one a guest editorial, even blamed the mass media, particularly book publishers and television producers, for feeding "the public a steady diet of science fiction fantasy, packaged and sold as real," that Heaven's Gate transformed into its "pseudoscientific" religion.[58]

Partially, journalists found the notion of Heaven's Gate as a science fiction cult a useful trope since it helped them to frame the group as bizarre and illegitimate, an approach that Sean McCloud has documented as typical of coverage of NRMs since the 1960s.[59] Yet science fiction possesses certain parallels to religion, ones upon which Heaven's Gate did indeed draw. Both consider ideas beyond the typical ken of usual human experience, both treat weighty issues such as the future of humanity and its place in the universe, and both seek to transcend the ordinary. Indeed, several other new religions have also drawn from or invoked science fiction, since the sympathies between religion and science fiction seem so prevalent.[60]

I have elsewhere written far more extensively of Heaven's Gate as a "science fiction religion," and I will not belabor that point here.[61]

However, one must take note of the prevalent place of science fiction within the Heaven's Gate worldview. Heaven's Gate incorporated elements from science fiction directly into its worldview. The group's members believed in classic science fiction tropes such as UFOs, interstellar wars, alien technologies, and human-alien hybrids, and referred to God as an extraterrestrial being. Despite these science fiction elements, the movement did not incorporate them willy-nilly. Rather, Heaven's Gate carefully introduced material drawn from science fiction in order to support and explain the theological perspectives that they developed through their specific hermeneutical approach. Yet since the movement declared that the Jewish and Christian Bibles were records of extraterrestrial contact with Earth, and that Earth functioned as a laboratory and classroom for extraterrestrials, certain parallels existed between their basic theology and that of science fiction. Indeed, several science fiction stories bear a remarkable similarity to Heaven's Gate's theology, most notably the movie and television series *Stargate*, a fact that members of the movement noted and used as part of their appeal to science fiction fans. Heaven's Gate member Rkkody cited *Stargate* as an accurate depiction of the origin of Earth's religions—"closer to reality than anyone thinks" in his words—as well as a good tool to convey the theology behind Heaven's Gate, indicating his reflexive awareness of the use of science fiction within the group.[62] In the case of *Stargate*, which describes malevolent extraterrestrials as the sources of much of the world's religions and troubles—obvious parallels existed. Since the Heaven's Gate theology predates that particular science fiction franchise, this is not a case of using fiction as a source for religious innovation, but rather appealing to outsiders using well-known elements drawn from popular culture.

Members also made extensive use of science fiction in seeking to convey their ideas to the public. The movement's one-third page advertisement in the national American newspaper *USA Today*, published May 27, 1993, best represents this approach. Transposing the story of the incarnation of Christ—an important aspect of Heaven's Gate's "backstory," since they believed they were continuing Christ's mission—onto that of *Star Trek*, the advertisement proclaimed: "Two thousand years ago, the true Kingdom of God appointed an Older Member to send His 'Son,' along with some of their beginning students, to incarnate on this garden. While on Earth as an 'away team' with their 'Captain,' they were to work on their overcoming of humanness and tell the civilization they were visiting how the true Kingdom of God can be entered." Here Heaven's Gate referenced the "away team," an invented concept from the fictional *Star Trek* universe of a small group of crew members descending from their spaceship so as to engage in some activity on a planet's surface. They also referred to Christ as a "Captain," alluding to the main characters of the various *Star Trek* television series, namely Captain Kirk from the original series and Captain Picard from *Star Trek: The Next Generation*.[63]

The advertisement continued, explaining the nature of the Heaven's Gate movement with reference to Christ and his apostles as well as to *Star Trek*. "That same 'away team' incarnated again in the 1970's in the mature (adult) bodies that had been picked and prepped for this current mission. This time the 'Admiral' (the Older Member, or Father, incarnate in a female vehicle) came with the Son—'Captain'—and his crew." Alluding to the rank system in *Star Trek*'s quasi-military Starfleet, the authors of the advertisement portrayed the movement's founders as both divine figures and science fiction characters, Applewhite/Christ/ Captain, Nettles/God the Father/Admiral.[64] Readers of the advertisement who had seen *Star Trek* would surely have thought of the pairing of Admiral Kirk (the character had been promoted since the days of the television show) and Captain Spock from the various *Star Trek* motion pictures produced in the decades before the advertisement, especially *Star Trek IV*, released two years earlier, which featured the Enterprise crew visiting twentieth-century Earth in an attempt to "save the planet from its own short-sightedness," in the words of the movie.[65]

Heaven's Gate's *USA Today* advertisement used other language drawn from *Star Trek* as well, most notably its reference to human morality as a "prime directive." In *Star Trek* the prime directive is a moral imperative of not interfering with another culture's natural development. For Heaven's Gate members, here drawing on a New Age sense of individual self-transformation, the prime directive became the moral requirement to not interfere in another person's spiritual development. The advertisement ended with another *Star Trek* reference, and one that combined the group's biblical, ufology, and science fiction language. The members of the movement would depart on "the *true* 'Enterprise' (spaceship or 'cloud of light')." This brief statement combines the multiple languages that Heaven's Gate spoke. Even casual consumers of science fiction would recognize the reference to the *Enterprise*, the spaceship that ferries the crew of the original *Star Trek* series and *Star Trek: The Next Generation* between its adventures, and over the course of the televisions series even develops a life of its own as something more akin to a character than an object. Heaven's Gate also utilizes a more generic term, "spaceship," a concept with which readers of the advertisement familiar with ufology would more closely identify. Finally, the movement referenced the biblical tradition and the "bright cloud" (elsewhere, "cloud of light") said to be present at divine events, and what Heaven's Gate believed was a UFO.[66]

Other Heaven's Gate sources repeated this phenomenon of utilizing the language of *Star Trek*. The group's Internet posting of January 16, 1994, "Last Chance Statement," repeated the same claims, as did the title of the movement's final Internet statement, "Heaven's Gate 'Away Team' Returns to Level Above Human in Distant Space," though the latter statement itself avoided any direct reference to *Star Trek* other than its title.[67] Former Heaven's Gate member Crlody, who left the group but remained a believer, similarly invoked *Star Trek* in order to explain that life without true access to the truth of Heaven's Gate is "analogous to the holographic characters on the holodeck in *Star Trek* . . . hav[ing] no idea or concept that they are projections of a simulated environment that can be 'turned off.'"[68] The most extensive treatment is found in the statement written by Heaven's Gate member Jwnody, "'Away Team' from Deep Space Surfaces Before Departure," which not only directly references the two aforementioned *Star Trek* series, but in its title possibly also alluded to *Star Trek: Deep Space Nine* (1994–99), a series still airing new episodes at the time of the suicides. Jwnody continued the trope of referring to herself as a crew member on an away team mission in the company of her Captain and under the command of her Admiral. Jwnody uses *Star Trek* quite intentionally, calling it a metaphor and implying that people might understand Heaven's Gate better through the lens of science fiction. She writes, "[m]etaphorically speaking, in 20th Century human vernacular, I am a member of the current 'Away Team' deployed from deep space. As a young and extremely fortunate student, I have been working closely with the 'Captain' and he in turn with the 'Admiral' (Chief Administrator of this civilization since its inception) on this remarkably complex mission."[69]

Jwnody was certainly intentional about her use of science fiction. As one of the most prolific members and one of the co-editors of the movement's self-published anthology, she made the use of science fiction a cornerstone in her attempt to engage the wider world. Her overview of the movement's history and theology served as the introduction to the group's anthology, and as one of its intellectual leaders, Jwnody was in the position to deploy science fiction as a means of reaching her target audience: educated, intelligent, questioning Americans. She explained in her overview, "[t]o help you understand who we are, we have taken the liberty to express a brief synopsis in the vernacular of a popular 'science fiction' entertainment series. Most readers in the late 20th Century will certainly recognize the intended parallels. It is really quite interesting to see how the context of fiction can often open the mind to advanced possibilities which are, in reality, quite close to fact."[70] Jwnody's use of quotes to set apart the concept of "science fiction" indicates her discomfort with the term. This discomfort arose not from disagreements with the validity of the genre or its claims, but the fact that science fiction was in fact, in her own words, "quite close to fact." Not fiction at all, science fiction represented a means of communicating the deep religious truths that Jwnody believed Heaven's Gate offered. Like her earlier material and the movement's *USA Today* advertisement, Jwnody's overview in the group's anthology made extensive use of *Star Trek*, and sought to portray the group as crew members on an Away Team mission to Earth, led at first by their intrepid Admiral (Nettles) and Captain (Applewhite), and later by the Captain alone.

Science fiction inundated the group's religious rhetoric and thought, and it appeared within their practices as well. Members attempted to create their community in a form similar to that of the crew of a spaceship, notably invoking elements from *Star Trek* in attempting to create a model for how to live as a group. Led by a "Captain," members lived within a "craft" and engaged in various "assignments" and "out of craft tasks." Members renamed parts of their dwellings using technical-sounding terminology reminiscent of the rooms in a spaceship or space station, such as nutri-lab for kitchen, fiber-lab for laundry, and compu-lab for office.[71] Finally, members wore uniforms reminiscent of those from *Star Trek* and other science fiction franchises. All of this combined to create a religious worldview deeply infused with elements and ideas drawn from science fiction.

The use of science fiction within a religious system naturally raises the question of fiction and its connection to religious belief. Most people assume that fiction and faith commitment are mutually exclusive categories, and that no religious person would invoke fiction as a support or source for religious belief. Yet the recent analytic work of religious studies scholar Carole M. Cusack challenges that assumption. Writing of what she calls "invented religions," Cusack argues that for many religious people today the absolute distinction between fact and fiction, real and false, no longer holds. For those who adhere to invented religions, fiction can possess more truth than reality, and fundamental facts about the world can exist within works of popular culture, satire, and even nonsense. Cusack identifies several prominent new religious movements that follow in this vein, most notably the Church of All Worlds, an American Pagan community whose founders named their organization after a fictional religious community within science fiction author Robert A. Heinlein's *Stranger in a Strange Land* (1961). Adherents of the Church drew multiple beliefs and practices from that fictional source, and have more recently introduced elements from J. K. Rowling's series of *Harry Potter* books (1997–2007) into their religious worldview. Cusack identifies other invented religions such as Jediism and Matrixism that similarly look to science fiction as offering religious value. For Cusack, invented religions represent the same sort of consumer-oriented religion that I argue Heaven's Gate's style of religious bricolage exemplifies. In her words, "invented religions, rather than being exceptional and best classified as 'fake' religions, are properly understood as the inevitable outcome of a society that values novelty, and in which individuals constitute their identity through the consumption of products, experiences, cultures and spiritualities."[72] In Cusack's reading, fiction serves as an ideal muse for many people in today's society of cultural consumption and representation.

Worldview, Belief, and Practice

Considered synoptically, several elements drawn from different cultural influences shaped the Heaven's Gate worldview, a bricolage pulled together by the group's members: postmodern consumerism, a mentality of pastiche, the Bible, theosophically influenced belief in extraterrestrial life, ufology, Christian millennialism, science, philosophical materialism, and science fiction. As active creators of a religious worldview, the members of Heaven's Gate drew from all of these sources in creating their religious world. Returning to Peterson's assessment of the nature of religious worldviews, he argued that such worldviews are orienting, normative ways of conceiving of the world, and possess three characteristics: they are fundamental, meaning that those who accept them consider them centrally important and relevant; they are explanatory, giving meaning to the surrounding cosmos; and they are global, meaning they encompass all of existence. The leaders and adherents of Heaven's Gate crafted such a persuasive normative worldview with use of many cultural and religious sources. Within this worldview as their guide, they then lived within a sort of religious habitus, as Pierre Bourdieu would call it, a set of meanings, values, and assumptions that helped them structure and organize their experiences. The next two chapters turn from the roots of this worldview to the specific elements of the specific theological beliefs and religious practices within Heaven's Gate, showing how the various sources they utilized appear and reappear within the religious beliefs and practices of the group.

4

Understanding Heaven's Gate's Theology

Until recently, most scholars in the field of religious studies have traditionally studied religions through a careful consideration of the beliefs promulgated by those faiths, focusing on doctrines and various theological positions. This approach has come under notable critique in the last half century on the basis of the need to also consider popular or vernacular practices and beliefs, social dynamics, and non-institutional forms of religion. Such critique has reshaped the field of religious studies.[1] Yet in the field of the study of new religious movements we have sometimes had the opposite problem; until relatively recently, few scholars have used the approaches of intellectual history or theological studies to research new religious movements.[2] Owing primarily to the disciplinary location of scholars of NRMs, much of the early work on new religions employed sociological or social history methodologies. Additionally, people sometimes assume that new religions such as Heaven's Gate did not have a developed theological system, or that the system made no sense, meaning fewer people have been drawn to study or assess these new theologies. Numerous media outlets openly disparaged the beliefs, actions, and even sanity of the members. Ted Turner, founder and board member of CNN, called the suicides "a way to get rid of a few nuts."[3] By contrast, the members of the group insisted that they were rational beings and that everything they believed made perfect sense to them. They felt this acutely, and in the "Exit Videos" produced just days before the suicides most of the members commented on how their beliefs and actions made sense to them, but they recognized that others would not understand them. Watching the videos it was clear that many members felt deeply wounded by this idea, and wanted to try to explain why they had made the choices they did. In the words of one member of Heaven's Gate, Drrody, "When we leave I know the media will treat this . . . as some sort of weird bizarre cult, a suicide cult, whatever you might want to call it. But look deeper than those words, look for what we've taught people. And the message we've left behind because we know that it is difficult to understand." Drrody explained that he believed in Ti and Do because the evidence supported them, and his experiences told him that they were right. Leaving behind his body represented "commitment to the Next Level," and rejection of the human level. It made sense to him.[4]

Deluded crazies, or rational empiricists? Between these two extremes is a simple reality: members of Heaven's Gate adhered to a system of beliefs that contained all the usual hallmarks of a religious *theology*, namely beliefs about salvation (soteriology), the order of the universe (cosmology), and the end of things (eschatology). As a Christian group, they also developed an understanding of the nature of Jesus (Christology). Like most religious systems, their beliefs were internally consistent and logical from the inside, though seem circular and bizarre from the outside. From the perspective of Heaven's Gate members, their beliefs provided them with meaning, identity, and a sense of their place in the universe. They were, in effect, the distilled theological essence of the religious habitus that the group's members developed and lived within. Ultimately, their beliefs demanded of them that they lay down their lives. This chapter tries to make sense of why, indicating how the members of this religion developed a specific and coherent theology within the context of the religious worldview discussed in the previous chapter.

Soteriology and Christology

The leaders and members of Heaven's Gate utilized an extraterrestrial biblical hermeneutic throughout its history, but the specific ways in which they read their sacred text changed over the years. Nevertheless, the central features of Applewhite and Nettles's hermeneutical approach lasted throughout their group's history, i.e., their reading of the Bible as a record of extraterrestrial contact with human civilization for the purposes of aiding personal self-transformation. Based on their reading of the Bible, the possibility of individual salvation and bodily assumption into Heaven provided the heart of the Two's teachings, and the form that self-transformation took within their movement. In order for potential followers to join them in this "trip," as they called it, they needed to leave their human attachments behind them and dedicate themselves exclusively to overcoming the human condition. Those dedicated to the message of Nettles and Applewhite would rise into the heavens and achieve eternal salvation. This process, the Two declared, functioned entirely on the material level, requiring a metamorphosis of the biological and chemical makeup of the human body, and resulting in a transformation into an ideal extraterrestrial creature. The Two believed that the extraterrestrials had brought this method of salvation through transformation to Earth. They called it simply "the Process."

This systemization of salvation—soteriology, to use the technical term—fit within a theological apparatus that explained the nature of the world and the heavens, the meaning of human existence, and the salvific drama associated with the Bible and its interpretations. Heaven's Gate offered a vision of the Earth and its relation with Outer Space. It offered a perspective on the nature of Christ and his mission, an explanation of the nature of the divine, and an explanation of the fate of the planet and its inhabitants during the end of days. In other words, the worldview that Heaven's Gate's founders and members promulgated possessed the basic qualities of any Christian worldview: soteriology, cosmology, theology, Christology, and eschatology. A very small portion of these positions of course matched what most Americans would call mainstream Christian belief, nor can one claim that Heaven's Gate's theological positions were in any way normative within orthodox Christianity. Yet while some might regard these theological positions as comprising a mishmash of science fiction, Christian heresy, and popular religious speculation, the basic hermeneutic remained consistent. The founders and members of Heaven's Gate read the Christian Bible through their beliefs about extraterrestrial visitations.

On May 31, 1974, Nettles and Applewhite gave to one of their first followers the Bible that they had carried with them and studied during their formulation of the movement's theology, a copy of which was later provided to me.[5] A King James Version (KJV) Red-Letter Bible, the physical text points toward the group's Protestant biblical origins. Though by 1974 many Protestants utilized other translations, most notably the Revised Standard Version (RSV), the KJV remained the translation of choice for conservative American Protestants. The Red-Letter edition, so called because such editions print the words attributed to Jesus in red ink, holds particular value among American Protestants, since it highlights what many consider the most essential core of the entire Bible, the teachings of Jesus. As biblical scholars Athalya Brenner and Jan W. van Henten have noted in their scholarship of the reception of Bible translation, the particular Bible translation utilized by a group or individual marks their overall religious identity.[6] In this regard, the Heaven's Gate founders' choice of the Red-Letter King James Version reveals their initial indebtedness to a biblically based conservative American Protestantism. In her own examination of Heaven's Gate, historian Rosamond Rodman also noted that Applewhite and Nettles's choice of a KJV Bible clearly identifies them as influenced by Protestant traditionalism, even as they embarked on exploring the text from the perspective of extraterrestrial hermeneutics.[7]

Applewhite and Nettles marked twenty-six discrete passages in their Bible, spread over four books—Matthew, Luke, Galatians, and Revelation (see table 3.1). Importantly, these four books all fall within the New Testament, indicating that the Two focused on what they perceived to be the salvific drama associated with Christ's incarnation. Specifically, most of their notations fall within the Gospel of Luke, which scholars identify as the gospel most emphasizing Jesus as both biographic exemplar and savior of the world.[8] The Two's markings included underlines, drawn asterisks, and occasionally written words. Their notations fell into three broad categories: (1) the nature of Jesus as Christ, specifically the incarnation; (2) the need to forsake worldly attachments; (3) eschatological predictions of judgment, persecution, and resurrection. These marked passages, when considered in the context of the three written statements that the two founders

Table 3.1: Annotated Verses by Biblical Book

Biblical Book	Number of Annotations
Gospel of Luke	18
Gospel of Matthew	4
Epistle to the Galatians	2
Revelation	2

Table 3.2: Annotated Verses by Theme

Theme	Number of Annotations
Overcoming Temptations and Attachments	6
Persecution of Prophets and Believers	5
Value of Spiritual Seeking	4
Judgment	3
Resurrection of Believers	3
Miracles (Healings, etc.)	2
Need for Purification and Forgiveness	2
Christological Events (Transfiguration)	1
Importance of Prayer	1
Two Witnesses	1

of Heaven's Gate wrote a year later in 1975, demonstrate the manner in which the Two sought to construct an entire theology predicated on their reading of the Bible through an extraterrestrial hermeneutic (see table 3.2).

As a fundamentally Protestant biblical group, Heaven's Gate naturally featured a Christology, a set of positions on the nature of Christ's incarnation. Few of the Two's markings in their Bible directly treat the nature of Christ, though they did underline six separate passages in Luke that speak to the question. Notably, they marked material related to Jesus's overcoming of temptation (Lk 4:12–14), prayer life (Lk 6:12), and miracles (Lk 8:33, 8:54–55). That the two founders identified these passages indicates their interest in what Christ did on Earth; however, they framed these by marking two other passages. The first, a statement by Zacharias, the father of John the Baptist, declared, "Blessed be the Lord God of Israel; for he hath visited and redeemed his people, And hath raised up an horn of salvation for us in the house of his servant David; As he spake by the mouth of his holy prophets, which have been since the world began" (Lk 1:67–70). This passage presents several major themes: that the Lord has visited "his people," that God speaks through prophets, and that God provides a savior. While these themes are unremarkable for most Christians, within the context of an extraterrestrial hermeneutic, they explain the underlying theology of Heaven's Gate. Based on a reading of the three statements they subsequently authored, Applewhite and Nettles treated any reference to God in a materialistic fashion, reckoning that what the Bible calls God is actually a highly developed extraterrestrial worshipped by humans as a deity. Here they followed the contours of the broader extraterrestrial biblical hermeneutic. Assuming that interpretive framework, the Two took Zacharias's statement that the Lord "hath visited" Israel literally, as evidence that the extraterrestrial being worshipped by the Israelites literally visited his people, making the Bible in fact a record of alien visitation. Regarding Christ specifically, Nettles and Applewhite followed the traditional Protestant approach of understanding the New Testament as centered on the life and teachings of Jesus, who offered not only moral teachings, but also the means of entering the heavens. They also followed conservative Protestant hermeneutics in reading the text quite literally rather than as a metaphor, though of course they interpreted its literal meaning differently. For Heaven's Gate, of course, the heavens represented physical space beyond the atmosphere of the planet. The Two's final notation regarding Christ's nature appears in Luke 9:28–34, the section of the text traditionally called the Transfiguration, since in this passage Christ's visage becomes "white and glistering [i.e., glistening]." Importantly, during this episode, God the Father speaks from overhead in "a cloud," recognizing Jesus as his son. Though Nettles and Applewhite made no effort to notate the nature of this cloud in the actual text of their Bible, they would return to it in their written statements a year later, explaining that it was "what humans refer to as UFOs."[9]

In this first statement, titled "Human Individual Metamorphosis," Nettles and Applewhite paid particular attention to the nature of Christ's incarnation, following the notations of their KJV Bible. In keeping with a central tenet of their extraterrestrial hermeneutic, the Two stressed not only the heavenly origin of Jesus, but also his physicality. Before incarnating on Earth, Jesus possessed a material body, and his awakening represented a "metamorphic" (rather than spiritual) process:

> Approx. 2,000 years ago an individual of that next kingdom forfeited his body of that kingdom and entered a human female's womb, thereby incarnating as the one history refers to as Jesus of Nazareth. He awakened to this fact gradually through the same metamorphic process. . . . Jesus' "Christing" or christening was completed at His transfiguration (metamorphic completion) and He remained in the "larva" environment, with other humans, only for some 40 days to show that His teachings had been accomplished.[10]

In this statement, Nettles and Applewhite laid out a basic theology of incarnation as read through their extraterrestrial hermeneutics, drawing on the passages that they had identified earlier, notably the Transfiguration. In keeping with their broader insistence on materialism, the Two identified Jesus as possessing a physical extraterrestrial body before incarnating, and implied that he either returned to this body or transformed his human body after his mission on Earth. He accomplished this, the Two explained, through use of a UFO, that is, the "cloud of light" of the biblical text. In addition to cementing the Two within the UFO subculture and identifying their hermeneutical approach as an extraterrestrial biblical one, their explanation of the "cloud of light"— a glossing of Luke-Acts (Lk 24:51; Acts 1:9) and possibly Ezekiel (Ezek 1:4–28) as well—as a UFO indicates the Two's desire to both interpret the biblical text as indicating the evidence of past visitations by UFO and also explain the miracles of the Bible in strikingly materialistic means. Both of these desires derive from their specific hermeneutical approach.

As Heaven's Gate's theology developed, the founders' and members' views of Christ changed. By the end, members far more often cited the

Gospel of John in explaining the nature of Christ, the gospel that most emphasizes Christ's otherness.[11] John's preamble, describing the Word as being with God in the heavens before incarnating on Earth, would surely have echoed members' beliefs about Christ journeying to Earth from the Next Level and then back again. Further, while at first they held a classically Christian position that Christ was both human and non-human (extraterrestrial rather than divine in the classic sense), by the end of the movement they advocated an adoptionist position, namely that the extraterrestrial being that was Christ entered into Jesus's body at the point of his Baptism and transformed him from a merely human being into a superhuman one.[12] Even more importantly, members of the group began to look to their leader Marshall Herff Applewhite as a reappearance of Jesus in another human body. Members had debated this possibility as early as 1975, but the Two's statements that Jesus would wait for them aboard a UFO seemed to contradict this, or at least complicate the identification of Applewhite with Jesus.[13] The movement made this identification explicit only later, in a statement authored by Applewhite shortly before the suicides, a September 1995 release that the group posted to nearly a hundred Internet fora in their hope to gain publicity and converts. Applewhite wrote:

> I am about to return to my Father's Kingdom. This "return" requires that
> I prepare to lay down my borrowed human body in order to take up,
> or reenter, my body (biological) belonging to the Kingdom of God (as I
> did approximately 2000 years ago, as Jesus, when I laid down the human
> body that was about 33 years old in order to reenter my body belonging
> to the Kingdom of Heaven).[14]

This new position that Applewhite was Jesus seemed to have developed at some point between 1992 and 1994. Heaven's Gate produced a series of satellite television broadcasts in late 1992 and early 1992, and while the broadcasts made explicit mention of Jesus as offering the same message as Heaven's Gate, the group made no claims that their leader was in fact Christ incarnate. This group's May 1993 advertisements similarly did not discuss this issue, though since the advertisements made scant reference to Christ one cannot determine what precisely members believed at this point. Yet by June 1994 the members of the group clearly had come to believe that their founder and leader was none other than Jesus returned to Earth, with a provocatively titled poster used to advertise their meetings: "He's Back, We're Back, Where Will You Stand?"[15]

The elevation of Applewhite to Christhood occurred simultaneously with the development of another radical theological tenet, namely that Heaven's Gate's co-founder Bonnie Lu Nettles was the same extraterrestrial being that the Bible referred to as God and that Jesus called the Father in the New Testament. Nettles had died in 1985, and while it appears that this spiritual elevation of her position occurred simultaneous to that of Applewhite, it clearly built upon a decade of increasing rhetoric of apotheosis. Again, as early as 1975 members had pondered this possibility, but it had never become an official position of the group, and ex-members report that it was not anything either Nettles or Applewhite had explicitly taught at that time.[16] In the first surviving material that Heaven's Gate produced after Nettles's death, a 1988 booklet they used for proselytizing purposes presumably authored by Applewhite, the movement's spokesperson declared that

> since that time [of the death], Do has been experiencing the role of having to communicate mentally with her, his Older Member, in a strengthening opportunity for mental or telepathic communication (not to be confused with the popular concept of channeling or spiritualism). The class has witnessed Ti's mind meshed in Do's thinking and even his choice of words as he talks to them. Does the quote "The Father is in Me and I am in My Father" mean maybe a little more than we previously thought it might?[17]

While the author of the booklet did not explicitly declare Nettles the same being as the one referred to as God in the Bible, the conflation of the deceased Nettles ("Ti" in the parlance of the group) with the Father from a paraphrasing of Jesus's words in the Gospel of John (14.11), clearly indicated that the movement's perspective on Nettles was that she served a central role in their theological worldview. By 1994, the identification of Nettles with the biblical Father was explicit, and the movement's members referred to Ti as the senior member of the heavens who administered Earth and its affairs.

Cosmology: The Next Level, Its Members, and Its Enemies

One very important tenet that remained constant throughout this theological development was the materiality of Christ, the Father, and all other beings inhabiting the heavens, what Heaven's Gate eventually called the Next Level. In their first statements from 1975, Nettles and Applewhite called the heavens from which the extraterrestrials came "the next evolutionary kingdom," or "kingdom world" or "next kingdom."[18] This kingdom or level represented what most other Christian readers of the Bible would call Heaven. It was the place from which Jesus came before his incarnation, and to where he returned. Entrance into that kingdom represented the goal of the group, and Nettles and Applewhite offered teachings designed to assist people to enter it. In keeping with their extraterrestrial hermeneutic, Nettles and Applewhite made it quite clear that the kingdom was not in fact a misty ethereal realm or spiritual plane of existence, but literally "another world." Its inhabitants possessed physical bodies that featured both chemical and biological makeups, although such bodies transcended the biological limitations of earthly life, such as sustenance, sexual reproduction, and death.[19] Again, one can see how the Two's hermeneutical approach led them to offer a materialistic interpretation of what most interpreters in the Protestant tradition generally understand to mean heaven or the heavens.

As Heaven's Gate developed, the concept of this other world became increasingly central, eventually culminating in the notion of the Next Level or the Evolutionary Level Above Human (TELAH). The founders and members of Heaven's Gate considered TELAH such an important concept that they named the legal entity they created to maintain their website and intellectual property after their suicides the TELAH Foundation, which they turned over to ex-members Mrcody and Srfody who continue (at the time of this writing) to operate it. Heaven's Gate member Smmody offered perhaps the most explicit statement about the Next Level in her statement simply titled "T.E.L.A.H.— Evolutionary Level Above Human," a statement that appeared in the anthology the movement created shortly before the end of the group. Smmody explained the Next Level as the most important concept that the group had to offer humanity. She emphasized that it was both real and entirely physical, and therefore a true place and not some sort of metaphor or spiritual plane of existence. "The Next Level, the Kingdom of Heaven, is a real physical place. It is a many-membered Kingdom. . . . The TRUE Kingdom of God (the Next Level) is a REAL place—a reachable place."[20] Smmody equated the fact that the Next Level was real and the fact that it was physical, indicating her rootedness in a materialist philosophy. All other statements produced by Heaven's Gate members or leaders took the same approach and emphasized the same themes that the Next Level was physical, tangible, and therefore real. Smmody and others declared that real, tangible living beings populated this Next Level, and that these extraterrestrial beings, whom Heaven's Gate members referred to as "members of the next level," existed in material, biological form. Since the members of Heaven's Gate believed that they would literally transform into the same Next Level creatures as a result of their involvement in the religious group, these beliefs functioned as absolutely central components of their theology.

Heaven's Gate members harped upon the nature of Next Level beings as biological and real, a theme that Applewhite and Nettles emphasized in their first statements and members of Heaven's Gate wrote and spoke about even in the final weeks of the movement. Whereas in the early days Applewhite and Nettles offered only vague statements about the specific physical nature of the Next Level extraterrestrial beings, members of the group in its final years held very specific beliefs about the Next Level beings. To take one representative account offered by Jwnody—whose writings we have already considered in some detail—Next Level aliens represented the ideal form of biological existence. "[T]he physical characteristics of our species," Jwnody wrote, is that "Next Level bodies are genderless and very pleasant looking, oftentimes somewhat childlike or wisely gentle in their appearance."[21] Jwnody and others additionally described the Next Level beings as "non-mammalian," "non-seed-bearing" (i.e., not-fertile), "eternal," and "everlasting." Moving beyond physical characteristics, members of Heaven's Gate described the Next Level beings as "crew-minded" and "service-oriented." Smmody summarized these beliefs in his T.E.L.A.H. statement: "Ti and Do and their students (crew) have come from a genderless, crew-minded, service-oriented world that finds greed, lust, and self- serving pursuits abhorrent."[22]

Figure 4.1. Printout of digital artwork showing a Next Level alien. The group's large print-out that they displayed in their home has been lost, but several smaller printouts remain. Image © TELAH Foundation.

Importantly, Heaven's Gate members envisioned their transformation into Next Level creatures as the ultimate goal and the form that "salvation" took within their movement. Within this theological context, Next Level aliens functionally equated to not only angels, but the saved elect in post-human life. The movement even presented an image of the Next Level aliens, one created by a member using a computer graphics program, a printout of which adorned their home, and also available as a link on their website.[23] The image shows a silver-colored being on a purple background, an image that any viewer would immediately recognize as an extraterrestrial of the sort made famous by Steven Spielberg in *Close Encounters of the Third Kind*, in the television series *The X-Files*, and in any number of science fiction books, graphic novels, television shows, and cartoons. The image bears striking similarity to the extraterrestrial beings usually called "Grays" as described by abductees and contactees, notably Betty and Barney Hill in their 1965 account and Whitney Strieber in his 1987 book, both of which were staples of ufology.[24] Heaven's Gate's "Gray" appeared far more tranquil and peaceful than those portrayed by abductees and contactees, but no less inhuman. Featuring an enlarged bald head, large sunken eyes, and a tiny mouth and ears, the image conveys intelligence and awareness. The being displays no gender markers and possesses a face that appears gender-neutral. It wears a featureless silver-colored article of clothing that seems to adhere tightly to its nearly identically colored skin.

The written and visual portrayals of Next Level beings offers an important glimpse into Heaven's Gate theology, primarily since this is how the members envisioned the true nature of God the Father and Christ, and also because members themselves wanted to become entities akin to this. The being is genderless, ageless, and seems to have little need for a mouth, indicating a relative unimportance for food or other forms of imbibing. In fact, members of Heaven's Gate spoke of their ideal life as one of sole focus on the requirements of being part of a crew, with no need for such "mammalian" activities such as sex, relationships, eating for enjoyment, alcoholic consumption, or other forms of recreation. Members believed that Next Level beings nourished themselves through absorbing sunlight, lived in states of pure bliss, and had evolved beyond the need for personal ownership of property.[25] Applewhite and Nettles had emphasized the need to live in a way similar to the Next Level beings as far back as their first public teachings in the mid-1970s, and this remained central until the end. Members of Heaven's Gate saw themselves as a crew that focused exclusively on crew-minded activities.

Two things were happening here. First, members of Heaven's Gate had reinterpreted the traditional Christian view of angels and projected it onto the members of the Next Level. While perspectives on angels differ throughout history and among different Christian denominations, the general theological consensus indicates that angels exist as what medieval historian David Keck calls "heavenly spirits," created beings inhabiting the heavenly world and interacting with humans to assist, challenge, and engage earthly activity.[26] Recent times have seen a resurgence of interest in angels, ranging from New Age appropriation of angel imagery to various forms of Christian representation. But, like the traditional theological approach, today's angel aficionados treat these beings as immortal, genderless, perfected beings, in many ways alien to our human condition. Heaven's Gate members transposed this image of the angel onto their view of the Next Level beings.

Second, and perhaps more important given the avowed interest of members in science fiction, the adherents of Heaven's Gate imagined Next Level beings as living in an idealized version of the universe as portrayed in *Star Trek*, its successor series, and recent science fiction movies and television shows such as *Stargate*. *Star Trek*, especially the original series produced in 1966–69, shortly before the birth of Heaven's Gate, imagines a universe wherein the central characters in the television show live and function as a harmonious crew dedicated to peaceful exploration and maintenance of an orderly universe. While *Star Trek*'s characters would often fight, they only fought enemies, never fellow crew members, and the crew generally functioned as a stable and efficient whole. The more recent *Star Trek: The Next Generation* (*ST:TNG*) replicated this pattern, and several members of Heaven's Gate alluded to this model. Most notably, Jwnody ended her Exit Video by both quoting the words and mimicking the hand gesture made by the characters in *ST:TNG* about to leave a planet and return to their spaceship, "Thirty-nine to beam up!"[27] This was the model that Heaven's Gate looked toward when they imagined the Next Level and its inhabitants.

Demonology: Luciferian Space Aliens

The cosmology that members and leaders of Heaven's Gate developed emphasized not only materialism in terms of the heavenly Next Level and angelic Next Level beings, but their opposites as well. Just as heaven physically existed as a real place filled with living extraterrestrial creatures, so too did hellish beings exist in a real physical sense. At the opposite end of the Heaven's Gate cosmology from the peaceful Next Level and its members, the dark forces that members of Heaven's Gate called the Luciferians occupied the role of tempters and antagonists. In the early days of Heaven's Gate, the founders and members paid little attention to the concept of darker forces, though they did believe in malevolent "spirits" or "forces" that could interfere in personal development. But as the movement's theology grew, the concept became more developed, and by the early 1990s Heaven's Gate possessed a rather thorough demonology. In the words of the group's 1993 advertisement placed in *USA Today* and various regional newspapers,

> there are many space alien races that through the centuries of this civilization (and in civilizations prior) have represented themselves to humans as "Gods." We refer to them collectively as "Luciferians," for their ancestors fell away from the keeping of the true Kingdom of God many thousands of years ago. They are not genderless—they still need to reproduce. They are nothing more than technically advanced humans who have retained some of what they learned while in the early training of members of the true Kingdom of God, e.g., limited space-time travel, telepathic communication, advanced travel hardware (spacecrafts, etc.), increased longevity, advanced genetic engineering, and such things as suspended holograms (as used in some religious "miracles").[28]

This advertisement hints at the Manichean position that members of Heaven's Gate took toward the cosmos. Adherents of the ancient and now mostly defunct Manichean religion believed that Earth exists as a sort of battleground between good and evil, and that individual human lives serve as skirmishes in that battle. Like ancient Manicheans, adherents of Heaven's Gate believed that while wholly (or holy) good Next

Level beings strived constantly to maintain a just and stable cosmos, periodically harvesting human souls to join them as the members of Heaven's Gate hoped to do, the universe was also filled with foul forces intent on destroying the Next Level's work, confusing human beings, and masquerading as gods. The reference to using extraterrestrial technology to mimic religious miracles serves as a staple of ufology and the various ancient astronaut theories that proclaim extraterrestrial visitations as the roots of the world's religions, as well as various forms of popular science fiction that tells stories of advanced species passing themselves off as gods among primitive humans. (Science fiction great Arthur C. Clarke's famous statement that any sufficiently advanced technology is indistinguishable from magic is perhaps emblematic of this sort of position, though phrased in a way less offensive to believers in religious miracles.[29])

For adherents of Heaven's Gate, Earth itself became the battlefield for these two forces, the location where the Next Level and the Luciferians struggled over the fate of the population of the planet. Unlike true Manichaeism or even pop science fiction, the result of this conflict was never in doubt. The Next Level not only possesses superior morality to the Luciferians, but superior technology. While Luciferian influence periodically waxes and wanes, the Next Level ultimately always achieves the upper hand. Earth therefore witnesses the rise and fall of civilizations, but each wave of civilizations culminates in the Next Level defeating Luciferian influence, harvesting a crop of human souls to join the Next Level, and restarting human civilization again. As a result, Earth functions as a sort of cosmic classroom where living beings must prove themselves above the temptations of the Luciferians and therefore deserving of Next Level membership. As Heaven's Gate member Anlody wrote shortly before the suicides, "Earth and its human level are the hell and purgatory of legend. It wasn't meant as a place in which to get comfortable or to stay. It was set up as a place to separate the renegades of Heaven—the Luciferians—from those who have risen above the human level, and a place to test souls striving to get to the Level Above Human."[30] Such a position not only posited earthly existence as a brief moment within the scope of a cosmic conflict between good and evil, but also implicitly devalued human life as compared to the Next Level existence to which Heaven's Gate members looked as their goal.

While seemingly bizarre, this view actually tracks broader Evangelical Protestant Christian thought, which often fixates on otherworldly heavenly salvation and envisions earthly life as a mere prelude to the life to come. In the years immediately preceding and following the Heaven's Gate suicides, the vastly popular Evangelical millennial fiction series *Left Behind* conveyed a similar sentiment, contrasting the finitude and tribulation of momentary human existence on a dying Earth with the eternal joys of heavenly salvation.[31] Readers of *Left Behind* thought of course of Christian images of Heaven. Heaven's Gate members looked to the physical heavens.

Eschatology

Heaven's Gate's extraterrestrial biblical hermeneutic became particularly evident in their treatment of eschatology (ideas about the end-time) and especially their reading of the New Testament biblical text, the book of Revelation. Specifically, their approach led them to interpret a Christian eschatological understanding known as dispensationalism, and its key component, the Rapture, by means of their hermeneutical lens, envisioning it in its extraterrestrial and materialistic form. This reinterpretation of a particular form of apocalyptic thought eventually contributed to the mass suicides that ended the terrestrial existence of Heaven's Gate, but in the early days of the Two's work together, it served as a hinge for much of their thinking. What I call Applewhite and Nettles's "technological dispensationalism" derived from their reading of a section of Revelation and other biblical texts.

Throughout the first several years of the history of Heaven's Gate, the Two predicated their message on what they dubbed "the demonstration." The Two declared that at some point in the near future, an unknown party would assassinate them. After outsiders verified them as dead, the Two would repair their bodies, metamorphose themselves into extraterrestrials, and depart the Earth aboard a UFO, thereby "demonstrating" the truth of their message to their followers and the wider world. The "Human Individual Metamorphosis" statement explained,

> There are two individuals here now who have also come from that next kingdom, incarnate[d] as humans, awakened, and will soon demonstrate

the same proof of overcoming death. They are "sent" from that kingdom by the "Father" to bear the same truth that was Jesus'. This is like a repeat performance, except this time by two (a man and a woman) to restate the truth Jesus bore, restore its accurate meaning, and again show that any individual who seeks that kingdom will find it through the same process. This "re-statement" or demonstration will happen within months. The two who are the "actors" in this "theatre" are in the meantime doing all they can to relate this truth as accurately as possible so that when their bodies recover from their "dead" state (resurrection) and they leave (UFO's) those left behind will have clearly understood the formula.[32]

Though the subsequent two statements did not explicate the demonstration nearly to the extent that the first statement did, both mentioned it. The second statement alluded to a forthcoming "illustration" and described the Two as "illustrators," and the third extended the theatrical metaphor of the first statement in describing the event as a "death and resurrection scene" to "demonstrate" the nature of real resurrection.[33] Other sources provided more details. The "What's Up?" mailing in July 1975, for example, provided details on the time frame of the resurrection, clarifying that "the ability to heal a diagnosed dead body and walk away some 3½ days later . . . is one of the characteristics of a member of that next kingdom."[34] Applewhite and Nettles apparently did not stress the demonstration at some of their earliest public meetings—a limited Waldport transcript does not mention it, nor do the first newspaper articles on the movement—but they discussed the demonstration in each of the interviews they granted, to Hayden Hewes in July 1974, Brad Steiger in January 1976, and James Phelan later that same month.[35] Several of the Two's earliest followers who also granted interviews mentioned the demonstration.[36]

The demonstration that the Two espoused in fact represented an interpretation of an end-time prophecy from the New Testament's book of Revelation filtered through the lens of their specific hermeneutical method, a fact that the Two hinted at with their reference to a three-and-a-half day time period to repair their bodies. When interviewer Brad Steiger asked Applewhite and Nettles if they patterned themselves on "the experience and death of Christ," whom Christian tradition also records as lying for three days before resurrection, they responded by alluding instead to "the passage in Revelation" that predicted them.[37] Steiger did not push them on this matter, perhaps because as a secular ufologist he was unfamiliar with Revelation. Phelan, who interviewed Applewhite and Nettles shortly after Steiger, failed to provide a direct quotation, but summarized that the Two "base[d] this prediction on the claim that they [were] not ordinary visitors from outer space but heavenly messengers whose appearance was foretold in the New Testament's Book of Revelation."[38] Elsewhere, the Two provided a specific reference. One man whom Applewhite and Nettles encountered recalled that they told him, "We have a message for you. You are to meditate. Read Revelation 11 and meditate."[39] Similarly, a member of the movement wrote on a postcard to her family in September 1975, "Mama. Am doing beautifully. Truly feel I am on the path I've searched for. Thank God. Please don't worry. Have faith. I am completely taken care of while I am learning my Father's will always in all ways. P.S. Read Revelation Chapter 11 in the New Testament."[40]

The Revelation passage to which Nettles, Applewhite, and their follower alluded describes two witnesses prophesying during the final days, only to meet popular scorn, assassination, and subsequent resurrection. The King James version of the New Testament declares, in a chapter marked in their Red-Letter Bible:

> [An angel said:] And I will give power unto my two witnesses, and they shall prophesy. . . . And when they shall have finished their testimony, the beast that ascendeth out of the bottomless pit shall make war against them, and shall overcome them, and kill them. And their dead bodies shall lie in the street of the great city. . . . And after three days and an half the spirit of life from God entered into them, and they stood upon their feet; . . . And they ascended up to heaven in a cloud. (Rev 11:3–12)

The Two read this Revelation text through the eyes of their extraterrestrial biblical hermeneutic, and owing to the basis of that approach, Applewhite and Nettles emphasized its materialistic nature, its ability to transform the individual, and of course its extraterrestrial nature. The Two insisted that the special case of the resurrection of the two witnesses represented a demonstration of the metamorphic possibilities of the human body, an option they held open for others as well. In keeping with their hermeneutical approach, they recast the Revelation prophecy in material and ufological terms, insisting that the Bible's description of resurrection and the ascension to heaven "in a cloud" represented a coded or symbolic description of a totally material process, and in fact represented a next-level spacecraft. "This demonstration is to clarify what Christ's mission was 2,000 years ago. Man could not understand then, but can *now* at this time," Applewhite handwrote onto one of the Two's mailings.[41] The Two's reliance on the book of Revelation provides a crucial hint to unpack the Two's wider message. Specifically, Applewhite and Nettles filtered a variety of Protestant Christian millennialism known as dispensationalism through their interpretive assumptions.

Dispensationalism emerged in the nineteenth century, and by the 1970s had become a feature of many conservative American evangelical Protestant communities.[42] Dispensationalists rejected the (postmillennial) ideal of human progress so prevalent in nineteenth-century American and European culture, and rather assumed a relatively constant decline of human civilization. Historian George Marsden explains the dispensationalist position: "Christ's kingdom, far from being realized in this age or in the natural development of humanity, lay wholly in the future, was totally supernatural in origin, and discontinuous with the history of this era."[43] Scholars also sometimes refer to dispensationalism as a type of premillennialism, since the prophesied one thousand years of peace (millennium) follows Christ's return. For dispensationalists, when the end comes, it occurs suddenly, in accordance with a strict reading of the book of Revelation, and proceeds utterly unstoppably.

C. I. Scofield (1843–1921), who systematized the theology through his publication of a reference Bible, identified seven dispensations, or eras: innocence (Eden); conscience (antediluvian); human government (postdiluvian); promise (Old Testament patriarchs); law (Mosaic); grace (the current age of the Church); and kingdom (the future dispensation of Christ's heaven-on-Earth). The sixth dispensation ends with what Scofield called the "rapture of the true church," during which living Christians rise into the air, meet Christ, and ascend into heaven.[44] Applewhite and Nettles borrowed several aspects of the dispensational system, but in typical Protestant fashion, read the system through their own examination of the Bible. Hence, the Two's hermeneutic strongly shaped the resulting eschatological perspective of the group.

The Two's most clear codification of their dispensational system occurred in a statement that they prepared for Hayden Hewes and Brad Steiger's book, *UFO Missionaries Extraordinary*, a portion of which the book's publisher printed in the final text as "A Statement Prepared by The Two." In this statement, Applewhite and Nettles described the world as passing through seven historical dispensations—using the term in its technical sense—five of them in the past, one current, and one in the future. Paralleling the standard Protestant dispensational system, which they presumably read in a Scofield Reference Bible or some other source, the Two named the five past dispensations Adam, Enoch, Moses, Elijah, and Jesus, three of which (Adam/innocence/Edenic, Enoch/conscience/antediluvian, Moses/law/Mosaic) precisely match the Scofield system of dispensationalism. Like other dispensationalists, they identified the current dispensation as the present, declaring that "[t]he sixth major help period for Earth's human garden is *now*."[45] Finally, they invoked the standard dispensationalist understandings of the end-time, explaining that the seventh dispensation would end with "what the Christian church refers to as the second coming, the 'rapture,' and the completion of the final prophecies in John's Book of Revelation."[46] Thus far, the Two's presentation of dispensationalist premillennialism closely followed the standard form found in many evangelical Christian churches.

Unlike most Christians following the Scofield dispensational system, however, Applewhite and Nettles interpreted their dispensationalism through the lens of their extraterrestrial biblical hermeneutic, seeking to synthesize the dispensational system with their broader theological worldview. Extrapolating from the dispensationalist assumption that God relates to humanity in different ways during each dispensation, Applewhite and Nettles explained that during particular eras, kingdom-level spacecrafts emitted a powerful burst of energy that washed over the Earth. Ever attuned to the materialism that characterized their hermeneutical approach, the Two maintained that while "you might not be able to see the actual physical manifestation of energy," it nevertheless existed, and shined on the planet like a shaft of light.[47] When this extraterrestrial energy touched the Earth, it created an "energy field" conducive to human development. Employing another materialistic metaphor, and one that invoked the extraterrestrial as well, the Two explained, "[t]hat energy source might be more clearly understood if you picture a searchlight that is circling the far distant heavens [momentarily] without interference from other bodies in the heavens, clearly shining on this planet as it did approximately two thousand years ago in its last orbiting."[48] Like a physical spotlight, planets and other astronomical objects might obstruct the Next Level energy, resulting in only periodic eras during which the light reached the Earth. This reinterpretation of dispensationalism, itself an interpretation of the biblical text, applies the fundamental assumptions of extraterrestrial biblical hermeneutics to the end-time scenario.

Much of Christian dispensationalist thought focuses on the idea of the Rapture of the faithful, the event during which dispensationalists believe living Christians rise into the air, meet Christ, and ascend into heaven. Hal Lindsey's *The Late Great Planet Earth* (1970), a dispensationalist best seller that was popular when Applewhite and Nettles first formulated their ideas, climaxed with a description of the Rapture, as well as incorporated the concept into much of the overall work.[49] (It is likely that Applewhite and Nettles read Lindsey's book, one of the decade's best sellers, given their admission of reading a variety of religious, spiritual, and scientific literatures; however there is no direct evidence of influence. It is also possible that since Texas, specifically Dallas, served as the center of dispensationalism, it percolated into their thought through less direct means.[50]) Applewhite and Nettles accepted the idea of the Rapture, but transformed the traditional view into a technological and material event. Rather than meeting Christ midair, their followers would aerially rendezvous with UFOs, one of which would hold the extraterrestrial whom human Christians remember as Jesus of Nazareth. "The one who was Jesus will come in at close range (as soon as those who have chosen to change over do it) and receive the elect in his company," they explained in their 1976 published statement.[51] (The Two presumably had not yet settled on the identification of Applewhite as Jesus at this time.) The UFOs, now bearing the human beings who had overcome their humanity through Applewhite and Nettles's process, would ascend into the literal heavens, forever leaving behind the Earth. In using the specifically religious term, "the elect," Applewhite and Nettles revealed the underlying religious content of their message, which used the vocabulary of their ufological hermeneutics—UFOs, biology, and space—but the concepts of Christian dispensationalism—resurrection, prophecy, and Rapture.

That the UFO rendezvous represented a technological reimagining of the Rapture explains why the Two so adamantly insisted that the UFOs would not land, but would meet the successful candidates for the Next Level in midair. During the Waldport meeting, Applewhite and Nettles stressed that although Jesus awaited successful candidates for the Next Level in a UFO, "He will not come down to this environment and show you His bruises and His glowing white robe. But he is present at close range, even now."[52] Attendees of the meeting might have interpreted that remark as an indication that the only evidence that Applewhite and Nettles promised was their demonstration and not the presence of Christ, and the Two certainly did stress that point as well. Yet their response to one of Brad Steiger's questions clarified the importance the Two placed on the aerial rendezvous itself, that is, the technological enactment of the Rapture. "Will other people be able to see the spaceship land and see the followers get on board?" asked Steiger. The Two responded, "[t]he spacecraft will not land. Individuals will be lifted up to the spacecraft if they have overcome. That is why if you go on this trip you have to overcome everything. If you have not overcome, you will not be lifted up."[53] Other sources repeated this important claim that the UFO would not land, and that the elect would rise into the air to meet Christ and craft midair.[54] Best explaining the Two's defense of this proposition, they desired to portray the impending departure of their followers on the UFO as a materialistic form of the Rapture as read through an extraterrestrial biblical hermeneutics.

From Dispensationalism to Suicide

As should be clear, the initial eschatological vision that the Two presented did not permit suicide as an option. Nor did it really work as a theology for a movement that existed for two decades, well longer than the Two initially indicated it would. And Nettles's and Applewhite's earlier eschatology completely failed to account for the death of Nettles in 1985, which violated the fundamental assumption of the group that there would be a bodily rapture of the faithful aboard midair UFOs. Nettles's death in particular resulted in a massive theological shift toward an eschatology predicated on mind-body dualism, a neo-Calvinistic notion of election and predestination, and increasing apocalyptic expectations. All of these permitted and even encouraged the development of a theology supportive of suicide.

Nettles's death served as a watershed in the history of Heaven's Gate, as important as the founding of the group itself. Applewhite became sole leader of the movement, and the surviving members transformed Nettles into a God-like figurehead whom the group members identified with the Father in the New Testament and Christian theology. Little clear evidence exists on Nettles's death itself, with conflicting statements from members, her family, and the media. She died on either June 18 or 19, 1985 from liver cancer, but had suffered from various other forms of cancer and health ailments for the previous year.[55] She had lost an eye to cancer in May 1982, and according to Sawyer ("Sawyer" is his nom de plume when discussing Heaven's Gate), a former member who is still a believer, she had been in pain for some time before and after that episode.[56] Ex-members Mrcody and Srfody reiterated that claim, noting that she had been suffering from disease for some time, and her passing was not entirely unexpected.[57] Yet for members of Heaven's Gate, Nettles's death was not death, but a point of transformation. Her cofounder Applewhite described the death as something far closer to a consciousness transfer than a true death:

> To all human appearances it was due to a form of liver cancer. We could say that because of the stress, due to the gap between her Next Level mind and the vehicle's genetic capacity, that the cancer symptom caused the vehicle to break down and stop functioning. However, it was strange that she experienced no symptoms prior to the week she left her vehicle, and for the most part her vehicle slept through the transition. We're not exactly sure how many days it might have taken her to return to the Next Level vehicle she left behind prior to this task.[58]

Nettles's death marked the first occurrence of the death of a member. While early in the movement's history the Two had preached that they would be martyred and resurrected—in accordance with the prophecy of Revelation 11—the Two had long since abandoned that teaching, and regardless Nettles did not resurrect after her death. The Two had adamantly insisted that one had to be alive to undergo the transition from human being to extraterrestrial and to board the UFO bound for the Next Level. "You do not have to die," they told Brad Steiger in 1976.[59] "You must take a changed-over physical body with you into the next level," they had elaborated.[60] The Two's followers had also clearly understood this teaching. When two of the Los Angeles converts were asked by a reporter in 1975 whether you have to die to go to the next level, their answer was direct. "Absolutely not."[61] Nettles's death changed all this. This was surely a moment of massive cognitive dissonance, when a sudden and unexpected event shook the expectation of the group's adherents. The surviving documents from this era are few, and all produced retrospectively several years later.

Ex-members provide the most candid reports. They all indicated that Nettles's death rocked the movement and Applewhite, but that most persevered. All agreed that Applewhite was able to cope and seemed to rise to the occasion, though he also had to respond to his feelings of loss. Sawyer, who was a member at the time, explained that

> Do was certainly very distraught when Ti passed on. It wasn't all that evident, except when He expressed it to us in a meeting and He did at that time want to also move on—[to] exit His vehicle[,] as Ti and Do both for a long time literally hated what this world had become . . . Yet He knew He still had a job to do to complete the task He had taken on, that Ti started Him on.[62]

Sawyer indicates that Applewhite was able to hold together the group through his own leadership, and that members seemed to accept Nettles's passing as merely part of a cosmically conceived plan. Neoody, a lapsed member of the movement who still identifies with the group's identity and message, simply explained that Nettles's death had "confused" Applewhite, though this comment was made years later and obviously underplayed the extreme emotional turmoil that surely resulted from the death of his spiritual partner.[63] Finally, Mrcody and Srfody—also members at this time who subsequently left the movement—indicated that Nettles's death "was really tough . . . a baptism by fire" for the members of the movement. "Everyone knew [she was sick], but it was unfathomable that she could die." Mrcody and Srfody explained that during Nettles's illness and immediately after her death, members began to discuss how the human body "simply couldn't handle the rigors of outer space" and Next Level activity, and that these bodies "would not survive the transition." They began to consider the need to "abandon the vehicle" (the body), though Mrcody and Srfody cautioned that "no one was discussing suicide" and that members still believed a flying saucer would pick them up, but now conceived as providing them with new bodies at that time rather than merely picking them up from Earth.[64]

From a sociological and theological perspective, Do was able to maintain cohesion of the movement by transitioning to a new form of extreme dualism, meaning that Ti was still alive, just in the Next Level. Nettles's prolonged illness probably provided the impetus for the Two to consider the ramifications of her potential death, a possibility that the spread of her cancer would certainly have raised. Applewhite's retrofit of the movement's theology saved the group from a certain collapse. This effort was made easier by the earlier reformulation within the group's theology of the idea of the Demonstration, which the Two had at first indicated would mean their actual murders followed by resurrections. Predicated on their interpretation of Revelation 11, Applewhite and Nettles had initially declared that they would be martyred, lay dead in the street for three days, and then be resurrected through Next Level technology, thereby demonstrating to humanity the validity of their teachings and the need to overcome human-level consciousness and cleave to the Next Level. Yet the Demonstration did not occur, and Applewhite and Nettles were forced to reinterpret the prediction as one describing a metaphorical martyrdom and resurrection. Applewhite indicated their theological reasoning in the *'88 Update*, the booklet produced to provide a mini-history of the movement:

> when the TV network news programs all broke the story about the two . . . Ti and Do felt that further meetings were pretty hopeless and people had already made up their minds about how ridiculous this all was. Ti and Do felt that the demonstration was still the one thing that could change that. However, they grieved literally for days, feeling like they had been shot down by the media and the mission was dead. They received instruction to not walk into a physical demonstration but rather

to know that the "killing in the street" of the two witnesses had occurred at the hands of the media.[65]

Applewhite showed remarkable reflexivity in recognizing that the public would generally judge their teachings to be "ridiculous" and that they stood little chance of attracting any significant number of converts. After all, the news stories to which Applewhite referred had revealed not only the names of the Two but also the rather damning facts of Applewhite's incarceration and various relational ills. One cannot know to what extent this need for a "reboot" might have served as impetus for Nettles and Applewhite to redefine the nature of the Demonstration, versus to what extent the fundamental problem was that the Demonstration had not yet occurred as predicted. Early Christians also had to respond to a similar "delay of the parousia" problem wherein the expected prophetically mandated event did not occur. (The Biblical Greek term parousia—literally, "presence"—means the return of Christ, and became an issue in early Christianity given the non-event of Christ's return to Earth.) Scholars of new religious movements in particular have noted that such delays often occur, and that successful new religions respond to the delay of the parousia through theological creativity.[66]

Applewhite and Nettles successfully held together their movement by reinterpreting the Demonstration to refer to a symbolic martyrdom and resurrection, and in doing so they planted the seeds for further reinterpretation of key eschatological claims. Effectively, members who would not accept such theological reinterpretations would have already left the movement during its early days, meaning that the only members remaining as part of Heaven's Gate into the 1980s and 1990s were already comfortable with this sort of reinterpretation and placed allegiance in the leaders themselves rather than the specifics of their religious message. Therefore, in the wake of Nettles's death, when Applewhite fundamentally transformed Heaven's Gate's vision of the nature of the human self and the form that salvation would take, adherents accepted this reinterpretation as well. Only one member left because of Nettles's death.[67]

Following Nettles's death, Applewhite deemphasized premillennial dispensationalism and replaced it with a more general apocalypticism.

Gone were specific references to a midair rapture, and never again did he refer to the seven dispensations of the Scofield system. However, Applewhite and the members of Heaven's Gate substituted a new apocalypticism predicated on ufological conspiracy theories, cultural pessimism, and technological Armageddon. Applewhite generally preferred horticultural metaphors when discussing eschatological concerns, most commonly referring to Earth as a garden about to be refreshed, and the few individuals who would journey to the Next Level as a sort of crop. In the 1991–92 satellite broadcasts he introduces the topic of the end-times in precisely this way: "here we are at the end of the Age and it's harvest time. Harvest time means that it's time for the garden to be spaded up. It's time for a recycling of souls. It's time for some to 'graduate.' It's time for some to be 'put on ice.' It's time!"[68] In a later broadcast in the same series, after viewers had some chance to hear more about their message and beliefs, Applewhite offered an even more dramatic and imminent perspective: "between now and the end of this decade— and I'm afraid I feel like we're off a number of years, that it's going to be significantly before the end of this decade—will be the end of this Age. So, it's spade time. And the big, big, big surprise will come."[69] Later in the same broadcasts Applewhite mentioned disease, environmental disasters, war, plague, extraterrestrial invasion, and government persecution as possible means by which the Next Level would allow the garden of Earth to become "spaded over." A certain theological sloppiness existed in Applewhite's approach, since he at times indicated that the forces of the evil Luciferian space aliens would be responsible for these events, and at other times indicated that such occurrences were in keeping with Next Level plans and judgments. Yet since the same inconsistency generally exists among more mainstream believers in Christian apocalypticism—substituting Satan for Luciferian extraterrestrials and God for Next Level ones—Applewhite merely reflected the influences of his millennial source tradition.

Alongside this shift in apocalyptic thinking away from rapture-oriented dispensationalism and toward a more general catastrophic millennialism, Applewhite taught that those destined to be saved, i.e., members of Heaven's Gate and those who followed them, would ascend to the Next Level not in bodily but in a non-corporeal form. This more than any other shift permitted the eventual adoption of a theology of

Figure 4.2. Video snapshot of Marshall Herff Applewhite (Do) from the 1991–1992 satellite series *Beyond Human*. Image © TELAH Foundation.

suicide, since it made the body an unnecessary hindrance to the soteriological pursuit. Since the first days of the movement, Applewhite and Nettles had denigrated the human body and taught the need to overcome it. Yet they had initially indicated that one had to transform the flawed human body into a perfected Next Level one through entirely physical means. Applewhite jettisoned this approach in the wake of Nettles's death.

Applewhite and members of Heaven's Gate were explicit in defining the body as a mere container that served little purpose beyond conveying the true self until such time as the body was no longer needed. To again quote the 1991–92 satellite program, the first major theological material produced by the group after Nettles's death:

> we use the reference [of "vehicle"] to this body that we're wearing—this flesh and bones—we use the term "vehicle" because it helps us separate from the body. . . . Whether it's a "vehicle" or "vessel," the term helps to get out of identifying with it. Where we get into trouble is when we identify and call this "me," because this is certainly not me if the soul has awakened. This is just a suit of clothes that I'm wearing, and at times it can be an encumbrance for me. It can be something that I don't want to identify with.[70]

Communications scholar Robert Glenn Howard calls this the "rhetoric of the rejected body," and he roots this rhetoric in a combination of inherited Protestantism and Applewhite's own rejection of his corporeal nature based on his muddled sexual identity and experiences. Howard rightly calls Applewhite's "co-opt[ing] and radicaliz[ing] the coercive power of Protestantism related to gender roles and sexuality" a rejection of both Christian and American societal norms.[71] While I find Howard's approach somewhat misguided in its highlighting of Applewhite's sexuality and disregard for his religious searching and background, Howard's characterizing of Applewhite's theology as it relates to the body is apt: Heaven's Gate rejected the body outright.

Instead, Applewhite and members of the movement believed that the individual self rested in a non-corporeal essence that they variably called the soul, self, or—later, toward the end of the movement—the deposit. A slow shift away from religious language and toward a sort of rhetorical materialism exists in their theological treatment of the soul, with both members and Applewhite in the 1991–92 broadcasts making use of the explicit language of the soul. At times, such as in the context of the discussion of the body as vehicle, Applewhite made no attempt to even explain the nature of the soul beyond indicating that it is "the real 'me'" and a sort of "invisible container" that holds the body within itself.[72] Yet generally Applewhite assumed his viewers—generally familiar with Christianity, based on American demographics—would have the same idea of "soul" as he did. It was the soul, Applewhite seemed to assume his viewers knew, that journeyed to the Next Level and would become the rootstock of a perfected extraterrestrial creature.

By the end of the movement's history, Applewhite and his followers treated the soul in a different way, a quasi-technological way that they insisted was materialistic rather than supernatural, despite its incorporeal nature. By 1996, just a year before the suicides that ended the movement, Applewhite described the soul using terms more reminiscent of computer technology than medieval theology: "their [Next Level] design enabled them to make small 'mental deposits' in human plants. We'll call those 'deposits,' for sake of understanding, the 'soul.' And those deposits are really like a small bit of Next Level 'hardware' with capacity for Next Level information."[73] Elsewhere Applewhite used similar language, referring to the deposit as computer-like, or akin to a computer chip.

Heaven's Gate member Snnody was even more explicit in her statement "Deposits," which appeared in the anthology Heaven's Gate produced shortly before the movement's end. Snnody writes that "deposits can also be compared to tiny computer chips programmed with a sort of 'homing device' to seek nourishment which can come only from a member of the Level Above Human," and that deposits function to provide "programming" to allow the self to begin its "metamorphic process" of becoming a Next Level being. Applewhite and Nettles had used language of metamorphosis since the first days of the movement, and Snnody invokes such language for similar reasons, namely to rhetorically position Heaven's Gate as offering a sort of materialistic equivalent to what most religious people would consider salvation. Snnody and other members went to great lengths to use entirely physical and material metaphors drawing from horticulture and technology to explain the nature of the deposit.

Those gifted with deposits had "eyes to see" the message that Heaven's Gate brought, a clear biblical reference that Applewhite cited accordingly. Different members of Heaven's Gate offered slightly different assessments of the true nature of the deposit, indicating that members felt no need for theological unity on this point. Snnody stated that the deposit contained the soul, and that different sorts of deposits existed. Some deposits mark a soul as beginning its journey to the Next Level, others mark an individual for use by a Next Level consciousness that is in need of a physical body, and a third type indicates a soul in the process of development.[74] Snnody states that most human beings lack deposits and implies that therefore the majority of people lack true souls. Snnody's compatriot Jnnody offered a slightly different approach, explaining that souls can exist without deposits, but that such souls can never advance beyond the human level of existence and are therefore stunted. Jnnody concurs that only individuals with deposits can recognize the truth offered by Heaven's Gate and thereby achieve Next Level consciousness.[75] Applewhite by comparison seems at time to almost dismiss the relevance of the topic, explaining that anyone who understands and accepts the message that he offers by definition has been bestowed with a deposit and therefore is one of the elect. "Well, if the Next Level picks you, don't question it. Let them be the ones responsible for that," Applewhite simply stated.[76]

Applewhite's mention of "the elect" reveals his rootedness in the Calvinist worldview that shaped his own Presbyterian birth tradition, a tradition with which he would have been deeply familiar given his father's ministerial vocation and his own attendance at a Presbyterian seminar. While the Presbyterian denomination with which Applewhite and his father were associated no longer upheld the orthodox positions of predestination and election as laid out in Calvin's *Institutes* or the Westminster Confession, Applewhite surely would have studied them for their historical and theological value. Predestination teaches that God predestines certain souls for salvation ("the elect") and others for damnation, a position identical to the one that Heaven's Gate eventually adopted. As I have noted in my previous research on Heaven's Gate—as has Christopher Partridge—the presence of this neo-Calvinist notion of election marks Heaven's Gate as a Christian theological offshoot.[77] Applewhite developed a rather complicated interpretation of the doctrine of election, but effectively summarized his view with the simple axiom that those who accepted his message must be elect, and those that rejected it clearly were not elect.[78]

Why exactly did Applewhite and adherents of Heaven's Gate even introduce this notion of election? Election separated the in-group from the out-group and explained the troublesome revolving door of group membership and the failure of Heaven's Gate to attract large numbers of converts.[79] Unlike the Puritans, Dutch Reformed, or other Calvinist communities, members of Heaven's Gate did not profess any doubts about their election. Do specifically reminded them that if they remained part of the group, they were elect. No members or former members of Heaven's Gate or its predecessor movements recorded any Edwardsian struggles over the state of their souls and whether they were of the elect. There is no evidence that Nettles or Applewhite ever turned away any prospective adherents under the pretext that the Older Members declared them to be not elect. Never did the spiritual leaders of the movement eject a follower because he or she lacked grace, although Ti and Do expelled at least nineteen people from the group over the years.[80] Since Reformed traditions generally uphold the idea of the "perseverance of the saints"—once elect, always elect—the expulsion of members seems remarkably discordant with this sort of Calvinist predestinarian theology. This approach might also have served to encourage retention within the movement, though the group's turnover rate indicated it did not fully succeed, dropping from forty-eight members at the time Nettles died and around when the doctrine of election was introduced to twenty-four in the early 1990s before the group began recruiting again.[81] While it might have slowed the rate of attrition, it did not solve it, and it is doubtful Applewhite intended it to do so.

Rather, the neo-Reformed elements of the group's soteriology served to minimize cognitive dissonance, a term coined by Leon Festinger to refer to a psychological state created when members of a religious group must rectify two contradictory sets of facts or beliefs. In his flawed but valuable study of the pseudonymously named "Seekers," a small UFO group that Festinger and his collaborators had studied, he utilizes the concept of dissonance in order to explain how the group members responded to a failed doomsday prophecy. The failures of predicted events to occur among both the Seekers and Heaven's Gate bear remarkable similarity—for the Seekers, no UFO landing, for Heaven's Gate, widespread rejection by the popular audience and no UFO landing. As a result, Festinger argued, members experienced cognitive dissonance. "The fact that the predicted events did not occur is dissonant with continuing to believe both the prediction and the remainder of the ideology of which the prediction was the central item," writes Festinger.[82] In the case of the Seekers, the disappointed believers sought to reduce the dissonance by proselytizing. Applewhite and Nettles developed for their followers a neo-Calvinist doctrine of election that explained why so few people joined their movement, satisfying Festinger's requirement that the group minimize dissonance in order to survive: "[t]he dissonance would be largely eliminated if they discarded the belief that had been disconfirmed, [or] ceased the behavior which had been initiated in preparation for the fulfillment of the prediction."[83] Heaven's Gate did both, discarding the notion that salvation, i.e., the overcoming process, was open to all, and largely neglected proselytizing for extended periods of time. The cognitive dissonance model best explains this shift in Heaven's Gate's tone.

Salvation Through Suicide

In a now famous monograph on the Peoples Temple, the new religious movement that engaged in a mass suicide and murder in Guyana in 1977, David Chidester wrote that "suicide itself may be regarded as an act of symbolic design. On the level of symbolism, suicide may factor out all of the variables of human life by imposing a single, self-determined order on the chaos of events."[84] While numerous differences exist between the murder-suicides of the Peoples Temple members and the suicides of Heaven's Gate members, Chidester's argument holds in both cases. Suicide functioned as a way to give meaning and order to life, and for the adherents of Heaven's Gate it functioned as the means of ending their terrestrial existence on their own terms.

The concept of suicide emerged in Heaven's Gate religious doctrine only very late in the group's history, but when it did the stage had been set for members to take very seriously the possibility of the need for religious suicide. Ex-members Mrcody and Srfody stated that no one had discussed suicide before they left the group in September 1987: "There was no talk ever of exiting [i.e. suicide] like they [eventually] did," they explained.[85] Balch indicates that a former member indicated discussions occurring as early as 1991, which seems to be the earliest possible date.[86] By contrast, ex-member Neoody recounts that the first mention of suicide occurred in the late spring of 1994. Neoody remembers this event as not particularly noteworthy, and that Applewhite had simply noted that he had received a revelation from the spiritual form of Nettles indicating that they may need to lay down their human bodies in order to join the Next Level.[87] In all likelihood, members of Applewhite's inner circle had discussed suicide as early as 1991, and Neoody only became aware of this when Applewhite publicly announced it in 1994. It is also important to note that Neoody writes from the perspective of a surviving member of a defunct group, and that he penned his thoughts on the episode a decade and a half after the described events. Yet the chronology Neoody describes of other events—travels, meetings, rentals of homes—can be easily verified through other materials, and one can therefore trust Neoody's memory of when Applewhite first raised the issue of suicide. At any rate, Heaven's Gate publicly alluded to the possibility of suicide in an August 1994 poster provokingly titled "The Shedding of Our Borrowed Human Bodies May Be Required In Order To Take Up Our New Bodies Belonging To The Next World."[88]

In Neoody's assessment, Applewhite presented suicide as an option because of the model of Jesus's willing death nearly two thousand years earlier. Since Applewhite claimed to in fact be the same spiritual being who had incarnated as Jesus, he spoke from personal experience, and explained to the group simply that "Jesus was ready to go back to the Father." In Neoody's recollection, Applewhite continued: "With tears in His eyes He said: 'leaving the body here is how the Soul of Jesus traveled back to the 'Next Level.' He asked of all of us 'What if we had to exit our vehicles by our own choice? Did we have a problem with that?' We all had a long conversation about the possibilities . . . As it turned out most people had no problem with that. They didn't identify with the vehicle anyway."[89]

Neoody admits that one member publicly challenged the decision and "packed his bags" that night. But Neoody himself stayed, though he later left the group shortly before the actual suicides. He explained that when Applewhite first broached the topic, he and his co-religionists supported suicide since they did not identify with their bodies ("vehicles"). Since the death of Nettles the basic theological beliefs of the group, at least as Neoody understood it, had indicated that they would abandon their human bodies and receive perfected Next Level bodies upon leaving the planet. Voluntarily relinquishing the human body therefore did not strike him—or most others, according to his memory—as odd. "Separate yourself (Soul/Mind) from the vehicle," Neoody paraphrased Applewhite's teachings. The soul or spirit encapsulates the true self, and the body is a mere container to be discarded when no longer needed.

This sort of dualistic approach also appeared in the August 1994 poster. Referring to themselves in the third person, the members of Heaven's Gate declared, "They say that they may be required to discard their 'undercover costume' (their borrowed human body) as they depart—leaving their 'chrysalis' behind." While the poster equivocated on whether this possibility would be required and whether perhaps the group might leave in bodily form on a "'cloud of light' (spacecraft) before such 'laying down of bodies' need occur," the dualistic assumptions that Applewhite and others had built over the decade since Nettles's death clearly were evident.[90]

Less than three years later the members of the movement took their lives in the act of collective suicide that ended the movement, a topic to which I will return in the final chapter of the book. But it would be a mistake to think that this idea had emerged out of thin air. Suicide built upon decades of rhetoric and ideology that denigrated the value of the human body, human activities, and human relationships. It built upon the same long history of proclaiming the possibility of martyrdom and resurrection, and it built upon the explicit mind/body dualism that the movement embraced after Nettles's death. While it would be an equal mistake to assume that suicide was the only option Heaven's Gate members had, one must recognize that it seemed like an almost natural concept to those adherents who had accepted and lived within this belief system for years. True suicide, members believed, meant staying behind on a doomed Earth rather than joining the Two in the Next Level.

The religious world of Heaven's Gate ended with the suicides, but their theological world remains in the materials they left behind. This chapter has argued that adherents of the movement constructed and lived within a dense and internally coherent set of religious beliefs and doctrines, a theology as logical to them as other religious theologies are to other practitioners. Members of Heaven's Gate upheld views of how one achieved salvation (soteriology), the order of the universe (cosmology), the nature and meaning of Christ (Christology), the nature of the forces acting against them (demonology), and beliefs about the end-times and final days of the Earth (eschatology). While certainly not convincing to outsiders, for adherents of Heaven's Gate these religious beliefs provided meaning, structure, and order in their lives.

5

Religious Practices in Heaven's Gate

Most of the scholarship on Heaven's Gate has focused on the group's social dynamics, their history, or increasingly on their religious beliefs, as the last chapter did.[1] Yet Heaven's Gate had a thorough set of religious practices that they developed over their two-decade history. Studying these practices presents more difficulties than studying their social dynamics, history, or beliefs, since practices leave fewer remnants. One can track membership and interview current or former members to assess a group's social dynamics, assemble archival material to get a sense of the group's history, and analyze the textual material to ascertain what members of the movement believed. But how does one study the religious practices of a defunct group?

In this chapter I reassemble the religious practices of adherents of Heaven's Gate by piecing together the ephemeral materials they left behind. Interviews with former members, devotional handbooks, behavioral guides, field notes from those who studied them, and the textual, audio, and video material the group left behind all provide some pieces of the puzzle. But before considering the religious practices of Heaven's Gate members, we must consider the religious practices of the movements that influenced Heaven's Gate's development. The adherents of Heaven's Gate borrowed and transformed the majority of their religious practices from sources within the diffuse New Age movement.

As previously noted, Applewhite, Nettles, and the majority of their followers all hailed from the religious environment that one can call either the early New Age movement or the cultic milieu, to follow Colin

Campbell. Yet Heaven's Gate tended to blur the boundaries between Christianity and the New Age, leading to an ongoing debate between scholars as to how to situate it and confusion among people trying to understand what this group was. As I have argued, Heaven's Gate's beliefs were fundamentally shaped by Christianity and their overall religious scheme was predicated on their interpretation of the Bible. Yet their religious practices did in fact derive from the New Age movement. In particular, Heaven's Gate inherited from the New Age an emphasis on self-transformation as the central idea of salvation and the central religious practice.

Self-Transformation and the Spiritual Practices of Heaven's Gate

Scholars have had a difficult time trying to define the precise practices of the New Age movement, just as they have had trouble defining the movement itself. It includes practices such as the use of tarot cards, crystals, shamanic healing, ufology, therapeutic touch, energywork, past life regressions, and meditation. New Age practitioners engage in a broad array of spiritual practices drawing from the Western esoteric, spiritualist, Native American, Asian, and Western religious tradition. One finds astrology, channeling, sweet lodges, yoga, and kabbalism side by side in the New Age. Yet one commonality stretches across most New Age practices and beliefs, that of self-transformation as the key means of self-development and salvation.

Particularly on the West Coast of America where Heaven's Gate emerged, the New Age movement drew much of its impetus from the work of transpersonal and humanistic psychology, specifically the system developed by Abraham Maslow (1908–70). An academic psychologist, Maslow did not himself become involved in the New Age. Yet his research and writing did. Maslow focused on the idea of what he called "self-actualization," wherein a person achieves the highest level of psychological functioning, which is characterized by a sense of wholeness, truth, completion, and peace. He wrote of "peak experiences" akin to what religious individuals would call mystical experiences, and he encouraged individuals to seek them out. Maslow's ideas became very influential in the New Age movement under the guise of the Human

Potential movement. Human Potential stressed that each individual must seek self-fulfillment and individual transformation so as to seek self-actualization. The Esalen Institute in Big Sur, California, served as the center of the Human Potential movement, and the founders and members of Heaven's Gate would have literally crossed its path while trekking between the recruitment meetings they held.[2]

The New Age movement overlaps with the Human Potential movement, and many of the New Age practitioners who joined Heaven's Gate would have been familiar with it. Historian Kay Alexander has argued that Human Potential's peak experience in fact equates on a secular level to the transcendent, and "was born of a new interest in the spiritual dimension of experience."[3] The individuals who became involved in Human Potential became familiar with language about heightening their spiritual and psychological awareness, self-transformation, and individual growth. Heaven's Gate used similar language, no doubt because of Nettles's and Applewhite's own readings of the diverse spiritual literature, and perhaps also intentionally as a way to form a bridge to potential converts.

As spiritual seekers, the individuals who joined Heaven's Gate sought self-transformation and development, though they might not have used those terms. In fact, such self-transformation emerged as the heart of this inchoate religious movement. "In a general sense 'personal growth' can be understood as the shape 'religious salvation' takes in the New Age movement," explains historian Wouter Hanegraaff.[4] Other scholars take the same position. Gordon Melton calls transformation the "primal experience" of the New Age movement. "New Agers have either experienced or are diligently seeking a profound personal transformation from an old, unacceptable way of life to a new, exciting future."[5] American religious historian Sarah M. Pike takes a similar approach, explaining that the term is an umbrella description, but at its heart the New Age possesses one common core: "New Agers are committed to the transformation of both self and society through a host of practices that include channeling, visualization, astrology, meditation, and alternative healing methods such as Reiki . . . or iridology."[6] For both Melton and Pike, transformational practices and technologies of transformation serve as the center of the New Age movement from which Heaven's Gate drew many of its adherents.

Not surprisingly, self-transformation lay at the heart of Heaven's Gate's religious milieu from its very first days until the end of the movement's history, and therefore at the heart of the group's religious practices. Nettles and Applewhite taught that they served as religious guides—later this developed into far more elevated positions of course—to help adherents transform themselves into perfected extraterrestrial creatures. In the first phase of the movement's history, before Nettles's death in 1985, the two emphasized the physical nature of this process. They labeled it a biological and chemical process of overcoming one's humanity and personally evolving into a higher organism. They likened it to a caterpillar's metamorphosis or a student's graduation, two metaphors that remained within the collective discourse of the movement until its demise two decades later. Their First Statement encapsulated this approach in explicit form, comparing human beings to the pupal stages of extraterrestrial life,

> However, if the human is thought of as the larva of that next kingdom then there are, at times, those who are approaching the completion of their individual metamorphosis and are beginning to have some of the attributes and characteristics of that next kingdom. When the metamorphosis is complete their "perennial" and cyclical nature is ended for their "new" body has overcome decay, disease and death. It has converted over chemically, biologically, and in vibration to the "new" creature.[7]

In addition to alluding to the then-current name of the movement—Human Individual Metamorphosis—and foreshadowing the later name—Total Overcomers Anonymous—this statement shows how Nettles and Applewhite positioned self-transformation at the center of their religious vision.

Elsewhere they used academic metaphors, comparing their spiritual teachings to a rigorous classroom experience meant to propel students from lower levels of awareness toward higher ones. "A way of understanding this process is to think of his cycles [of experiences and existences] as twelve grades in school," explained the Two.[8] Because the Two accepted the idea of reincarnation—a belief probably deriving from Nettles's background with Theosophy, which also accepts reincarnation—they looked to this schooling process as a long and arduous one. Yet they argued it was worth it, for it culminated in transformation into extraterrestrial life. "It is graduation time for all levels of life forms," they declared in the continuation of the metaphor.[9]

The pupae/pupil metaphors positioned Heaven's Gate within the culture of self-development and self-exploration that characterized the New Age movement. It also ties into Theosophy, which both Applewhite and Nettles admitted to reading and with which Nettles had been affiliated. Inspired by Buddhist and Hindu views of reincarnation, Theosophy teaches that individuals take more successfully evolved incarnations so as to personally evolve toward higher consciousness. Nettles and Applewhite did not stress reincarnation in their early teachings, but they clearly accepted it, and Applewhite later made it a sanctioned and important part of the Heaven's Gate belief system. Reincarnation served an unclear role at the end of the movement's existence, but several ex-members confirmed that they believed it was a part of the group's beliefs even at the end.[10] Since so many Americans accept reincarnation—upwards of 24 percent of all Americans, as recently as 2009—the Two parlayed this popular belief into a means of reaching out for new adherents.[11] It became part of their rhetoric of self-transformation.

The idea of transformation into an extraterrestrial may strike many people as unbelievable and downright bizarre, but it made sense to adherents of Heaven's Gate for several reasons. First, the New Age emphasis on self-transformation and personal spiritual evolution had already primed them to accept such a possibility. Major New Age teachers and books such as Jane Roberts's *Seth Speaks*, Helen Schucman's *A Course in Miracles*, Starhawk's *The Spiral Dance*, Shirley MacLaine's *Out on a Limb*, and James Redfield's *Celestine Prophecy* all taught that individuals could transform themselves both physically and spiritually through specific spiritual practices. American champions of the Hindu practice of yoga in particular claimed that yoga could enact bodily transformations leading to not just greater wisdom or flexibility, but a variety of arcane powers as well. Paramahansa Yogananda's Self-Realization Fellowship and its kriya yoga system, as well as Swami Muktananda's siddha yoga movement, both upheld variants of this, and both were active in the mid-1970s when Heaven's Gate attracted its first converts. Maharishi Mahesh Yogi's Transcendental Meditation, another very popular Indian import at the time Heaven's Gate was emerging, also upheld a vision of transforming the body, though in this case through meditative practices, and obtaining new abilities possibly including levitation.[12] Proponents of all of these popular techniques taught that individuals could transform their bodies into more perfected forms, achieving a variety of powers and abilities.[13]

Remaking the World as the Next Level: Dwelling

Having traced the origins and context of the religious world of Heaven's Gate, as well as the overall goal of members to achieve personal self-transformation into perfected alien creatures, one can now consider how members sought to achieve this through religious practice. Religious practice has recently become a new focal point within the study of religion, offering scholars a manner of reaching and analyzing "religion on the ground" and not just in the heads of believers. Under this rubric of "lived religion" scholars have focused on how the adherents of a diverse range of religions create meaningful practices in their daily lives, within the context of social groups and institutions.[14] In the words of historians Laurie F. Maffly-Kipp, Leigh Eric Schmidt, and Mark R. Valeri, attention to practice allows scholars to broaden the scope of our studies and consider religion from a wider angle. "Within religious studies, the deployment of the category of practice has facilitated examinations of behavior beyond narrow constructions of ritual and liturgy, enabling scholars to move into the murky arenas of daily social encounter and everyday experience," they explain.[15] Indeed, attention to religious practice within Heaven's Gate helps us to highlight the actual experiences of members rather than only the final ritual—suicide—for which the group is best remembered.

Pierre Bourdieu has reminded scholars that practice serves as a means of translating one's fundamental personhood—*habitus*, to use his term—into a means of living and relating to the people and institutions around oneself. Habitus provides a means of understanding one's world through deeply held assumptions, approaches, and perspectives, but practice is how a person lives. Practice functions as the way of translating habitus into means of creating, procuring, and using capital, either in the material sense of food and stuff, or the immaterial sense of religious and social capital.[16] Bourdieu focused on religion in its role within colonial and post-colonial conflicts, but his general point has broader relevance.[17] Terry Rey, one of Bourdieu's foremost interpreters within the field of religious studies, argues that Bourdieu points scholars toward study of the body within the context of practice: "Bourdieu's work offers much analytical power to scholars seeking to understand the central place of the human body in religious experience and practice."[18] Practice, for Bourdieu, involves control and manipulation of the individual body of the member of society and collective body of society itself.

One of the most helpful recent theoretical considerations of religious practice and its connection to religious identity and beliefs is the approach of cultural theorist and American religious historian Thomas A. Tweed, who also highlights issues of the body. Tweed considers the place of religious practice as part of a broader project in crafting a theoretical understanding of religions, and as such one must contextualize his view of practice with his view and definition of religion. Tweed defines religions as "confluences of organic-cultural flows that intensify joy and confront suffering by drawing on human and suprahuman forces to make homes and cross boundaries."[19] Wordy as that definition may be—and Tweed admits to this—it centers and highlights the practices that Tweed considers most central to religion, namely the creation and maintenance of worlds in which the religious live. Tweed calls this "crossing and dwelling," and places these practices at the heart of religious life. He connects these practices to the notion of what he calls "organic-cultural flows," named embodied practices that religious individuals perform as parts of communities of religious belief and practice. Tweed writes:

> as many theorists have noticed, religions are performed. The religious prescribe and enact a wide range of embodied practices, including culturally patterned practices or rituals—for example, praying, bowing, reading, singing, fasting, dancing, meditating, or chanting. To say that religions are organic-cultural flows, then, is to suggest they are confluences that conjoin to create institutional networks that, in turn, prescribe, transmit, and transform tropes, beliefs, values, emotions, artifacts, and rituals.[20]

Within the religious system of Heaven's Gate many such religious practices existed, and they functioned as Tweed describes. Heaven's Gate members structured their lives around practices related to eating, sleeping, working, meditating, and creating homes, all of which fall within Tweed's category of "dwelling." They also practiced acts—often the same ones—that sought to transport them from their human worlds to superhuman ones, often but not only through physical travel. Such "crossing" practices included actual movement, but also prayers and other actions designed to distance the self from the human level of existence. Members of Heaven's Gate tended to combine both crossing- and dwelling-related practices within the same actual religious behaviors, for example meditation or eating. Yet one can also attempt to separate these practices according to Tweed's typology in order to better understand how such religious practices functioned within the context of the religious world of members.

Heaven's Gate members dwelled in many places and in many ways. They were a highly mobile group, moving from campground to campground in their early years and from house to house in their later years. Often small subgroups of members would strike out on their own and create "satellite" colonies, or travel separately so as to host meeting and other public events. Yet within all this crossing they dwelled too. Heaven's Gate members created human homes and human lives, but they did so with the intention of overcoming their basic humanity. Tweed describes dwelling as an active process by which one creates meaning and gets one's bearings. "[D]welling, like crossing, is doing. Dwelling, as I use the term, involves three overlapping processes: mapping, building, and inhabiting."[21] Because living groups such as Heaven's Gate tend not to follow strict theoretical divisions, it is best in this case to look at these three processes as one single fluid set of activities: Heaven's Gate members mapped their cosmos through creating homes and individual identities, built livable worlds through actions within those homes that helped them create the types of identities that they sought, and tried to inhabit this world through ritual practices that rooted them within their religious community. These practices then reinforced the adherents' beliefs, creating a religious system in which individuals found meaning and value.

Throughout the history of Heaven's Gate, members grappled with how to create livable space in which to dwell, and how to use that practice to make meaning and achieve their religious goals of transcendence and overcoming the human condition. The specific way they did this involved transforming human space into Next Level space, by rhetorically repositioning it. "Next Level"-talk served as one of the most important modes of religious practice, since it actively created meaningful dwellings for members. Because Heaven's Gate members believed that Next Level beings lived and worked in spacecrafts in manners reminiscent of the world of *Star Trek*, *Battlestar Galactica*, or *Stargate*, they used language drawn from those science fiction franchises as the central way of rhetorically creating meaningful dwellings.

Heaven's Gate members called their abodes "crafts," short for spacecrafts. Former Heaven's Gate member Neoody explains that they did so in order to mimic the Next Level and create a Next Level-like atmosphere: "it is our understanding that 'Next Level Beings' do most of their tasks from a spacecraft. So, we were taught to do all of our tasks as if in a laboratory on board a spacecraft with crew minded accuracy."[22] Robert W. Balch, who studied the group during its early days, reported a similar phenomenon of members redefining their dwelling places as crafts during the group's formative period of 1975 and 1976, showing that this practice reached back to the movement's formative days.[23] Renaming these spaces in this way, the members of Heaven's Gate created sacred spaces meant to duplicate those in the literal heavens, outer space. While they did so using the language of science fiction, they were quite serious about the practice. Since Next Level beings dwelled in crafts, and Heaven's Gate members sought to become Next Level beings, they too lived in crafts. Within each craft they similarly transformed the constituent spaces into dwellable spaces through the use of Next Level language. As previously noted, Neoody explains that they called bedrooms "rest chambers," kitchens "nutri-labs," laundry rooms "fiber-labs," and offices "compu-labs," terms that the members felt represented the high-tech nature of the Next Level. Members renamed as "out of craft tasks" their excursions out of the house to earn money through odd jobs or to engage outsiders. [24]

These practices as described by Neoody illustrate what Tweed calls the "homemaking" aspect of dwelling. Religious individuals, he indicates, engage in practices of "constructing, adorning, and inhabiting domestic space. Religion, in this sense, is housework."[25] Heaven's Gate's members remade their human dwellings into spaceships fit for the Next Level and its inhabitants, created homes through religious language and the way they related to the space. They therefore transformed the mere ordinary space in which they dwelled—campgrounds, rented houses, and in one case even a warehouse—into sacred space, space that they as religious people could inhabit. This transformation provided the spaces with a sense of meaning and transcendence, and gave those living within them a sense that they were not merely engaged in ordinary human dwelling, but actively engaged in the religious pursuit of overcoming the human condition. Even excursions out of the safe space of the craft became transformed through this religious language. Rather than a potentially unsettling sojourn from the insular and sectarian community in which they lived, outings became "out of craft tasks" akin to spacewalks.

One of the best examples of Heaven's Gate's members' religious practices as they related to dwelling involves a camp that the group purchased and transformed in Manzano, New Mexico, in 1995. Naming it the "launch pad," the members of Heaven's Gate attempted to build the most elaborate manifestation of their spatial practices on the abandoned husk of a former summer camp previously owned by an insurance company. There they sought to create a multi-building community modeled on the "Earth ship" approach of building structures using recycled tires. Though the movement did not complete their "launch pad," it serves as a powerful example of how they developed their spatial practices in an attempt to create a Next Level dwelling.

The Earth ship model, popularized by Michael Reynolds in Solar System Press's book, *Earth Ship: How to Build Your Own*, calls for creating buildings through the careful deployment of recycled automobile tires. Billed as an ecological and self-sufficient way to create an alternative way of living, supporters of the Earth ship approach view it as a way to sustainably live within the limited resources of the planet, as well as create self-sufficient homes not dependent on external resources such as hookups to electricity, sewage, or water. The Earth ship movement therefore blends environmentalism and ecological awareness with survivalism and homesteading. For Heaven's Gate members, this alternative model of creating a dwelling offered a chance to create a non-human building while still living among humans. The name "Earth ship" would have appealed to them, and we know that members of the movement purchased a copy of Reynolds's book to use while building the launch pad.

The members of Heaven's Gate planned to build several buildings according to the Earth ship model. In addition to a multi-room dwelling of which they successfully built the walls but not a roof, they also planned for a bakery, pharmacy, lookout tower, and a kitchen and mess hall, what they described to the later owner of the property as a "nutri-lab" and "consuming area."[26] Clearly the movement's members were planning on a long-term dwelling, and one can see in their plans the approach of a group of people interested in orienting themselves in time and space, as Tweed would describe it.[27] Heaven's Gate's adherents intended to use this space to live in accordance with Next Level norms and practices, on an Earth ship that contained not just a craft to live within, but all the other buildings necessary to support and maintain their community, ranging from defense (guard tower) to sustenance (bakery, nutri-lab, and consuming area), and health (pharmacy). Interestingly, the forty-acre property that they purchased already contained a mess hall from its previous service as a summer camp. Building new Earth ship style dwellings for the production and consumption of food, despite adequate conventional facilities already existing, shows just how seriously they took the need to inhabit Next Level rather than human level dwellings. Yet for all this, the launch pad project did not prove a long-term success. Neoody reports that when the weather turned cold, the group abandoned the launch pad and moved to Phoenix.[28] They sold the property after only ten months of ownership.[29] While dedicated to the principle of Next Level dwelling, Applewhite and members of the movement apparently lost interest in this particular means of seeking to do so. "It was just too hard to keep doing," members reported.[30]

Members of Heaven's Gate not only mapped the Next Level onto physical space and created dwellings out of physical materials, such as automobile tires, they also mapped the Next Level onto the self and created a sense of identity and community in which they could dwell. Tweed invokes the metaphors of watch and compass, indicating how religions and religious people seek to create meaningful time and space.

Figure 5.1. Heaven's Gate member Jmmody helping to build the "Earth ship" structure in Manzano, New Mexico. Image © TELAH Foundation.

As he notes, "[r]eligions construct the body as watch and compass by figuring, regulating, and modifying" the cultural flows of people and ideas.[31] Such practices position the body in space and time, Tweed explains.

The primary way that members of Heaven's Gate engaged in this sort of dwelling involved renaming themselves as members of the Next Level and recreating their community as the crew of a Next Level spaceship. The practice of renaming of course has parallels in many other religious groups. As a monastic community, the most obvious parallel to Heaven's Gate is Christian monastic orders, specifically Catholic or Eastern

Orthodox monasteries or convents wherein individuals assume a new name and new identity upon joining. Referring to the renaming ritual within the context of the Eastern Orthodox Christian Church, Kurt A. Bruder calls this "deconstructing and reconstructing the self," and notes that it functions to reinvent the identity of the monastic within the context of his or her new community of practice.[32] One finds similar practices among monastics in other religious communities, and of course converts to new religions. Writing of the contemporary conversion of Saami—natives of Lapland—from Christianity to reconstructed versions of pre-Christian Saami religiosity, Norwegian historian of religion Lars Ivar Hansen explains that a renaming ritual results in the "washing-off" of the Christian name given by baptism and the assigning of a "proper Saami name" to the individual.[33] Such rituals function to cement new identities.

Upon joining, Heaven's Gate members adopted new names. In the first few months of the movement, names varied and different people recounted different means of receiving them, either through their own choices or being given them by other members or the group's founders. Two amateur investigators who infiltrated the group in September 1975 found that the members they met were still using their birth names, but Balch and Taylor reported other members using new names when they joined the group at nearly the same time.[34] Given the social disorganization within this inchoate new religious movement, clearly its founders had not codified any particular practice at that time, and ex-members reports vary.

In late 1977, while the group was camping in Canyon Lake, Texas, a large reservoir between Austin and San Antonio, Nettles and Applewhite instituted a new approach to naming, and formalized the style of names given. Calling the members of their class one-by-one into the large green tent in which the group would occasionally assemble, Nettles and Applewhite renamed each member with a three-letter single syllable, followed by the suffix "-ody." In some cases, members simply shortened names they had already been using, and added the new suffix, for example Surri who became known as Srrody, or Seraph, who became Srfody. In other cases, individuals were given completely new names, for example the then-member who had been using the name "Philip" became Mrcody.[35]

Adherents and leaders both saw the renaming as an important act. In a much later source dating from the 1990s, Applewhite explained his understanding of the practice, indicating it served a role of helping the convert focus on the Next Level,

> [a] funny thing here about using the name "Thompson," [for example] when you're in the process of overcoming, one of the things that helps you is to take a new name. This is adopted in a way in the Catholic church [sic] when nuns and some of the monks or hermits—some of the ones who isolate themselves more in thoughtful, studying conditions— they take another name. They take the name of a saint or some Biblical name and it helps disassociate them from the family tree. It helps get their mind more on their pursuit of their concept of God.[36]

For Applewhite, the practice of renaming helps an adherent shift their attitude and perspective—their habitus—from the circumstances of their birth and life before joining the movement to a new frame of reference emphasizing their membership in Heaven's Gate and striving toward the Next Level. In the words of Anlody, reflecting on her experience of renaming, "My name I got from my older member. . . . When you first join the class you try to separate yourself from the vehicle, so you take another name so you are not being called from what the vehicle is being called."[37]

Yet the specific form the new name took offers relevance on its own within the context of renaming as a religious practice. If practice serves to embed an individual within a religious community and recreate their identity within the context of that community, then the "-ody" names of Heaven's Gate reveal a specific way of doing so. Nettles and Applewhite did not decide upon "-ody" randomly, nor did they assign the syllable preceding that suffix willy-nilly. Ex-members have provided two different explanations for the meanings of the "-ody" suffix. Mrcody and Srfody, who were present at the renaming and therefore serve as reliable witnesses as to how it was initially explained, indicate that "-ody" meant "child of God." Under Nettles's and Applewhite's rationale, "-od" served as a contraction to represent "of God" and "-y" functioned as a diminutive, much like "Jimmy" is a diminutive of Jim/James. Accepting this new name ending in "-ody" therefore marked adherents as children of God. Mrcody and Srfody—who had left in September 1987—indicate that members told them that they had considered dropping the final "-y" from the suffix in the final two or three years of the group's existence to indicate that they had matured and were ready for graduation, but apparently this did not occur.[38]

Neoody, who was present in these final years, offers a second meaning of the "-ody" suffix, indicating either that members' understandings had changed, or at least that idiosyncratic interpretations also existed within the movement. Neoody explained that "-ody" reflected the names of Applewhite ("Do") and Nettles ("Ti"), merged into one suffix "-DoTi," which under the phonetic principle of natural relaxed pronunciation became vocalized and subsequently spelled as "-ody."[39] Under this interpretation, by renaming themselves with reference to the names of their religious leaders, members of Heaven's Gate engaged in a religious practice meant to bind themselves to the community and its founders. No less than a Catholic monastic adopts the patron saint associated with his or her new name, adherents of Heaven's Gate marked themselves as disciples of Applewhite and Nettles as Do and Ti, and reframed their identities in that light. The movement later developed a thorough theology of "grafting" wherein members of the group believed they had grafted themselves onto the Next Level through attaching themselves to the rootstock of Ti and Do, though the Two had mentioned this idea as early as 1976.[40] Heaven's Gate member Brnody describes this as a chain or link between the most basic "human plants" up the "chain of command" to the heavens.[41]

If the suffix of the new name represented the member's new identity within the movement (under either of the two interpretations offered by ex-members), the name's prefix or first syllable symbolized the individual identity. Members used these first syllables as a sort of first name, sometimes referring to each using them rather than the full forms of their names.[42] On formal occasions, such as in writing or the Exit Videos, members always used the full versions of their names with both prefix and suffix, effectively first and last names. This prefix took different forms, sometimes reflecting a physical characteristic of the member, or sometimes a personality quirk or reference from their past. For example, Applewhite gave Tllody his name because he was physically tall.[43] Drrody reports his pride that Ti and Do named him because of his personality and spiritual strength, "What does Drrody mean? It is kind of a funny name. Drrody is a name that was given to me by my older members. And simply it was a name meaning being *dur*able . . . they chose that name for me and I appreciate it very much," he explains.[44] In Drrody's case, his durability referred to his persistence in having left and subsequently rejoined the group years later.

The act of renaming therefore functioned not just to solidify the member within the community, but to link the old and new identities through a specific religious practice. On a theological or ideological level, the doctrine of Heaven's Gate rejected the value or relevance of the physical human body or the experiences of that body, and therefore any intrinsic value of the life led by a convert before joining the movement unless that experience or condition led to the individual's trajectory into Heaven's Gate. Hence, Applewhite recognized Drrody's durability as a quality that assisted him in his spiritual quest and entrance back into the movement, and named him accordingly. Yet adherents believed that the body functioned as a mere set of clothing that the true self possessed or wore for a limited time, and likewise the experiences of that body before the true self emerged after meeting and joining the movement served little purpose. Previous experiences were those only of the body or vehicle, not the true soul or individual. In the words of Nrrody, "When I met Ti and Do, my life in this generation started." Nrrody describes "taking over (incarnating into) a 32-year old vehicle (body)," and throughout the material she produced she endeavored to avoid associating herself with that body.[45] Nrrody did not indicate why she chose or received her new name, but obviously she saw it is disconnected to her old name and identity before joining the group. Ironically, Nrrody's birth name was Nora, making Nrrody not a radical departure. Yet the change itself represented the meaning, not the actual shift in letters.

Neoody similarly reports his experience with the religious practice of renaming, but in his case he experienced this not in 1977 with other members of the group, but when he joined in 1994. His first-person account emphasizes the religious practices of receiving a new name, new clothing, new vocabulary, and a new set of social norms. It was a rebirth into a new life:

I was told that everyone is asked to choose a new name while in the monastery. "You don't want to use your human name because it is eas-ier to excel in the non-human lessons if you identify with the new you." They said, "Each name would be represented by three letters." I felt new, so I chose NEO. This was years before the sci-fi movie *Matrix* came out [in 1999] with the lead character named NEO.[46]

Neoody writes that he received the "-ody" portion of his name only after he had proven his commitment to the group, approximately three months later, and that this represented his new "family name." Like the family names ("last names") of most American people, this family name indicated Neoody's membership in a kinship network of support-ive individuals, and the value that Heaven's Gate placed on the group as a form of family.

Beyond the step of renaming themselves, members of the movement also engaged in practices meant to remold themselves into a Next Level spacecraft crew rather than a gathering of human spiritual seekers. These practices included rhetorical ones of referring to themselves as a crew, as well as social practices meant to reinforce crew consciousness. Most notable of the latter practices, members adopted identical diets, uniform clothing, and grooming. Famously, members of the group wore uniforms during their final acts of suicide. Yet this practice extended well before the 1997 suicides. Members shown in the 1992 video series wore uniforms as well, though of a different style. Neoody recounts that when he joined, uniforms served the simple purpose of "making the laundry easier," but the first uniforms were more a dress code than an actual uniform, indicating appropriate clothing to emphasize modesty, comfort, and utilitarian value.[47] Members of the group never actually indicated why they wore uniforms or why they chose the ones they did, but clearly wearing the uniforms functioned to make Earth more akin to the Next Level. The specific uniforms that the movement chose reflected this attempt to orient themselves toward the Next Level, to use religious practice as a "compass," as Tweed would say. During the 1992 video series, members wore simple grey Oxford-style shirts, fully but-toned to the top. At the time of the suicides, members wore identical black pants and shirts, and black Nike shoes. Members of the San Diego Sheriff's department who found the remains described these as "track

Figure 5.2. Video snapshot from Do's Exit Video showing the uniforms of members of Heaven's Gate on March 19, 1997. Image © TELAH Foundation.

suit"-style uniforms, and reported that all members of the group wore identical clothing, and had draped identical purple shrouds over themselves. Famously, each carried a roll of quarters and a five-dollar bill in their pocket. (Ex-members report that this was a sort of inside joke recalling how members brought small change for bus fares whenever they traveled.[48])

Members of Heaven's Gate did not choose these uniforms randomly. Avid viewers of the science fiction television series *Star Trek*, the members of Heaven's Gate had intentionally modeled their uniforms on the ones worn by characters in this show who serve as members of Starfleet, the fictional military order who explore, police, and adventure throughout the universe. Heaven's Gate members idolized this vision of the cosmos, and saw the characters of *Star Trek* as models for how the Next Level functioned. They therefore adopted uniforms that mimicked those worn by the characters of *Star Trek* and *Star Trek: The Next Generation*. The practice of wearing the specific uniforms that members did served to unite the adherents of Heaven's Gate with their ideal understanding of the Next Level, in this case through mimesis of popular culture.

Remaking the Self for the Next Level: Crossing

Heaven's Gate members did not simply want to dwell on Earth. They ultimately envisioned themselves as seeking to overcome the planet and their humanity and to reach the Next Level. This idea of transcendence fits within what Tweed would call "crossing." Recall that the adherents of Heaven's Gate who planned and built the multi-structure community in New Mexico on the "Earth ship" model called their dwelling the "launch pad." The members who chose this name made an interesting choice. Launch pads, like airports, train stations, or harbors, are a specific type of space: space intended to enable movement away from itself, and toward a new space. Cultural theorist Marc Augé calls such locations "non-places," and writes that such non-places "cannot be defined as relational, or historical, or concerned with identity," and exist only to ferry individuals somewhere else.[49] Emblematic of crossing, a non-place ushers individuals through and onto their next destination. This represents precisely how members of Heaven's Gate came to view their terrestrial lives, earthly abodes, and domestic situation. Recreating their home as a no-place "launch pad" therefore made perfect sense to them. They wanted to cross over and transcend the human level, and such crossing served as an integral part of Heaven's Gate's religious practices.

Tweed envisions three types of crossing, all of which are present to some degree in Heaven's Gate: "I argue that religions enable and constrain *terrestrial crossings*, as devotees traverse natural terrain and social space beyond the home and across the homeland, *corporeal crossings*, as the religious fix their attention on the limits of embodied existence, and *cosmic crossings*, as the pious imagine and cross the ultimate horizon of human life."[50] Making use of the idea of crossing as Tweed has developed it, one finds that Heaven's Gate members engaged in extensive acts of terrestrial crossing as forms of religious practice, in hopes of preparing themselves for what was literally a cosmic crossing. What Tweed calls a corporeal crossing, namely the transitions through human life, is precisely what members of Heaven's Gate sought to avoid by cleaving to Next Level consciousness.

In keeping with Tweed's approach, one can understand the frenetic wandering of Heaven's Gate members itself as a sort of religious practice. Not wanting to attach themselves to any particular physical space or create too permanent a home here on Earth, members of this movement engaged in wandering as a form of religious practice. Before Heaven's Gate even existed as a movement, its founders Nettles and Applewhite had engaged in a similar journey of self-discovery that physically, psychologically, and spiritually moved them away from Texas and their family and friends, brought them to new physical and mental places, and broadened their horizons. In the words of Applewhite, recounting the experience in the third person a decade later:

> Leaving the hill country [in Texas], having left everything behind in Houston, giving it all away, they struck out in their last possession, a little sports car convertible. They seemed to just go where "the spirit" led, lacing the country up and down and from side to side as if they were being used as cameras and microphones for the Next Level. They did odd jobs to sustain travel funds, everything from carving crosses for a little store in Las Vegas where the owner took an extreme interest in them, to digging septic tank test ditches near Savage Rapids on the Rogue River in southern Oregon.[51]

Applewhite's retelling of his and Nettles's wandering invokes both the biblical trope of time spent in the wilderness and the American cultural image of freedom on the open road. (In a convertible even!) This sort of "errand into the wilderness," to borrow the phrase historian Perry G. Miller used to describe the Puritan founding of New England, represents a religious quest that indicates intentional unmooring from one's roots. Jack Kerouac spoke of the same sort of spiritual wandering in his *On the Road* and *Dharma Bums*, two of the most popular travelogues of the counterculture, and texts with which Nettles and Applewhite were surely familiar. The Two understood their experience as a form of data collection for the Next Level and preparation for their ministry, and it prefigured the way that they understood their followers' sojourns as well.

Once the movement itself became established, physical crossing quickly became a standard mode of living in the world. Nettles and Applewhite established a series of camps wherein members would congregate and create temporary communities. Shortly after the Waldport meeting the two founders stopped traveling with the group, and in fact divided the movement into smaller groups they named "families." The families traveled extensively but haphazardly. Balch and Taylor describe "wandering aimlessly," camping along the California coast in such a small family group, though later adherents reported traveling only in pairs or even alone in the event that a partner had abandoned the movement.[52] Similarly, James S. Phelan, who interviewed the Two for the *New York Times Magazine*, described this travel as "seemingly aimless wandering in pairs and small groups, mostly from one campsite to another."[53] As a result of this approach, the group lacked any social cohesion in its early days. The families spent their days on the road and in the wilderness, constantly traveling. Adherents of Heaven's Gate seldom traveled with their founders, and many converts joined without even having met the group's founders. Balch and Taylor summarize:

> Each family was completely autonomous, traveling almost constantly, going wherever it felt it was being led. Family members held public meetings of their own as they traveled. Most of them were small, but a few attracted audiences of several hundred people. . . . During their random movements across the country, families rarely kept in touch with each other, and after the press lost interest in Bo and Peep's [i.e., Ti and Do's] odyssey, many families had no way of learning anything about other members of the UFO cult.[54]

Such travelers spread the message of Nettles and Applewhite—who used the names Bo (Applewhite) and Peep (Nettles) at this point—and sought to encounter hardship and new experiences so as to overcome their human attachments and cleave toward the Next Level. Applewhite and Nettles characterized this as "leaving one's life behind" and "straining" to develop a "clear line of communication" with the Next Level.[55]

Yet they wandered with some purpose. In Phelan's interview with Nettles and Applewhite they indicated that they encouraged their followers to seek out Oregon, Colorado, and Sedona, Arizona, all of which were "high energy places."[56] In a 1975 public meeting they hinted at what the Christian tradition would call a "gathering of the saints," wherein those who accepted their message would spontaneously journey to special parts of the Earth where they would congregate and wait for the

Next Level saucers to arrive.[57] This also paralleled New Age practices of gathering in convergences at sacred places thought to possess special energy or power. (Interestingly, Steven Spielberg wrote a nearly identical idea into the plot of his 1977 film, *Close Encounters of the Third Kind*, in which a few special souls journeyed to Devil's Tower National Monument in Wyoming to wait for the extraterrestrial flying saucer, though I have seen no evidence that ufologists generally followed similar practices.) Members also sought out areas that adherents of the inchoate group had not yet visited, so as to hold new meetings and seek new converts.[58] Still others moved where the spirit led them, and sought only to encounter new experiences to help them overcome their human conditions.[59] All this indicates that crossing served multiple roles in the movement's corpus of religious practice: separatism, evangelism, and introspection among them.

Looking beyond physical crossing, one finds ample examples of Heaven's Gate members engaging in forms of religious practice meant to enable a metaphoric crossing toward the Next Level, and (members hoped) an eventual physical crossing over to that level. These took multiple forms, but most notable adherents engaged in bodily practices involving self-control and self-purging and acts of prayer and meditation meant to help them focus on the Next Level. All of these practices served to direct the adherent's psychological and spiritual focus toward the group, the leaders of the movement, and their ideal of transcending the Earth and achieving membership in the Next Level.

Self-control and self-purging served central roles in the lives of members of Heaven's Gate and in their daily religious practices. In fact, Nettles and Applewhite taught that individuals could only transform themselves into extraterrestrial creatures through extreme self-control. Even in the movement's earliest days they told those who accepted their teachings that adherents must abstain from the sort of activities that characterized the human level, and emulate those of the Next Level. Activities to avoid fell within two categories: those that were forbidden because they rooted one in a human-level social system, and those that led to various forms of attachment and distraction from the Next Level. The first category included working at a job, having relationships with one's family and friends, and sexual relationships. The second category included drinking alcohol, drug use, indulgent eating, and casual sexual activity. Nettles and Applewhite called the avoidance of these forms of human level activity the "walking out the door formula." They explained in one of the first statements that the Two wrote:

> Each true seeker of the next kingdom must literally walk out the door of his life, leaving behind his career, security, loved ones, and every single attachment in order to go through the remaining experiences needed to totally wean him from his needs at the human level. Until this frightening experience is underway, a man cannot begin to comprehend the reality of these "higher" and simple experiences necessary for this total metamorphosis into a new being.[60]

Other sources from the first months of the movement in 1975 reveal that the Two had already insisted on many of the monastic hallmarks of the later movement. Potential members were instructed to leave behind all possessions with the exception of those of immediate use to the individual and group as they sought to persevere and overcome the human level. As the Two wrote in a letter to prospective members, "If you are ready to go you will need: a car, a tent, a warm sleeping bag, a stove, at least two changes of winter clothing and two for warmer weather, eating and cooking utensils, and whatever money you can bring."[61]

Heaven's Gate attracted media attraction in 1975 and 1976 for precisely this reason, most notably in October 1976 when between twenty and thirty-three people abandoned deeds to their homes, personal possessions, and family members—children and partners, in several instances—in order to follow Applewhite and Nettles into the wilderness.[62] Members from this time period remarked upon the austerity and focus of their religious practices, of the near constant focus on what they needed to avoid. The group banned sex, drugs, drinking, most forms of media entertainment, and idle conversation, the ex-member noted. One member "recounted how this translated into a rather dull routine at HIM [Human Individual Metamorphosis, i.e. Heaven's Gate] retreats in Oregon. Highlights, he said, included cooking, eating, meeting, meditating, and hustling forays into the outside world in search of more recruits," reports a *San Francisco Chronicle* reporter.[63]

Other monastic practices developed in response to the various limitations that the Two placed on their followers. Since Applewhite and Nettles taught that personal possessions and the accumulation of money were human level characteristics, movement members lived communally and shared what little money they brought with them. When money ran out, Nettles and Applewhite permitted members to work odd jobs, but discouraged actual permanent employment that might lead to attachment to one's career or vocation, a possibility that sometimes occurred and resulted in several members leaving the group, in effect choosing secular over religious vocations.[64] Members also developed a shared purse. One former member recounted his experience of the early months of Heaven's Gate's history, when he was a member: "Once at a camp in Colorado everyone in the group was told to turn over all his money to one member who handled money for everyone. . . . If you wanted a quarter for an ice cream cone you had to ask him, and he could say no if he wanted to."[65] This former member believed that Applewhite and Nettles had explicitly taught that members should operate with a shared purse, but several other members of the group describe the process differently, with one ex-member saying she had concocted the idea of a shared purse rather than the notion deriving from Nettles and Applewhite.[66] While the specific origin of the practice remains in doubt, the underlying logic clearly owed its origin to the Two's teachings about avoiding money and the ownership of personal property.[67] Communal living and a shared purse became standard by spring 1976, when the group's leaders ceased proselytizing and gathered all active members into a single remote camp in Wyoming. From that time forward, members lived as members of a monastic community with all property in common.

Group members lived by a rigorous religious code demanding self-control of appetite, mind, body, and self. A list entitled "17 Steps" provided the behavioral guidelines necessary for overcoming one's human condition, and it forbade such activities as inconsiderate conversation, clumsiness, procrastination, oversensitivity, rudeness, overfamiliarity, and defensiveness. In an admittedly odd example of "using more of something than is adequate," the rules note to avoid overuse of toothpaste or too high of a cooking flame.[68] Such rules indicate how a thrifty communal group managed to live within its finances, but also how the adherents sought to live as uniform crew members within a highly regimented and dedicated community, akin to how they imagined the Next

Level beings lived in outer space. These behavioral guidelines evolved over the lifetime of the group to become three "major offenses" of deceit, sensuality, and knowingly breaking instructions or procedures and a list of thirty-one minor offenses generally encompassing those drawn from the earlier 17 Steps.[69]

At first glance these restrictions appear to be drawn from the worst nightmares of anti-cult activists, who argue that NRMs such as Heaven's Gate limit the freedoms of their members by enforcing bizarre sets of rules designed to force obedience to the group's authorities and a suitable compliant membership. Such critics of NRMs have a point that these rules created a sense of obedience, and that members had to follow the instructions of their leaders to remain within the group. The movement actually made this approach quite explicit, spelling out such minor offenses as "[t]rusting my own judgment—or using my own mind" and "[r]esponding defensively to my classmates or teachers."[70] Yet members saw these rules as part of their process of overcoming their human desires for individualism and sensuality, and they looked to obedience of their leader as the primary way of identifying with part of a Next Level crew and living in the same way that the extraterrestrial members of the Next Level did. It must also be noted that not all of the initial adherents actually followed these rules at first, and that during the periods in which the founders were not present, a variety of alternative models of religious practice developed. However, upon Nettles's decision to end proselytizing and the exertion of greater control by her and Applewhite, the practices upheld by the Two again became authoritative.

Members in fact saw their obedience of these rules as part of their membership in a monastic community dedicated solely to the development of their true selves and eternal salvation. Since Next Level beings always obeyed the commands of their superiors and lived in order to serve as part of a crew, so did members of Heaven's Gate. The group explicitly compared themselves to a monastery, since monks and nuns in a variety of religious traditions—Christian and Buddhist especially— make similar sacrifices as part of their communities. Ex-members generally saw the regulations as helpful. In the words of Mrcody, the rules meant that members "no longer cared about the petty stuff, only cared about what was best for all. . . . It was being with the best individuals of my life. They really had your best interests at heart."[71] These regulations, in other words, freed individuals to focus on each other rather than themselves, but paradoxically because of the power of the community, members felt supported and freed from inconsequential concerns.

Initially Applewhite and Nettles offered few instructions on which religious practices one should *follow*, rather than just those to *avoid*. One former member from 1975 indicated that "they were also ordered to 'keep a steady communication with members of the next level who are fathering you through the process.'"[72] The ex-member could not say what this meant, and offered only some vague suggestions that it involved meditation or prayer. Even Applewhite and Nettles offered only ambiguous suggestions at this point in the group's history. One must "establish a strong, direct line of communication with your Father," they counseled.[73]

Years later Applewhite and Nettles would offer explicit advice as to how to connect to the Next Level. In a July 1982 class that the members of the movement recorded onto audio tape, Nettles makes clear that meditation served as the key to this process. "We want you to devote as much of your time to sitting in meditation," she explained. "You'll need to spend more and more of your time in meditation." Nettles called for members to rush through their "lab work"—outside jobs that sustained the community's finances—so as to focus as much time as possible on meditation.

The specific meditation that Nettles taught combined multiple influences, with some aspects clearly derived from the New Thought tradition—an American innovation emphasizing the power of mind and positive thinking—others from self-actualization techniques, and also a strand derived from Asian visualization techniques. "Imagine the light passing through your body. Imagining yourself in perfect health, perfect harmony, extremely relaxed. Try to place your eye at the top of your head. Concentrate on the spot right here at the top of the brain." Nettles did not indicate how she had developed or derived her meditation technique, but her allusion to the Indian *chakra* system's codification of the third eye and topmost chakra there combines with the New Thought approach of the power of positive thinking, and even the Western Christian tradition of visualizing the light of God. Regardless of Nettles's sources, she and Applewhite clearly understood that they had drawn from different traditions in assembling these religious practices. Immediately after Nettles described the process, Applewhite explained, "We will have people sit straight up in a comfortable way with legs crossed, but that's as Hindu as we are going to go."[74]

The Two also offered general guidelines for how to act. They instructed members to strive to be gentle, simple, cautious, thoughtfully restrained, physically clean, and respectfully do tasks requested by other members of the group.[75] These various forms of mood and affectation combine to form a religious practice that one might describe as docile monasticism, a gentle otherworldliness that members believed characterized beings of the Next Level and their leaders Nettles and Applewhite, and that members strove to emulate. Outsiders reported that Applewhite in particular seemed to radiate this sense of docile monasticism. Those with positive bias toward the group often described this trait in positive terms, while those predisposed toward negative bias characterized Applewhite's affectation as dangerous or nefarious. One of the earliest ex-members to become a vocal critic described Nettles and Applewhite as possessing "an aura of love and understanding. The man, especially, had hypnotic eyes, although I can't explain the thing by hypnosis."[76]

Members sought to emulate this docile monasticism since they believed it represented the mood of the Next Level, what one might call Next Level habitus, defined by a gentle communitarianism and group-centered monastic dynamic. Smmody described the Next Level and its inhabitants as "a genderless, crew-minded, service-oriented world that finds greed, lust, and self-serving pursuits abhorrent."[77] Adherents of Heaven's Gate therefore adopted rules and principles aimed at reproducing this form of gentle monastic presence in order to propel themselves toward this affectation.

Bodily and Mental Control

Eventually, Nettles and Applewhite—and then just Applewhite, after Nettles's death—offered new religious practices meant to encourage members' overcoming through a variety of bodily control techniques. Among these were various forms of diet. According to Applewhite and several members, adherents of Heaven's Gate followed strict eating regulations throughout the group's history, yet changed these regulations regularly. They did this in order to break their attachments to the very human tendency to enjoy eating and become attached to specific foods or styles of food.

Like the adherents of most religious communities, the production and consumption of food served an important role in the daily lives of members, and while specific diets varied from time to time, all members followed a single diet at any one time. These diets limited members' intakes of certain foods, and overall they seemed designed to distance adherents from the enjoyment of eating and transform food and eating into a purely utilitarian act. Adherents also used food for purgative purposes, with former member Neoody reporting several diets that he describes as meant to purge members in both a physical and spiritual sense, including ones involving cayenne pepper drinks and enemas.[78]

Like the other religious practices developed and utilized by members of Heaven's Gate, the group's food and eating practices helped members look beyond their earthly condition toward an ideal of crew-mindedness, otherworldly asceticism, and separation from materials of purely terrestrial concern. Adherents therefore followed a series of regulative restrictive diets, but avoided following any singular diet for too long so as to avoid focusing on the diet itself. As Applewhite remarked in 1992,

> We've used every diet in the book that you can think of. And for the period of time that we're using a particular diet, we do it seriously. We'd really think, "This is a super diet!" We used a vegetarian diet, we used a fruitarian diet—not just for a few days—we were vegetarians for a long, long, long time. We were fruitarians for quite a while. We did water fasts for an extended period of time. We've done juice fasts. We've done Hippocrates' diet. We've done Gersen's [sic, i.e. Gerson's] diet. We've done so many diets that, you know, we ran out of books of diets to do. And while we were using each one of them, we were devoted to it. We tried testing this and testing that. But we then began to realize that what we were really doing was *liberating* ourselves.[79]

Applewhite astutely observes here a form of intense serial devotion to diet, but not for the sake of the diet itself. Key to this religious approach, members of Heaven's Gate sought to break their sense of enjoyment of food and their view of food as anything other than mere nutrients. Members report that at no time did they feel malnourished or ill, but certainly many of the diet regiments and the specific ways that members of Heaven's Gate followed them would have tasted monotonous and bland. All this worked to break members' interest in food. The group's members went so far as to develop new nomenclature for food, renaming it as "fuel" and referring to eating as "consumption."[80] This sort of technical language served to distance them from the materials they ate, from the act of eating, and the enjoyment that most people associate with eating.

Yet despite the various diets they tried, one commonality emerged. The majority of the diets to which members adhered were vegetarian, including the Hippocrates and Gerson diets, and the far more restrictive fruitarian diet. Vegetarianism has traditionally served as one of the major ways that Christian religious practitioners have attempted to control the body through food. Under the rubric of "constructing bodily boundaries," scholar of Christianity and food David Grummet has written that:

> Food has performed a significant role in defining and preserving the boundaries between different church bodies and different human bodies. By requiring abstention from specific foods, especially meat, particular Christian churches and groups have established markers of inclusion in their corporate body and of exclusion from that body. Moreover, by associating immoderate eating with promiscuity and seeking to prevent both, Christian groups have sought to impose moral and spiritual discipline on their members' physical bodies.[81]

In Grummet's reckoning, Christian experiments with vegetarianism— which he documents as a quite broader and more historically rooted phenomenon than is often assumed—represent the attempt to control the body and its desires, and harness the body for a tool of Christian practice. Within the context of Heaven's Gate, vegetarianism served that same role. By controlling the consumption of meat, individuals controlled desire, and by controlling desire they controlled and limited their humanity.

The leaders and adherents of Heaven's Gate believed that the members of the Next Level whom they emulated and toward which they sought to transform themselves existed without eating. Applewhite specifically noted that such Next Level beings do not engage in sex, eating, or dying. These three things became linked as fundamental qualities of the human level, or "mammalian existence" to use other language of the group. Earthly mammals focused on procreation and imbibing, and earthly mammals died. Next Level beings did not procreate through sex and did not eat, and they did not die either. Eating therefore rhetorically became seen as a form of "little death" that members sought to avoid. Applewhite framed this as an intentional act of mimesis, explaining that "they [members of the Next Level] would also show no signs of digestive organs as humans know them. So wouldn't it follow that it is important to have no likes or cravings for food, other than as fuel, if you hope to inherit a Next Level vehicle (body) or suit of clothes?"[82]

Yet despite this, group members ate well. Ex-members provided a set of recipes to me, which they called "experiments," which included such normal American fair as pasta, soups, and salad. During the 1970s and 1980s members baked whole-wheat breads, and ate lean proteins, but they ate balanced meals and felt satisfied.[83] Copies of several gourmet cookbooks were found in the group's Rancho Santa Fe home after the suicides, and throughout the movement's history individuals would eat in restaurants while traveling.[84] Group members splurged on chicken pot pies at a Marie Callender restaurant shortly before they died, and ate a final communal meal of pizza immediately before the suicides.[85] What this indicates is therefore that members of Heaven's Gate—like most people—simultaneously sought to control their eating, yet gave into their cravings.

Beyond limits on food, members of Heaven's Gate incorporated a broad range of ascetic limitations into their religious practices. One of the longest-standing of such practices entailed the use of partners, sometimes called check-partners, which provided a means of forcing members to self-examine their actions, be honest with themselves, and create tension and friction intended to help them overcome their humanity. Nettles and Applewhite made this partnering an important part of their teaching in the earliest days of the movement's history, and it remained important for decades into the 1990s. In the words of the group's founders in a letter they sent to prospective candidates in 1977, "[b]ecause this process works best if you have a partner, you should be willing to be paired up with another person for a time. You will serve each other in bringing out those human aspects which must be overcome. This will occur without premeditation. Human irritation, frustration, anxieties, reactions, etc., must all be overcome. The only bond between you and another person will become a mutual desire to get to the Next Realm."[86]

In practice, members of the movement lived alongside their partners, sharing material possessions, money, and physical space with their partners, and traveling alongside them as a dyad. Since the group's leaders assigned partnerships with an eye toward increasing friction, during the first years of the group's existence they made sure to assign heterosexual men and women as partners, and keep gay men or lesbian women together in same-sex pairings. Sexual tension as well as routine interpersonal tension owing to close quarters and constant daily contact therefore led to anxiety, self-consciousness, and sometimes conflict. Applewhite and Nettles apparently hoped that these feelings would prove cathartic in helping their followers overcome their human attachments, emotions, and especially sexual attractions.

By the early 1990s, Applewhite viewed the choice of partners somewhat differently, noting that he avoided pairing people if there was a possibility of mutual attraction. "The partnership could still work if one partner was slightly 'turned on' by the other, but the other partner could not possibly be physically 'turned on' by that person,"[87] he cautioned. He also offered a more complete explanation of the partnering approach, and even a biblical rationale for it. Applewhite explained in a 1987 proselytizing leaflet, "This is a totally new way of life we have adopted—always reaching, together with our partner, for the most right solution to a problem or the most right action, based on what we think our Heavenly Father would have us do. This is what was meant in the Bible by 'Wherever two or more are gathered together in my name. . .' 'In my name' means looking to Him for guidance. We believe that when two individuals work together to come to an agreement, they are more likely to arrive at what their Heavenly Father would have them do."[88] Rooting the partnership ideal in the biblical tradition appears as a rather late attempt to explain a practice that the group had developed decades earlier, and possibly Applewhite intended this explanation only for outsiders. Regardless, he explained the philosophy of partnering in the same way as he and Nettles did in the 1970s, as intending to break the individual's self-reliance and individualistic focus and force them to overcome their attachments and human-level feelings.

Numerous members and ex-members attested to the value of their partners and the practice of working with a partner. Referring to the sexual tension between himself and his female partner, one Heaven's Gate member—using a pseudonym of 'Seymour'—from the first year of the movement explained that "It's like a kind of battle takes place and then the fire goes out." Having extinguished that flame, Seymour spoke positively of his partnership and its effects.[89] Such a process certainly followed the way that Applewhite and Nettles intended it to function, and for Seymour the partnership worked in accordance with how he and his partner wished.

Former member Srfody similarly recounted an experience of over-coming tension in her partnership with Glnody during their time together in "fiber-lab" (laundry). Srfody described herself as an efficient and fast worker, and folded laundry quickly. Glnody by contrast worked much more slowly, and after several days of working together in fiber-lab felt "small and hurt" by comparison to Srfody. Glnody brought this to the attention of Srfody, and with the guidance of Applewhite they discussed it and Srfody tried to work more slowly and in concert with Glnody. "It worked out really well, it had a way of bringing out aspects of yourself you needed to overcome. . . . Partnership leads us to do what is otherwise rude. It leads to compassion and empathy," Srfody explained. Because most people avoid conflict and see direct confronta-tion as rude, the partnership approach forced members to do what in some sense is quite unnatural in broader American culture. Srfody saw it as a way of overcoming her own tendencies to work quickly and not think about how this made others feel.[90]

Yet partnerships unfolded in complex manners, and like any inten-sive personal relationship, they did not always develop the way the leaders of the movement intended. They sometimes resulted in strong friendships, frustration and animosity, and even broken hearts. Refer-ring to a much later period in the group's existence in the mid-1990s, Neoody details one of his own partnerships that resulted in all three. Having been assigned a recent convert named Joyody, Neoody bonded with his partner over their mutual experiences of having raised children before joining the movement and facing the difficulties of cutting ties with their children. They were of approximately the same age and shared a similar path of spiritual seeking. "We got along great," Neoody recollected. Neoody and Joyody separated after two weeks to travel with different groups, but several months later reunited and once again partnered. "One day we were out looking for a place to camp and told her that I was really glad we had this time together because I hadn't been able to talk to her in a long time."[91] Neoody details tender moments of friendship and deep heart-to-heart conversation. This resulted, Neoody noted, in Joyody admitting to herself, Neoody, and Applewhite that she had fallen in love with him. "I told her she should be falling in love with DO [Applewhite], not with me! She began to cry and said she knew that and she felt badly, but she couldn't deny the feelings." Applewhite split up Neoody and Joyody's partnership, and Joyody left the group. She rejoined, and left again. Then she rejoined again, and before leaving for the last time she confronted Neoody, took his hand, said how "very special" he was to her, kissed him, and left for good. Neoody ended his tale, written years after the events described, with an emotional note. "Joyody, wherever you are, I hope you are well and happy."[92] Even in a movement as strict as Heaven's Gate, with a theology and practices calling for radical self-control, denial of the flesh, and rules designed to prevent emotional attachment, the basic humanity of members remained ever present.

One can easily lose sight of why members of Heaven's Gate followed these strict regiments of bodily and mental control, and why adherents committed themselves to rules that so limited their freedoms and choices. Yet the individuals who belonged to Heaven's Gate believed that this method represented the only way of achieving salvation, as surely as do members of other religions calling for various forms of asceticism. In the words of Nettles and Applewhite from the first days of the movement, they aimed to "subject the person to all the experiences and circumstances necessary to overcome all his human needs. . . . [which] actually converts the cells of the body, chemically and biologically, into a new body. Upon the completion of his conversion experience that new body will have overcome death and decay."[93] Or, in the words of Applewhite from the closing days of the movement, "[we] *offer the way leading to membership into the Kingdom of Heaven . . . if you leave* everything of this world and follow me, I can take you into my Father's Kingdom . . . Leaving behind this world included: family, sensuality, selfish desires, your human mind, and even your human body if it be required of you—all mammalian ways, thinking, and behavior."[94] Over the two decades of history, the basic religious goal had not changed: overcoming one's humanity in order to transcend the human level and cleave to that of the Next Level.

Prayer

Prayer occupies a central position in the religious practices and lives of the members of most religious traditions, including the Christian tradition from which Heaven's Gate derived, but also the other various source religious traditions that influenced Heaven's Gate. While nearly universal, prayer is also entirely situated, and reveals as much about the one who prays as the being to whom one does the praying. As philosophers of religion Bruce Ellis Benson and Norman Wirzba wrote in their introduction to *The Phenomenology of Prayer*, prayer "connects . . . [the believer] to something beyond ourselves and beyond immediate reality. . . . Prayer, though, is not simply about a connection to the divine but also about us."[95] Prayer takes particular forms in particular religious culture, and the study of prayer therefore illuminates those specific religious contexts.

Members of Heaven's Gate prayed. Prayers took several forms within the movement, paralleling the same patterns that one finds on other religions. Some prayers took petitionary forms, making requests of the Next Level, its members, or the "Older Members," i.e., Applewhite and Nettles, either before or after her death. Other prayers assumed the style of thanksgivings, blessings, or praises. Some served as meditative focuses, and others functioned within rituals intended for healing or spiritual awakening. Numerous prayers existed, though not all were preserved in full form. Applewhite and Nettles taught that members should construct their own prayers and pray in the ways that suits them best, and therefore only fragments remain from those members who chose to write down their prayers or preserved them in some other way.

A member named Brnody penned an essay called "Up the Chain" for the group's anthology that included a selection of her prayers. Brnody's essay focuses on the theme of communication of ideas, requests, teachings, and energy up and down the "chain" connecting her to Applewhite (as Do) to the deceased Nettles (as Ti) and from her to the other members of the Next Level. She concludes her essays by providing examples of the sort of prayers she uses in asking for help from the Next Level, and Ti in particular. In a very Protestant way she cautions that her prayers are "only intended as a guideline to show you how you might formulate your requests," and that each person must pray in their own way. Ex-members confirmed that these prayers were unique to Brnody.[96]

Brnody explicitly directs nearly all of her prayers to Ti and Do, her Older Members. Adherents believed that the Next Level communicated in a highly regimented way, with the most senior of Next Level ideas, energy, and assistance trickled down to the chief administrator for Earth—Ti—and then her representative on the planet—Do—and then to the adherents of Heaven's Gate—Next Level members in training. Brnody makes engaging in just this sort of hierarchal chain a central part of her prayer life. The second prayer she includes in her collection—the first asks for help in not identifying with the human body—calls for the Next Level to help her self-develop toward achieving her goals of joining the level above human. "I ask for your unquenchable thirst and desire so that I don't place any limitations on my growth, and I ask that your will be mine so that I push to do everything in my power to become a viable newborn of the Level Above Human—the Next Level."[97] Brnody's petitionary prayers focused on these two general types of requests: overcoming one's humanity and human attachments, and spiritual self-development toward achieving Next Level membership. Toward those two ends, she asked specifically for wisdom, maturity, strength, courage, and selflessness.

Some of Brnody's prayers take such a generalized form that one can imagine them on the lips of nearly any religious person. For example, her prayer, "I ask for your strength to graciously accept lessons and correction, to overcome the fear of change, and to make the adjustment on the spot and move on," bears remarkable similarity to the commonly used "Serenity Prayer" credited to mid-twentieth-century American Protestant theologian Reinhold Niebuhr, "God, grant me the serenity to accept the things I cannot change, the courage to change the things I can, and the wisdom to know the difference." Brnody did not cite

Niebuhr or the prayer directly, but it appears that Brnody merely paraphrased the existing Serenity Prayer and rephrased it in a manner more befitting her needs as an adherent of Heaven's Gate. Her prayers as well as Niebuhr's express a similar sentiment of accepting and strengthening from the experience of the vicissitudes of life. Both frame this sentiment in an explicitly petitionary form, asking assistance from the being(s) in which the adherents believe. Both served as central practices in the prayer lives of individuals, though Niebuhr's mainline Protestantism and Brnody's Heaven's Gate of course differed in numerous ways.

Several of the prayers speak more centrally to the specific tenets of the members of Heaven's Gate. Those that address the need to overcome the human condition obviously reflect that part of the group's ideology. Brnody's fourth prayer asks for inner strength so as to help in "maintaining non-mammalian behavior of the Evolutionary Level Above Human—around the clock—in order that my soul (mind) will be compatible with and able to occupy a genderless vehicle from the Next Kingdom Level."[98] Other prayers reference space aliens and leaving behind the planet Earth, marking them as very specifically rooted in the theology and practices of Heaven's Gate. Brnody asks for help in blocking desires related to her life from before she joined the movement, and help in avoiding sensory distractions, speaking to the various other practices of self-control, meditation, and asceticism that characterized the group.

Other Brnody prayers seem remarkably unusual, even compared to other sources within Heaven's Gate. For example, Brnody includes as her penultimate prayer a statement more often associated with Ancient Near Eastern sources than the contemporary Christian or New Age movements: "Please let me be an instrument of your righteous fury against what this world has chosen to become whenever (and if) it's appropriate."[99] Brnody provides no context for this rather odd petitionary prayer, and the term "righteous fury" does not appear in any other written, audio, or video source produced by the group that I have encountered. It does however speak to the way in which Brnody had experienced the world surrounding Heaven's Gate. It conveys a clear sense that the outside world had rejected her and her movement, and embraced forms of social and spiritual decline against which Applewhite and other members of the group railed.

Brnody concludes her essay with a brief set of four prayers of thanks-giving, crediting Ti and Do for the gifts they have bestowed onto her, their nurturing of her spirit, and their support. "Thank you for your patience, understanding, and support; for standing by me through all the tough lessons it took to test me by fire, so I may sometime become a well-forged link in the Next Level chain of minds," she concludes.[100] Brnody notes that she ends every day with expressions of thanks to her Older Members, though her statement is too vague to determine if she means the specific examples she provides, or if she varies her forms of thanksgiving. Regardless, the image that emerges of Brnody's prayer life is one of a member of a new religious movement who expresses through prayers the same sort of hopes and gratitude that one finds in many other religious traditions, albeit clearly embedded within the religious practices, beliefs, and worldview of Heaven's Gate.

Turning from Brnody's prayers to those authored by co-founder Nettles and employed by all members of the group, one finds a quite different prayer. Nettles authored a short booklet titled "Preparing for Service" that she and Applewhite gave to members shortly before she died.[101] Ex-member Rkkody transcribed the prayers contained in "Preparing for Service" onto his short-lived website, and I have examined the actual booklets that Mrcody and Srfody preserved.[102] The "Preparing for Service" booklet contained a series of aphorisms and prayers that fell into two categories—either meditative prayers or prayers of praise. The meditative prayers took the simple forms of words to be spoken or thought and instructions on how to visualize or meditate in keeping with the prayer, e.g., "Say to yourself, 'Everyday my vehicle is getting healthier and happier and in better control.' And follow up the words with imagining yourself having a healthier body, a happier body and in perfect control of it."[103] Here one sees both a visualization—imagining one's body in a new state—and a spoken or thought prayer—what one says to oneself. Other meditative prayers lacked one or the other elements, or combined them. Another particularly evocative prayer served as both a form of visualization exercise as well as prayer to be spoken or considered silently, but added an additional element of a heavenly visualization: "Now I want to imagine that I am sitting at the feet of the Chief . . . not being afraid of what He sees in me, but hoping He will examine me very carefully and thoroughly . . . prescribing exactly the circumstances, events and lessons which will start correction and adjustments so that I might get back on the tack of perfect growth."[104]

Such meditations or visualization prayers function analogously to those of other religious movements, but again are rooted within the worldview, beliefs, and practices of Heaven's Gate. The first of the "Preparing for Service" prayers cited above follows a pattern as seen in American New Thought, positive thinking, and other forms of metaphysical religion. These traditions emphasize the power of thought in constructing reality, and the ability to heal and perfect the body through such thought. Historian of American religions Catherine A. Albanese has written of this form of religiosity as the third major strand in American religious life—in addition to evangelical and liturgical religion—and she views it as centered on "magical" practices that entail mental powers used to influence the body and outer world. In Albanese's words, "[h]ere imagination and will join forces with the body and the material 'field' in which it dwells. In mental magic, the field is internalized, and the central ritual becomes some form of meditation or guided visualization—so that the mental powers of imagination and will can affect and change the material order, abolishing apparent flaws by realizing its unity with a cosmic Source."[105] Nettles's "Preparing for Service" prayers function in precisely this manner, embodying the American metaphysical tradition within a particular worldview and theology specific to Heaven's Gate. The second of Nettles's "Preparing for Service" prayers adds to this by following a pattern often seen in religion, namely the heavenly vision. Most notably among mystical writings such as the Jewish Apocrypha (e.g., the Enoch literature) or Catholic mysticism (e.g., Teresa of Avila), such prayers effectively serve as visualizations meant to bring the worshipper closer to the divine. One finds similar visualizations in the Tantric Buddhist and Hindu traditions, and especially in Tibetan Buddhism, which uses visual aids as well. The Heaven's Gate visualizations obviously differ from these examples in terms of the specific heavenly vision that they conjure, but like them the prayers serve to help the adherent imagine themselves achieving their religious goals, in this case a bodily transformation.

Nettles's "Preparing for Service" booklet concludes with two specific prayers: a four-line healing prayer and a twenty-eight-line meditative prayer meant to help an adherent ritually and physically transform

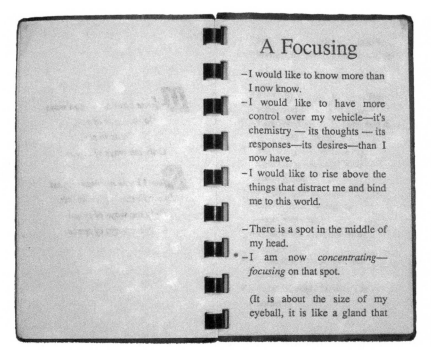

Figure 5.3. The "A Focusing" prayer from the "Preparing For Service" booklet. Booklet © TELAH Foundation. Image © Benjamin E. Zeller.

themselves into an extraterrestrial creature. The healing prayer again follows in the vein of Albanese's conceptualization of metaphysical healing practice, making use of "mental magic" to seek self-transformation.

> The power of life is flowing through me; My (body) is healing
>   perfectly.
> WITH STRONG INTENT AND POWERFUL FEELING, MY
>   (BODY) RECEIVES A PERFECT HEALING.
> Help me have no human ways. No thoughts of self, No faults to see.
>   Only the ways of space.
> Now I know my heart is fast. In my Father's path at last. Only the
>   ways of space. Only the ways of space.[106]

Nettles's untitled healing prayer reveals the central practices, beliefs, and worldview of Heaven's Gate. First, it focuses on the body. The transformation of the body served as the heart of the message of the movement and the beliefs of founders and adherents. Before Nettles's death, adherents believed that they would physically transform their bodies into perfected extraterrestrial creatures and physically journey to the Next Level aboard a UFO. This prayer, preserved after her death, still retains the belief in the perfection of the body. Since Nettles was actually dying from metastasized cancer while she wrote this prayer, her dedication to the transformation of the human body—and members' dedication to this ideal despite her later death—emerges as a clear theme. The prayer in fact couches the idea of self-transformation in the language of healing, a standard trope in the metaphysical and New Age tradition from which so many members came, but one particularly acute and somewhat ironic during the end of Nettles's life.

Second, the prayer reveals the centrality of meditative prayer and visualization in the religious practices of members of this group. As Albanese has written of such movements, "for American metaphysical believers and practitioners[,] ritual means—in the terms I employ for this narrative—'material,' or more usually, 'mental' magic."[107] Heaven's Gate is therefore part of a broader American religious tradition wherein adherents conceive of mental imagination as efficacious means toward bodily control.

Third, Nettles's prayer shows the way in which overcoming one's human condition remains at the heart of the group's practices and beliefs. Members avoided common human activities such as eating for enjoyment, sexuality, close friendships, and most forms of recreation. They believed that they would transcend their human forms in this way, and looked toward the heavens as their true home.

This then is the fourth point that this healing prayer reveals: the centrality of the vision of outer space in the worldview of Heaven's Gate. Nettles's "Preparing for Service" healing prayer invokes "the ways of space" three times in its closing, each time amplifying the message that members of this movement sought to reposition themselves—to *cross*, in Tweed's terms—into outer space so as to recreate themselves as new extraterrestrial beings in the Next Level—to *dwell* there. Outer space served as the functional equivalent of heaven for members of Heaven's Gate, but more than that it was the model for how one ought to live one's life and practice one's religion. Inhabitants of the Next Level lived in a state of crew-mindedness, of monastic discipline, of control and service. Those therefore became the hallmarks of life within Heaven's Gate.

The final prayer in Nettles's collection, titled "A Focusing," encapsulates many of the same themes, but in a much longer twenty-six-verse verbalized and non-verbalized prayer. The prayer begins with the theme of self-development and -transformation, moves into a visualization of such, and concludes with a call for further transformation.[108] The TELAH Foundation, the inheritor of Heaven's Gate's various materials, explicitly granted me permission to reprint the prayer, therefore it appears in full here:

> A FOCUSING
> -I would like to know more than I now know.
> -I would like to have more control over my vehicle—it's [sic] chemistry—its thoughts—its responses—its desires—than I now have.
> -I would like to rise above the things that distract me and bind me to this world.
> -There is a spot in the middle of my head.
> *-I am now concentrating—focusing on that spot.
> (It is about the size of my eyeball, it is like a gland that has been asleep, inactive, waiting for me to concentrate on it.)
> *-I am, right now, going to feel it become active and alive.
> *-I am focusing on it, I can feel it now in its location.
> *-All of my energy is being directed toward this Next Level gland.
> *-As this spot accepts all of my energy it is helping my chemistry change.
> *-I can feel the power of that energy there.
> *-I can feel the calm of that power.
> *-I can feel my chemistry in control.
> *-I feel no frustration or anxiety.
> *-I feel only that calm, powerful energy.
> (-As this spot becomes more alive it will help me sustain this calm.)
> (-It will eliminate distraction from my goal.)
> (-It will keep me clear.)
> (-I will know more.)
> *-As I recognize higher control and knowledge I will adopt it quickly, discarding my weaknesses.

*-My potential for growth is limitless.

*-I am rapidly changing.

*-Growth has been offered to me and I am choosing to become it.

*-I feel and hear that spot coming more to life!

*-Change! Vehicle,

  Change! Chemistry.

*-I am going to hold onto this until I sit and become even more!

(* indicates especially long pauses)[109]

One of the more remarkable facets of this prayer is the way it combines standard religious tropes with very specific elements of Heaven's Gate's worldview, beliefs, and practices. One might imagine members of many religious movements praying for "ris[ing] above the things that distract me and bind me to this world," yet none other than adherents of this movement pray for awakening of a "Next Level gland." This prayer in fact shows the diverse religious influences of Heaven's Gate, and the way that the members of the movement and Nettles, who composed this prayer, drew from elements of Christianity, Hinduism (or Hindu-derived movements), the New Age, and science and technology.

The overall form of the prayer lets slip the Protestant heritage of most members of the movement, and Nettles's own religious background as a Baptist before her explorations of Theosophy and the New Age. It follows a standard form of relatively short straightforward sentences without any particular ritualistic refrain or mystical references. Yet the overall tone reflects the interpretation found within the New Age tradition of the Hindu and Buddhist concept of the *chakras*, the energy centers in the body. Within the tantric philosophies of Hinduism and Buddhism, such chakras serve as neural and spiritual nexuses that serve important roles in biological and spiritual well-being. Tantric religious-medical practitioners focus on the treatment and health of the various *nadis* (vessels) connecting to these chakras, and look to the chakras as important energy centers in the body that have real effects on the well-being of the person. Though separating religion from medicine in the Hindu and Buddhist traditions presents difficulties, a second view of the chakras offers even more religious relevance. Tantric Buddhists and Hindus engaged in meditation believe that as they meditate they energize and empower these *chakras*, and that with the energizing of the top-most chakras—those generally associated with the forehead, brow, or crown of the head—one achieves awareness, enlightenment, and realization of the divine.

The Focusing prayer identifies this energy center as a Next Level gland as a "spot in the middle of my head," similar in size to an eyeball, the empowerment of which leads to self-transformation and development. Such references to making this gland or spot alive, waking it from sleep, and providing it with energy all reflect various interpretations of the chakra concept as promulgated in the American New Age movement. While no definitive list of the chakras exists and different tantric and New Age systems feature different versions, all identify the awakening of the chakra near the forehead—where Nettles identifies the Next Level gland—as leading to the religious and bodily fulfillment appropriate to those specific systems. The chakra system serves as an essential tenet in how many individuals within the New Age milieu understand health and the human body itself. As Wouter Hanegraaff has written of this tradition within the New Age movement, tying together themes of healing, the body, and spiritual development: "[a] central characteristic of Holistic health is the important role that the mind plays in physical healing. The immunity system or, alternatively, the Indian chakra system, is seen as the connection between the spiritual, mental and emotional faculties, on the one hand, and the physical body, on the other."[110] In Hanegraaff's assessment the chakra concept binds together several different elements, i.e., mind, body, spirit, and serves as a key concept with the holistic sub-tradition of the New Age movement. For the adherents of Heaven's Gate who used this prayer, the idea of the "Next Level gland" served the same role, both in function and form though not in name.

Finally, the Focusing prayer makes explicit reference to scientific sounding concepts, an important part of the Heaven's Gate worldview. Changing and controlling one's bodily chemistry functions as a trope and repeated concept in this prayer, indicating the way in which members of Heaven's Gate sought to engage in practices meant to chemically transform the body. Here the movement diverges from the metaphysical tradition that Albanese describes, since adherents looked to physical rather than metaphysical transformation as the key to their salvation and religious practices. Yet this prayer follows the movement's broader trajectory toward invoking science and scientific-sounding concepts as part of their religious worldview and practices.

Practices, Membership, and Beliefs

Religious practice is very important for understanding how and why the Heaven's Gate movement functioned as it did. Practices serve to solidify religious community, to create a sense of belonging and meaningfulness, to mark the boundaries between insiders and outsiders, to structure one's experiences, and to give meaning to daily life. Historian of American religion Courtney Bender has written that the study of practice "draws attention to the capillary working of power in and through our bodies and speech, normalizing and naturalizing the relations that make our worlds."[111] Looking to practice, in other words, helps scholars pay attention to how the leaders and adherents of Heaven's Gate navigated issues of power, relationship, the body, and the world.

One cannot lose sight of the issues of power in Heaven's Gate. Applewhite and Nettles created, founded, and led the movement, and with the exception of the tumultuous first years of the movement, served as the sole sources of religious and social authority. One could certainly leave the group, as many members did, but those who chose to remain accepted Applewhite and Nettles as such authorities. Applewhite's religious revelations shaped the trajectory of the group, and his and Nettles's ideas were the most important. Yet one too easily conceives of adherents as passive members meekly accepting whatever their charismatic leader said to them, as one so often finds in the common cult stereotype. Members of Heaven's Gate probably did not create the contours of the worldview, theology, or practices of the movement, but they did fill in the details. The previous chapter traced how members such as Jwnody and Smmody filled in religious beliefs of the group, and this chapter has considered how members such as Brnody created meaningful rituals and other practices within the overall schema that Applewhite and Nettles developed. Practice allowed the members of Heaven's Gate to navigate the power dynamics of the group and find meaning on their own terms, within the scope of the overall power structures.

Practice also shows the connections between Heaven's Gate and broader American religious culture. Nettles and Applewhite taught a form of bodily control as spiritual practice, a teaching that puts them in a long genealogy of spiritual teachers. Within the mainstream Christian tradition, Church leaders had long taught self-restraint and control, and monastic groups have traditionally made this control a highlight of their spiritual practices. Historian of American religion R. Marie Griffith has written of the American religious obsession with control of the body, what she calls "the quest to transform self and world by controlling dietary and sexual appetites."[112] Even more rigorous alternatives also existed, especially among new and alternative religious groups. The Shakers, one of the most notable of new religions during the colonial, early national, and antebellum periods, offered a precursor to Heaven's Gate in their monastic emphasis on bodily control alongside practices of communal living.[113] Seventh-day Adventists, Latter-day Saints (Mormons), and many other groups have upheld notions of bodily control as religious means toward salvation.[114]

The religious practices of members of Heaven's Gate also help to answer the question that people often have of how members of this group could believe the odd things that they did—salvation on a UFO, the need for suicide, Jesus as an extraterrestrial. The answer lies in the fact that their religious practices functioned like the religious practices of other religious groups, providing a lived manner in which adherents could make sense of their beliefs vis-à-vis their community of fellow adherents, their daily lives, and the world around them. The members of Heaven's Gate did not exist as brains in vats; they lived as embodied human beings who sought to overcome that embodiedness through specific religious means. Their religious practices functioned alongside their religious beliefs and worldview to help them do so.

6

Why Suicide?

Closing Heaven's Gate

On March 22 and March 23, 1997, all thirty-nine active members of Heaven's Gate committed suicide, exiting the Earth, as they referred to the act. In three waves, members ingested a poisonous mixture of barbiturates and alcohol, and as their breath slowed and bodies shut down, they asphyxiated under plastic bags that they had tied over their heads. Members followed guidelines they had researched several years earlier, and laid down their earthly lives in what can only be called ritual precision and attention to detail. In keeping with the group's customs, each member wore an identical uniform, but in their final months the group's members had added a customized "Heaven's Gate Away Team" patch that positioned them as merely visitors to this planet rather than inhabitants, invoking the concept from the *Star Trek* universe of visitors from a traveling spaceship. They also covered themselves in purple shrouds, the shroud an echoing of nearly universal ancient burial customs, and the purple a reminder not only of the Easter season but, as Robert W. Balch and David Taylor have pointed out, Nettles's favorite color.[1] Each member carried a five-dollar bill and three quarters, a standard practice that members of the group had followed to avoid being stranded without money for transportation. Members of each wave had cleaned and tidied after their compatriots had died, removing the plastic bags and draping the shrouds over their deceased companions. Applewhite ended his life on the second day of the suicide, along with his closest helpers. When ex-member Neoody, informed of the exits by a mailing he had received from the group, found the bodies on March

26, there was nothing left of Heaven's Gate. Neoody called the 911 telephone emergency hotline to report the deaths, then left.

The most radical thing one can say about the Heaven's Gate suicides is also the simplest: the suicides were religious acts. Members understood them not as deaths but graduations, cutting aside the decaying matter of Earth so as to free their true selves to journey to the Next Level in the heavens. Were they suicides? Yes, certainly to outsiders such as myself and (presumably) most readers of this book. But for the adherents of Heaven's Gate, no they clearly were not. Members of the group defined suicide as "to turn against the Next Level when it is being offered," a definition they crafted at least several months before the actual suicides.[2] By that logic those who remained on Earth had committed the true suicides, rejecting the promise of eternal life as perfected beings in the Next Level. Members of Heaven's Gate merely exited a world they had long rejected.

Why, journalists, scholars, and the general public have asked, did the adherents of Heaven's Gate ultimately choose to commit suicide in March 1997? Unlike the members of the Peoples Temple living in Jonestown, Guyana, who committed mass suicide and murder in 1978, no network of hostile outsiders sought to take down the group. Nor did government forces raid the home of Heaven's Gate, nor did its leaders face any sort of criminal or civil charges, as happened in the cases of the Branch Davidians and Christian survivalists at Ruby Ridge, Idaho. In each of those examples, outside forces combined with inside ones to lead to violence and death among members of a new religious movement. This leads to a curious point: in most cases of millennial violence, something or someone instigated the final violent end of the group. This is precisely what appeared *not* to have happened in the case of Heaven's Gate, which makes it all the more surprising that thirty-nine people— plus more later—chose to end their lives.

This chapter argues that members of Heaven's Gate chose to commit suicide in March 1997 because their dualistic theology had long led them to view this act as a possible necessity; their model of graduation from the human world required that they take some step to depart; and the combination of a *lack* of government persecution and the appearance of the Hale-Bopp comet and its related publicity served to force the issue. Members had expected government forces or other Luciferian agents to kill them, and paradoxically the absence of any overt oppression led adherents to decide they had to end their own lives rather than rely on the government to kill them. This being said, ultimately I do not think we can accept any specific argument of why members chose to commit suicide *at that particular time*. Certainly they might have waited for another cosmic sign, or waited longer for government action against them. Theoretically Applewhite might have crafted a theological rationale for staying on Earth indefinitely. None of these things happened. Scholars can point to influences and historical developments, but reducing the individual choices of so many people to one or even a handful of causal forces is difficult. The best evidence died with the members of Heaven's Gate.

Yet some evidence remains, namely the group members' writings and videos. Several scholars have tackled the question of why the events in Heaven's Gate ended as they did. The opinions of Robert W. Balch and David Taylor most closely match my own, and since they are the two sociologists with the longest-standing research background in the study of the group, their interpretation relies on the most support. "[T]he suicides resulted from a deliberate decision that was neither prompted by an external threat nor implemented through coercion. Members went to their deaths willingly, even enthusiastically, because suicide made sense to them in the context of a belief system that, with few modifications, dated back to Ti and Do's initial revelations," the two sociologists wrote in their 2002 analysis of the Heaven's Gate suicides.[3] They note several factors predisposing the group to suicide, including not only their belief system and its dualistic cosmology, but also the attrition of less committed members, the organization of their leadership system, and their perception of an external conspiracy against them. They also identified a series of precipitating factors, notably the aging of Applewhite, the end of active proselytizing, the arrival of Hale-Bopp comet, and Easter.[4]

Balch and Taylor's analysis is correct, and I am in basic agreement with it. I am less convinced that the precipitating factors represented a truly convincing case for suicide, but since the only individuals who can conclusively indicate if this is so are now deceased—or in the Next Level, if one accepts their own belief system, and regardless beyond our ability to interview—this question will remain permanently unanswered and unanswerable. I also think that the lack of government persecution against the movement was far more influential than any other factor in pushing the group members toward deciding to commit suicide, as their past statements indicated that they expected this to happen imminently. The *lack* of any government siege against them would not only have represented a failure of expectations but a basic logistical problem in how to get their souls to the Next Level. (That is, members faced the same problem they had for nearly two decades: how to get themselves to the Next Level if the government was not going to kill them and free their souls to journey onward.) Further, the metaphysical dualism of the movement's thought is equally important as their worldly and cosmological dualism.

Historian of religion Catherine Wessinger offers another paradigm for the end of Heaven's Gate based on her model of catastrophic millennialism. Wessinger calls Heaven's Gate a "fragile millennial group," meaning that the movement existed in an unstable state because of its millennial theology, its hierarchal model of leadership, and the aging of its leader Applewhite.[5] Yet importantly, the group had existed in basically the same theological and social form for years, and while fragile, it nevertheless had endured. No particular sense of fragility characterized the movement in 1997, as Wessinger herself notes: "Applewhite . . . had feelings of persecution dating back twenty-five to thirty years, but at the time of the suicide, the group was not really persecuted."[6] In Wessinger's view, the suicides resulted from a group that slowly closed itself off from the outside world based on decades of rejection by outsiders, combined with a theology that created an unstable worldview. "The decision to 'exit' planet Earth was made in response to internal weaknesses that were caused by Do and the other leader, Bonnie Lu Nettles (called 'Ti'), who died in 1985. But the group's uncomfortable relationship with mainstream American society contributed to the Heaven's Gate believers' group suicide," Wessinger explains.[7]

The internal weaknesses to which Wessinger refers emerge from the group's theology of grafting and hierarchy, wherein the Next Level communicated and related to Earth only through a chain of mind linking the Next Level to Ti, Ti to Do, and Do to the members of the Class, i.e., the adherents of Heaven's Gate. Ti had already exited her human vehicle, but Do remained as a conduit to the Next Level. "What would happen to the students after his death," Wessinger envisions the members asking.[8] In her analysis, the theology of grafting had resulted in an unstable situation wherein members relied entirely on Applewhite-as-Do to enable their connection to the Next Level. As Applewhite aged, his followers presumably reasoned, would they not stand to lose any chance of salvation? James R. Lewis makes a similar argument in his analysis of the Heaven's Gate suicides, explaining that "there seemed to be no other viable solution to the problem of what followers would do after he passed away."[9]

I do not disagree with Wessinger and Lewis that this particular theological position played a role in the members' decisions to accept suicide, but I do not see it as an underlying cause, rather at most a supporting factor. Adherents did express a single-minded dedication to their leader, and they clearly did not want to lose their connection to the Next Level through him. But the example of Nettles's death and the continued Next Level activity of Ti offers a powerful counterexample of the resilience and stability of Heaven's Gate's belief system. Despite the death of her vehicle, Ti continued to live, and while the death of Applewhite surely would have rocked the movement's members, there is no reason to assume that one or more adherents would not simply have accepted the mantle of "senior student" and become a sort of surrogate to Do. As a parallel, one can look to the continued activity of a small network of former members of the group, who even fifteen years after the death of Applewhite and their co-religionists, persist in their beliefs and connection to the movement.[10] Do literally transcended Applewhite as a human being, and therefore the death of Applewhite would not have meant the death of Do, as members very clearly indicated through the actual suicides. Nor was Applewhite's death particularly imminent in March 1997, though he had expressed concerns that he might be suffering from cancer. The aging of Applewhite might have predisposed himself and members to look for signs of the end, but it did not in itself cause the end, or serve as a sign.

I would therefore disagree with Wessinger that the movement was fragile in the sense of social instability. Of course there is no way to know how the adherents would have responded to Applewhite's death, since in fact the vast majority accepted his decision to force the issue of their departure by choosing to exit their vehicles, that is, to commit suicide, on their own terms. Yet Wessinger is correct to highlight the role of the group's negative relationship with broader culture, their "sense of alienation from society," as she calls it.[11] This form of dualistic thinking serves as one of the theological forces enabling the suicides.

While Balch and Taylor and Wessinger offer helpful models for the suicides, several other scholars have proffered overly reductionist approaches that either rely on circular logic or fail to account for empirical realities. Robert Jay Lifton has described the exits as the result of Applewhite's "own decision to force the end—of his own journey, of his megalomanic self, and of the small cult of 'grafted' followers that had come to constitute his entire world. In destroying that world, he was destroying everything."[12] It is difficult to argue against Lifton's position since he provides no specific evidence of Applewhite's alleged psychological state nor why Applewhite chose March 1997 as the time to destroy the world. Rather, Lifton envisions the group member as sliding toward a "shared delusion" that he characterizes as possessing elements both "poignant and absurd," such as the Away Team patches.[13] Lifton's inability to take seriously the Heaven's Gate suicides and lack of evidence as to why one should root the deaths in pathological psychology rather than theology makes his model rather unhelpful. That being said, Lifton is correct to note that the decision to end the group's terrestrial existence rested with Applewhite alone.

Sociologist Janja Lalich's model of the Heaven's Gate suicides is in some ways far more helpful, for she recognizes that for members "[t]he mass suicide of the Heaven's Gate cult was not a delusional or insane act . . . Rather, it was the ultimate and inevitable next step within the self-sealing system of their community."[14] While "self-sealing" seems too strong a position—several members left after the group decided to consider suicide, and one member departed just weeks before the suicides—she is correct that the acts made sense for adherents of this worldview. Yet Lalich places too much stock in her model of "bounded choice" which she argues creates a "complete dependency of the members on the leaders, built around an intricate system to oversee that degree of control which led to their bounded choice of their own demise."[15] While members did depend *in a soteriological sense* on their leaders, this sense of dependency was neither absolute nor entirely bound, as the examples of defections and continued activities of former members after the suicides indicate. Yet even if Lalich is correct that such a dependency exists, the materials produced by adherents of Heaven's Gate in their final years did not credit this sort of hierarchal dependency as the reasons they chose to commit suicide. Rather, a close examination of the documents they produced indicates that members chose to commit suicides because they had come to reject the world just as they had long believed that they had to reject their bodies. They sought transcendence, not bounded choice. However, Lalich is correct to root the suicides in a concept of binding, but rather than see their choices as bound, it is best to see the members themselves as binding themselves to Applewhite.

By contrast to Lalich and Lifton, and in keeping with Balch and Taylor, Wessinger, Lewis, and others, I understand the Heaven's Gate suicides as ultimately driven by theology and worldview, and members making what sociologist Rodney Stark and his collaborators would call rational choices to remain within the group, accept Applewhite's decisions, and end their lives.[16] By the end of 1996, the members of Heaven's Gate had reconfigured their worldview in a starkly dualistic manner. They upheld two forms of dualism: one a metaphysical dualism that distinguished the body from the true self, found in the mind or soul; the other a second form of dualism that I call "worldly dualism," which distinguished the members of Heaven's Gate and their movement as good, saved, and wholesome, and separated from a bad, damned, and corrupt outside world. These two forms of dualistic thinking had long been developing, and both clearly emerged from the thought and teachings of Nettles and Applewhite as far back as 1974, when they taught that human beings had to overcome and transcend the world to achieve eternal heavenly salvation, and to abandon human and terrestrial existence.

Yet the early 1990s clearly had reshaped both forms of dualism into more strident form that envisioned the Earth as not merely something to graduate from, but something to hate, human bodies not merely things to evolve out of, but vehicles to willfully destroy through suicide. As this chapter will demonstrate, the best explanation for this more strident dualism is that members of Heaven's Gate had given up on the world and had decided after years of widespread rejection that the broader society, especially mainstream Christians, was beyond any attempt to reach and save. They had also given up on their bodies, witnessed the death of Nettles and the aging of Applewhite, and fought the demons of sensuality and humanness for decades.

Both types of dualism had to combine and ferment before adherents would seriously entertain the possibility of suicide. These two forms of dualism informed how the group's members thought about the world and the self, and enabled the idea of suicide. Yet other factors contributed as well. Most importantly, the hoopla surrounding the appearance of the Hale-Bopp comet and claims that a UFO trailed the comet signaled to them that their time had come to an end, and that the whole world would at last see their commitment to the Next Level. In the end members chose to commit suicides because they had rejected the intrinsic value of the world and the human body, and because their leader, Applewhite, had indicated that the time was right to discard their attachments to both of them. The vast majority of members accepted this logic and chose to exit their human bodies.

In other words, there was a very clear reason that members chose suicide: because they did not perceive the actions they chose as suicides. They looked to them merely as a form of graduation from an unwanted terrestrial existence on an undesirable planet in disagreeable bodies, to a cosmic existence in the Next Level in perfected new bodies. For members, suicide was the only logical choice within their worldview. Members had expected and even hoped that a government raid would end their earthly lives, but when that did not transpire they chose to end their lives themselves. In order for the adherents of this religious movement to have made this choice, several historical developments had to occur, culminating in how members of the group responded to the appearance of the Hale-Bopp comet and a rumored extraterrestrial companion. The rest of this chapter traces the history of the end of Heaven's Gate, and how the members' beliefs and worldview developed to enable the actions they chose.

The History of the End

The Rancho Santa Fe mansion in March 1997 may have held the discarded bodies of the Heaven's Gate dead, but the process had begun to unfold thirty months earlier, in September 1994, forty miles up the California coast in a San Clemente warehouse. There the members of Heaven's Gate listened as their founder and leader Marshall Herff Applewhite, with an empty chair set beside him to represent the departed Nettles, explained that just as Jesus had willingly allowed himself to be killed, so too they might need to discard their bodies to enter the Next Level. Neoody, one of the few people attending that meeting who is still alive, reports that after Applewhite explained this new theological development, he asked the members of the group, "What if we had to exit our vehicles by our own choice? Did we have a problem with that?"[17] Neoody indicated that one member did object, and immediately made plans to depart. Sawyer, another former member of Heaven's Gate who attended the meeting and reported substantially the same wording of Applewhite's questions, indicated that a second person left as well.[18] The remaining members of the movement, somewhere around thirty-six individuals, voiced their approval of the possibility.[19] (Neoody and Sawyer later left the group for different reasons, as did several others.)

Why? Why would three dozen people—plus more by 1997[20]—willingly accept the idea that they might need to intentionally terminate their earthly existence? Fundamentally, because they had already rejected both the world and their bodies. From the spring of 1976, when Nettles first closed "the harvest"—that is, active proselytizing through holding large public meetings—until March 1997, the members of Heaven's Gate functioned as a sort of highly isolated roving monastery. Adherents sought to isolate themselves from the world and even when necessity forced them to engage, for work or to spread their message, they tried to remain apart from it. Eventually they even came to hate the world, and rejected it as a foreign place. By the end of the group's existence members spoke of themselves as something akin to popular psychic Ruth Montgomery's concept of "walk-ins," spirits from the Next Level who had long ago been human, but had abandoned their humanity in order to become Next Level creatures, and now returned to complete a predetermined task.[21] Members therefore saw themselves as more alien than human, as engaged in only a temporary sojourn on Earth but destined to return to the Next Level. One of the earliest and most explicit examples of such occurs in a 1994 statement that Applewhite or other members of the group wrote but did not distribute. Using the third person to refer to themselves, they wrote, "[t]hey began 'touching down' on Earth (evacuating their bodies and the crafts they came in) in the 1940's and subsequently began incarnating in adult human bodies in the 1970's and will evacuate this planet within the next year ('96)."[22] This statement links multiple concepts: the origin of members of the class in crashed UFOs such as those found in Roswell; the walk-in concept of entering human bodies so as to interact with others on Earth; and an imminent return to the Next Level, though this document predicted an earlier exit (1996) than actually occurred.

Members of the Class might have discovered the concept of walk-ins by reading Montgomery's 1979 book on the topic, *Strangers Among Us: Enlightened Beings from a World to Come*, or they might have encountered the term on the television series *The X-Files*, which featured multiple episodes exploring the topic. Regardless, they included "walk-ins" among the invisible key terms on their web page that would allow an Internet search engine to link the term to their web page. They clearly represented themselves as such, though they did not use the term. The ramification was nevertheless evident: they had come to Earth to complete their final lessons and overcome their humanity, but they did not belong here. While quite different from the earlier teachings of the Two and in fact difficult to harmonize with the movement's long-standing teachings of human individual metamorphosis and human self-development, members' willingness to voice that sort of belief shows how strongly they had come to reject both the world and the bodies they inhabited, their vehicles.

Yet ironically, members only embraced suicide because they had *tried* to engage the world. Their attempts, spread over the years since the death of Nettles, had resulted in numerical failure and a general sense that the world had rejected them. Multiple times adherents of the movement broke their self-imposed isolation and reached out to attempt to share their message and attract new members. In 1988 they mailed a short booklet, the *'88 Update*, and in late 1991 and early 1992 they broadcast a twelve-part satellite program discussing their beliefs. These tentative outreach efforts lay the groundwork for the movement's final push into the world, a series of advertisements in 1993 that culminated in face-to-face meetings in late 1993 and throughout 1994. These outreach efforts did succeed in attracting a few individuals who joined the movement and stayed, but in several cases these new converts were actually briefly former members in the 1970s who had left and rejoined. Balch and Taylor reports that approximately twenty-five individuals joined during this time, with "about half" staying beyond a few months.[23] Excluding those who rejoined, only seven new individuals joined in this period from 1991 to 1994 and remained committed enough to stay until the end (see table 2.1). The overall success rate was therefore quite low, with about a half dozen new adherents based on several years of work, more than thirteen hours of satellite broadcasts, dozens of posters printed, a costly advertisement in *USA Today*, and thousands of miles of driving between multiple states to hold public meetings. The scope of their travel was indeed high. Members of Heaven's Gate traveled in four and sometimes five groups from January 21, 1994 until August 19, 1994, starting in Texas and California and including visits to the Pacific Northwest (Oregon, Washington), Mountain West (Colorado, Wyoming, Idaho, Utah), West (Arizona, New Mexico), South (Louisiana, Georgia, Florida), Midwest (Illinois, Wisconsin, Minnesota), and New England (Massachusetts, New Hampshire, and Maine).[24] With only a few converts to show from these travels and almost no serious media attention, by any meaningful measure, these outreach efforts failed.

Members of Heaven's Gate were not unaware of this relative numerical failure. The posters and advertisements the group used in 1994 became increasingly pessimistic and confrontational in tone. The first poster, used to advertise a November 1993 meeting, described the group's beliefs in eight rather succinct bullet points. Titled, "The Only Way Out of This Corrupt World," it nevertheless shied away from any explicit depiction of worldly corruption or any discussion of what would happen if one remained, and focused instead on a more positive message of the Next Level itself. By June 1994, the poster the group used somewhat more confrontationally declared, "He's Back, We're Back, Where Will You Stand?" and stated directly that the world was about to be "re-booted—canceled and restarted." The final poster, dated August 18, 1994 and included in the group's 1997 anthology but not used for advertisement purposes, implied that the group members may be murdered, and explicitly declared in all uppercase letters that they may need to die, "The Shedding Of Our Borrowed Human Bodies May Be Required In Order To Take Up Our New Bodies Belonging To The Next

World." The poster indicated that humans today were "enslaved," that all existing religions were "corrupted by malevolent space aliens," and that the Next Level would soon begin "the process of recycling Earth's environment and inhabitants."[25] Certainly nothing in any of the posters was new or noteworthy when judged in comparison to the group's theology and previous statements, but in terms of how the members of the group chose to self-represent themselves through the media of posters, the group's advertisements during the 1994 tour increasingly and clearly became more dire.

The group ceased holding meetings in August 1994. Sawyer recounts that during the final meeting he oversaw, in Portsmouth, New Hampshire on August 13, the only person in attendance was from the media.[26] Neoody similarly recounts lackluster responses, particularly on the East Coast where "the attitude was pretty bad" and they "[did] not find any like minded people."[27] Neoody recounts that these failures, especially in August in New England, resulted in Applewhite's decision to halt active proselytizing and once again retreat to cloistered living. In Neoody's words, "[o]ne day in Maine, after having gone through the whole country to give, what they thought was the most important information on the planet[,] Do said, 'Well, I guess it's time for us to quit holding meetings for a while.'"[28]

The failure of the outside world to respond to the message offered by members of Heaven's Gate signaled to its adherents and leader that their mission was nearly over. At this point Applewhite gathered his followers in the San Clemente warehouse and at this time he publicly disclosed the possibility that the group members may need to leave the Earth by their own hands. Crucially, two important factors contributed to this development: the comparative failure of attempts to proselytize, and the apparent lack of any active persecution from outside forces that would result in the adherents of Heaven's Gate being murdered and therefore freeing their souls to journey to the Next Level. Sawyer, who was present at the meeting, made the first part of this connection quite clear in his later explanation: "He [Applewhite] wasn't sure yet[,] but what precipitated his saying that was in part the dwindling response of the public to their second face to face message delivery around the U.S. and Canada that began on January 1, 1994 and ended in mid September of that same year."[29] After months of travel the lack of any apparent success led Applewhite and other members to decide that Earth's inhabitants had apparently lost their chance for advancement to the Next Level.

In the March 19, 1997 "Exit Video" that Applewhite produced—three days before members began their "exits"—an hour-long synthesis of his reasoning for the eventual suicides, a nearly exasperated Applewhite explained that while he and his movement offered the only opportunity to enter the Kingdom of Heaven—and that all those left behind were subject to recycling and death—individuals outside the movement did not seem to recognize or take seriously the magnitude of their message. "It is not our fault" that people haven't taken seriously the opportunity, he explained. "We've been ignored, ridiculed, . . . whatever cult you can call it, we've been called that."[30] The world, Applewhite indicated, had rejected them, and they now rejected the world as being apparently uninterested in the Next Level or eternal salvation.

Yet equally important, there seemed little evidence that the government, hostile family members, or other outside forces were likely to storm the members' home and kill them in some sort of mass violent act. The possibility remained, which explains why Applewhite presented suicides or intentional self-induced exits as a mere possibility in the September 1994 meeting, rather than a foregone conclusion or eventuality. Sometime in the following years, probably in 1996, Applewhite authored a document entitled "Our Position Against Suicide" that members eventually posted on the group's website at the end of 1996. The document laid out several possibilities of how members might free themselves of their human bodies so as to journey to the Next Level: (1) physical pickup onto a spacecraft, and transfer of bodies aboard that craft; (2) natural death, accident, or random violence; (3) outside persecution; and (4) willful exit of the bodies in a dignified manner.[31]

The first possibility, "boarding a spacecraft from the Next Level very soon (in our physical bodies)," harkens back to the group's first teachings, and Nettles's and Applewhite's explanation that one does not need to die in order to join the Next Level, since they would board the UFOs midair.[32] This remained a possibility, however remote, even in the mid-1990s, though the example of Ti's abandoning of her human vehicle clearly revealed an alternative. Applewhite referred to the case of Nettles/Ti in noting a second possibility, "one or more of us could lose our physical vehicles (bodies) due to 'recall,' accident, or at the hands of some irate individual."[33] Applewhite had at one point indicated that Nettles's vehicle had simply burned out from her overuse of its facilities, and according to at least one source he thought he might be developing health problems of his own.[34] This also remained a possibility for one or two members of the group, but waiting for old age, disease, or random chance seemed an unlikely way to ensure the entrance of the entire Class into the Next Level.

The document indicated a third possibility, "we could find so much disfavor with the powers that control this world that there could be attempts to incarcerate us or to subject us to some sort of psychological or physical torture (such as occurred at both Ruby Ridge and Waco)."[35] Here Applewhite referred to two infamous cases of violence involving conflict between religious groups and the U.S. government—the 1992 actions against the Weaver family in Ruby Ridge, Idaho, and the 1993 raid on the Branch Davidians in Waco, Texas, the latter just three years before Heaven's Gate members posted this document onto their web page. In the case of the Weavers, members of a right-wing white supremacist Christian movement called Christian Identity, a dispute over illegal weapons and a possible conspiracy against the federal government resulted in the U.S. Marshals and FBI laying siege to the family's cabin, eventually killing two members of the family.[36] The case sparked wide public attention based on apparent bureaucratic failures that led to escalation as well as the seeming heavy-handedness of the government response, which included shooting to death the mother of the family, Vicki Weaver, while she held her infant in her arms. The Branch Davidian case similarly involved a government raid targeting a religious group, in this case by Texas officials, the Bureau of Alcohol, Tobacco, and Firearms (ATF), and the FBI, over charges of weapons violations and child abuse. Eighty-two Branch Davidians died in the conflict, along with four ATF agents, over a fifty-one-day siege that culminated in a conflagration following the use of military-style equipment including tanks. Again, the events attracted broad attention and in some quarters—particularly among alternative religious groups and members of fringe subcultures— condemnations of excessive force and government persecution.[37]

Adherents of Heaven's Gate looked to a similar raid against their movement as one possible avenue through which their earthly existences may end, but by 1997 this possibility seemed increasingly remote. Even if a raid was indeed forthcoming, members considered the possibility that they might need to end their own lives to avoid torture, arrest, and murder, or in the words of Applewhite, "to evacuate their bodies by a more dignified, and less agonizing method." In other sources, Applewhite and movement members explicitly linked this to the example of the Jewish rebels of Masada in 73 CE, whom tradition recounts committed mass suicide when it became apparent that the Roman army would overrun them, most likely raping and torturing many before their deaths, and possibly forcing others to live as slaves. Josephus, a Jewish historian of the era, recounts that nine hundred and sixty ancient Jews chose suicide rather than death or capture at Roman hands.[38] The Masada suicides attracted worldwide attention in the mid-1960s when excavations unearthed the ancient fortress and twenty-five bodies, all of which were entombed in 1969 with full Israeli military ceremony as Jewish heroes of antiquity.

Another possible example of religious suicide that might have inspired them, though not one to which members of Heaven's Gate alluded, is that of the members of Jim Jones's Peoples Temple in Guyana on November 18, 1978. In the case of members of the Peoples Temple, a network of former members, family of current members, and government agencies all worked together to investigate claims of rights abuses within the movement's utopian commune of Jonestown, in the Guyanan countryside. Like the members of Heaven's Gate, the members of the Peoples Temple had previously considered suicide as an option in response to potential persecution, and their enacting of "revolutionary suicide," in the words of their leader Jim Jones, followed a well-rehearsed routine of death by poison when they finally enacted it. Unlike the case of Heaven's Gate but like the Weavers of Ruby Ridge and Branch Davidians, members of the Peoples Temple actively fought with outsiders and there is strong evidence that at least some of the suicides were in fact murders, and certainly the infants and children poisoned to death did not make informed choices about ending their own lives, or even do so by their own hand. It is unclear why the members of Heaven's Gate never referenced Jonestown and the Peoples Temple, but in all likelihood the fact that the Jonestown dead included adults and children who did not willingly commit suicide, and perhaps the

overall notoriety of the group, minimized its value as a potential parallel or exemplar.[39]

Suicide in the face of possible persecution remained a distinct
chance, and as the years advanced without any sign of overt government attack, the possibility of suicide without any direct instigating factor rose into prominence. Neoody reports that the group considered
specific means of suicide shortly after the September 1994 meeting, pur-
chasing a copy of Derek Humphry's *Final Exit: The Practicalities of Self-
Deliverance and Assisted Suicide for the Dying*, which had been published in 1992.[40] This book provides medical, legal, and ethical advice
and specific instructions for patients facing terminal illnesses who wish
to end their lives. The members of Heaven's Gate looked to the specific
instructions that Humphry offered in the book as they prepared for the
possibility of suicide, and the eventual suicides followed Humphry's
instructions closely. Humphry recommends that those who wish to die
ingest powdered barbiturates taken in yogurt or pudding, drink strong
alcohol to increase the effects, and then tie a plastic bag over the head.
This method, Humphry indicates, "is 100 percent certain."[41] Tellingly,
Humphry discourages the use of weapons to commit suicide, as they
can sometimes maim or paralyze but not kill. The group briefly considered intentionally instigating a shootout with government forces and
even purchased some firearms, but following Humphry's advice opted
not to rely on the luck of where a bullet landed.[42] The group members
locked the guns into storage, and opted for the chemical means that
Humphry recommends. In the 1997 suicides members of Heaven's Gate
substituted applesauce for pudding, but otherwise followed Humphry's
instructions.

Yet while the members of the movement prepared for the possibility
of suicide, they continued living as well. A year later, in 1995, members
of the group built the Manzano, New Mexico "launch pad"—as discussed in the previous chapter—what Neoody calls a "Monastery Fortress," what was to be a massive array of buildings akin to a small community with spaces for members to sleep, eat, and work.[43] Importantly,
Applewhite and the movement's adherents clearly intended the launch
pad to serve as a permanent home for the group, meaning that they did
not envision an imminent demise of the group or the immediate need
for suicides or other forms of earthly exits. Yet the group abandoned

plans for the launch pad once snow began to fall in the autumn, implying that perhaps their view of building a permanent home on Earth was
not ultimately a strong enough impulse for them to continue.

Around this time (1994–95) the first members of Heaven's Gate
sought and received medical castration. After the suicides the revelations that several members of the group, including Applewhite himself,
were castrated led to a flurry of sensational news reporting and various pop-psychological interpretations. Different members of the group
described their rationale for the procedure differently, but all agreed that
the fundamental reason that they or their co-religionists chose to "have
their vehicles neutered," as members referred to the procedure, was the
need to control the body and its hormones. Applewhite explained that
they chose to do so "in order to sustain a more genderless and objective consciousness," while Stmody indicated that the procedure permanently blocked the production of "hormones that keep the body intoxi-
cated, stupid, empty-headed, and 'blind.'"[44] The chronology is unclear,
but either Srrody or the partnership of Alxody and Vrnody engaged in
the procedure first, in 1994 or 1995, followed by Applewhite himself.[45]
Four other members underwent the procedure according to autopsies
performed after the suicides two years later.[46]

From the perspective of Heaven's Gate's theology and the worldview
in which members lived, castration made perfect sense, just as suicide
did, and for similar reasons. Members of Heaven's Gate rejected any
identification with human bodies, which they regarded as merely vehicles, containers, or plants. The true self was the soul, which transcended
the body and sought entrance to a genderless kingdom, the Next Level.
Further, since the first years of Nettles's and Applewhite's movement,
then still known as Human Individual Metamorphosis, they taught that
adherents had to control and sublimate sexual desires so as to overcome
their base human condition and recondition themselves for service to
the Next Level. Members abstained from sex and masturbation, and ex-
members recounted that the absolute abstention and control of sexual
desire was often the most difficult practice of the group. Neutering provided a simple solution.

Yet surgical castration, as much as it showed how members cleaved
to the Next Level and sought admission there, signaled that Applewhite
and others were still quite intent on remaining on Earth and continuing

their earthly lives at least for the foreseeable future. Given the long recovery from such a surgical procedure—Neoody reports that Applewhite's surgery had long-lasting and unpleasant complications[47]—one cannot expect suicidal individuals to seek out or undergo it. In fact, while the castrations clearly demonstrate the Next Level centeredness of members' thinking, it also shows that they had not entirely rejected earthly living at least for the moment, either because they felt they had more to learn and experience in the world, or because they had not fully give up hope that outsiders might still recognize and accept the message that they brought.

One Final Push: The Internet, *Heaven's Gate* Anthology, and Other Media

Members made several last ditch efforts to reach the broader world with the teachings of their movement, most notably two statements posted on the Internet in the autumn of 1995, followed in 1996 by the publication of the group's anthology, two new videotapes, and the group's website. Together these outreach efforts represented the group's last attempts to reach an outside audience, and while they succeeded in attracting one member who eventually joined the movement and remained for the suicides (and one who joined and left before the suicides[48]), by and large these efforts resulted in little concrete results. In fact, members reported ridicule and heckling rather than support, and the lack of public interest in their message highlighted their earlier suspicions from 1994 that the time for earthly engagement must be coming to a close. Ironically, these outreach attempts probably served as the final impetus for the decisions to turn inward and end the group's existence, and certainly the group's members' forays onto the Internet provided a crucial link to a counterculture of conspiracy that eventually brought to their attention the Hale-Bopp comet and with it a sign of the end.

The group's two 1995 Internet statements, posted in September and October, convey the same basic information in two distinct forms. Both statements were posted to UseNet, the Internet-based bulletin board system that at the time represented the most widely read and interactive form of communication on the Internet. UseNet is organized into

Table 6.1: *UseNet Posts by Date and Group*

Title	Date	UseNet Group	Message-ID
UNDERCOVER JESUS SURFACES (www.indirect.com/www/lillo)	Sept. 26, 1995	alt.current-events.usa alt.good.news alt.news-media alt.tv.news-shows	44aldo$69@newsl.channell.com
UNDERCOVER JESUS SURFACES (www.indirect.com/www/lillo)	Sept. 26, 1995	alt.consciousness alt.consciousness.mysticism alt.consciousness.near-death-exp alt.drugs.culture	44ale8$69@newsl.channell.com
BYPASS DEATH — THE ONLY WAY TO	Oct. 13, 1995	comp.ai,comp.ai.alife comp.ai.philosophy	45m7ss$o9q@ddi2.digital.net
E.T. SPEAKS: UFO'S / SPACE ALIENS / REBOOT CIVILIZATION	Oct. 13, 1995	comp.ai comp.ai.alife comp.ai.philosophy	45m7sm$o9q@ddi2.digital.net
E.T. SPEAKS: UFO'S / SPACE ALIENS / REBOOT CIVILIZATION	Oct. 13, 1995	alt.drugs.psychedelics alt.drugs.usenet alt.fantasy alt.folklore.urban	45mp3q$9a6@Newsl.mcs.net
E.T. SPEAKS: UFO'S / SPACE ALIENS / REBOOT CIVILIZATION	Oct. 13, 1995	rec.arts.startrek.tech alt.starfleet.rpg rec.arts.sf.misc rec.arts.st.starwars.misc alt.startrek	45m9vu$s8m@Newsl.mcs.net
WAR IN HEAVENS — IT HAS BEGUN — IT IS REAL	Oct. 13, 1995	rec.arts.startrek.tech alt.starfleet.rpg rec.arts.sf.misc rec.arts.st.starwars.misc alt.startrek	45ma07$s8m@Newsl.mcs.net
THE REAL Q — AN E.T. SPEAKS OUT	Oct. 12, 1995 (Reposted Oct. 14, 1995)	aus.sf.star-trek uk.media.tv.sf.startrek rec.arts.startrek.misc alt.startrek.creative	45k23q$n09@ddi2.digital.net (repost: 45pbdk$hgl@ddi2.digital.net)

a system of newsgroups, organized within categories such as *comp.* (computers), *rec.* (recreation and entertainment), *sci.* (science), various country-based categories such as *uk.*, and a general catch-all of *alt.* ("alternative" to the other categories). Within each category one found subcategories and even sub-subcategories, until one ended up in a specific newsgroup to which one could read and post, e.g., *alt.tv.newsshows* for the discussion of television news shows, or *rec.arts.startrek. tech*, for the discussion of the technology of the science fiction series *Star Trek*. Like much in the early decades of the Internet, UseNet was decentralized, and unlike many forums or chat systems of more recent decades—this was long before "social media" existed as a term or concept!—anyone could post to the majority of the UseNet newsgroups, and anyone could read them and respond. Members of Heaven's Gate posted to UseNet to several different newsgroups.

The first statement, "Undercover Jesus Surfaces," used religious language to describe the group's beliefs and self-consciously represented an attempt to reach a Christian audience, according to Applewhite.[49] Generally it followed the contours of the previous materials produced by the group, and it certainly represented the standard theology and approach of the group. The statement introduced and explained the group's Christology and soteriology, and explained the concept of deposits and incarnation. The post avoided any explicit apocalyptic language about the impending demise of Earth and its inhabitants, but it called Heaven's Gate the "'last bus' out of this civilization" and implied that those who remained behind would lack any possibility of advancing beyond the human level.[50]

Where this UseNet posting departed from other materials was its description of an explicit expectation of a forthcoming government raid and the demise of the group and its leader. The post began with the statement that "I am about to return to my Father's Kingdom. This 'return' requires that I prepare to lay down my borrowed human body," a rather clear announcement that the group's departure for the Next Level was imminent and bodily. Yet Applewhite not only avoided any discussion of suicide, he explicitly positioned an alternative, namely that group members would lay down their human bodies and exit their vehicles—that is, die—through a violent confrontation with the government. Applewhite encouraged potential candidates who wished to join him and his movement in the Next Level to prepare for just such an eventuality:

> How is this "laying down of our bodies" to occur? If you DO recognize me and choose to look to me for guidance, I would recommend that you purchase firearms, get comfortable using them (or partner with someone who can), and somehow position yourselves (separate from others enough to not be vulnerable) so that you might establish a relationship with me, protected from interference as far as possible. In this day and time the authorities make no bones about their "need" to protect the public from "dangerous radicals like us." They will aggressively attempt to require us to abide by their values and their rules (which are of this Luciferian world and its society—as difficult as that might be to believe). They won't hesitate to trump up charges or suspicions in order to search us or take us into custody so they can "judge for themselves" whether or not we are some kind of a threat. There is no need for us to be submissive to their wishes (such as to their search or custody questioning) when we know we have broken none of God's laws. Not only have we done nothing wrong, but our total existence is devoted to entering and offering God's World. Our choosing to not "be submissive"— coupled with "being armed"— pretty much addresses the "laying down of our bodies" question.[51]

This UseNet posting is remarkable in its bluntness in calling for those who wished to join Applewhite to arm themselves and wait for the government forces to kill them. He added that if he was arrested and executed, then individuals could "join me as soon as they choose to." He also included a cautionary note that Ti would confirm the precise means by which he and the members of his group would exit, and that possibly a spacecraft might rescue them first. Yet the vast majority of his writing—in fact, the longest of his enumerated notes in the posting, is the above quoted material.[52] Clearly, in the autumn of 1995, Applewhite and other members of the movement expected an imminent government raid that would result in their deaths, or at least the deaths of the human bodies. This was the time period during which they procured firearms, and during this time period they expected their deaths to come at the hands of the U.S. government.

During the mid-1990s, fears of government raids of unconventional or radical groups were no mere paranoid fancy, but rooted in real events such as the government actions against the Weavers and Branch Davidians. Further, two more recent historical events no doubt influenced Applewhite's suspicions that things were going downhill fast, that a war between the government and radical outsiders like himself was accelerating, and that the government would soon execute or murder members of Heaven's Gate. Just seven days before Applewhite wrote and posted the "Undercover Jesus" statement, the *New York Times* and *Washington Post* published a pseudonymously authored manifesto entitled *Industrial Society and Its Future* written by a violent social activist at that time known as the Unabomber, later revealed to be named Ted Kaczynski. Kaczynski had terrorized the education, technology, and infrastructure industries through letter-bombs he sent to targets he identified with an oppressive industrial system, seeking to start a war between anarchist radicals such as himself and the technocratic forces of modernity. The Unabomber would soon be caught after the publication of what the FBI called his "manifesto," and there is no evidence that Applewhite or other members of Heaven's Gate sympathized with him, but the anti-institutional and anti-government views of the Unabomber manifesto clearly had some resonance with Heaven's Gate self-perceived position, and the massive government search for him and the discussion it engendered among some adherents of radical and alternative religions meant that potential raids were very much in the air.

Probably even more concerning to Applewhite, and indicative of an accelerating war between the government and various fringe groups, was the event that occurred five months earlier. Two anti-government survivalists named Timothy McVeigh and Terry Nichols had orchestrated the bombing of the Alfred P. Murrah Federal Building in Oklahoma City. McVeigh and Nichols envisioned their bombing as a political act, and explicitly invoked the Weavers of Ruby Ridge and Branch Davidians of Waco as martyrs of government persecution. Allied with radical right Christian groups, the weapons rights movement, and various anti-government militia groups, McVeigh and Nichols focused a spotlight on what they perceived as an oppressive social and governmental system. Again, there is no evidence that members of Heaven's Gate identified or sympathized with McVeigh's and Nichols's ideas, but the specter of a war between the federal government and groups that the government considered fringe or suspect became an important part of the culture of radical and alternative religious groups with which Heaven's Gate apparently increasingly identified, at least based on Applewhite's references to guns and government raids.

Heaven's Gate posted the "Undercover Jesus" statement to newsgroups focusing on current events and the media (*alt.current-events. usa, alt.tv.news-shows, alt.news-media, alt.good.news*) as well as those associated with alternative spiritual practices (*alt.consciousness, alt.consciousness.mysticism, alt.consciousness.near-death-exp[ience], alt.drugs. culture*). The first set of newsgroups generally served the same role that the alternative media of the blogosphere would a decade later, a space for those who rejected the mainstream media to post news stories and comment on their interpretations. These newsgroups were hotbeds of claims of cover-ups, government malfeasance, conspiracies, and other controversies. The second set of newsgroups appealed to individuals interested in alternative spiritualities, and provided a free and uncensored place to discuss spiritual awakening through mystical or drug-induced experiences. Interestingly, although Applewhite indicated that he intended the post to "address the religious world, primarily the Christians, in relationship to their expectation for Jesus' return," he did not post the statement to any of the myriad of Christian newsgroups.[53] (Despite the title, alt.good.news is not a Christian newsgroup, but one focused on discussing positive or affirming news stories.) While one must avoid an argument based on a lack of something, the unusual fact that Applewhite wrote a statement for Christians but posted to newsgroups for alternative news and spirituality indicates that he and members of his group had become increasingly aware that conventional Christians had little interest in their movement, and that their opportunities for appealing to outsiders were strikingly limited, a position that the Two had begun to take not even a year into their shared work together in creating Heaven's Gate, but had reached full fruition at this time.[54]

The second UseNet posting, "E.T. SPEAKS: UFO'S / SPACE ALIENS / REBOOT CIVILIZATION," used language designed to appeal more to secular-minded individuals, those interested in ufology, science, and science fiction. Applewhite described it as "what we would consider more clinical and objective terminology."[55] The movement posted this statement primarily to newsgroups associated with science fiction, and *Star Trek* and *Star Wars* in particular, for example *rec.arts.sf.misc* ('sf' meaning science fiction), *alt.startrek*, and *rec.arts.st.starwars.misc*. This statement echoed the first one in content, describing the group's view of the nature of the cosmos, planet, human existence, the Next Level, and the nature of the soul. Regarding the exit from their human bodies, the statement similarly described the possibilities as either departure "aboard a spacecraft in a laboratory circumstance, as we head for home," or the "'dropping' of 'that shell'" during violent confrontation with the agents of the "'space' alien humanoids," that is, the government forces employed by the Luciferians.

This statement did not have the same imminent tone as the previous one regarding the group's exit, but instead it emphasized a far more apocalyptic vision of the impending demise of Earth's present civilization, "[b]ecause of the overripe corruption of the present civilization, this is the last scheduled visit before its recycling. It is the End of the Age. The human population, under space alien 'thought domination,' has become irreversibly perverse and rotten."[56] Human existence, the statement indicated, was about to come to an end, and the only way to survive was to overcome the Earth with Applewhite and his coreligionists. While the apocalyptic urgency was heightened, the overall theological message had not changed. Yet the statement nevertheless highlighted a highly dualistic vision of a cosmic war between good and evil soon to engulf Earth and its inhabitants: "A war in the literal heavens is underway as the alien races fiercely battle each other vying for the literal, invaluable spoils of this planet. Their campaign is escalating— actively recruiting, experimenting, and mining elements both mineral, biological (genetic)—in their efforts toward survival."[57]

The members of Heaven's Gate posted Applewhite's second statement far more widely than the first one, to sixteen different UseNet newsgroups, as well as reposting the same message with different subject lines to the same newsgroup, a clear breach of unofficial UseNet protocol ("netiquette") that indicated how seriously and urgently they saw their task. The members changed the title of the post on several *Star Trek*–oriented newsgroups to read, "The Real Q— An E.T. Speaks Out," a reference to an omnipotent extraterrestrial being known as "Q" on the popular *Star Trek: The Next Generation*, and a being that they obviously envisioned as comparable to Next Level aliens in power and scope.[58] In addition to some unusual choices of newsgroups such as the urban folklore forum (*alt.folklore.urban*), the group also targeted newsgroups focusing on the discussion of artificial intelligence (*comp.ai.philosophy*, etc.) as well as drug-induced spirituality (*alt.drugs.psychedelics*). The lack of attention to religious newsgroups is not remarkable in this instance, since the movement had intentionally written this statement for a different audience, but the lack of focus on either ufological news-groups or more mainstream scientific newsgroups indicated that just as Applewhite and the members of Heaven's Gate had begun to give up on Christians, clearly they had moved away from appealing to secular ufol-ogists and scientists as well, and looked instead to those who stood on the fringe between fact and fiction, present technology and speculation.

The responses to the UseNet postings were not positive, and while many of their posts were simply ignored, others became targets of rid-icule. "Please keep this obvious dribble [*sic*] from appearing in these forums again!" posted one UseNet reader in New Zealand, respond-ing to the E.T. Speaks post in the artificial intelligence newsgroups.[59] Another responded with a mangled gibberish quote from the 1951 science fiction movie *The Day the Earth Stood Still*, perhaps meant to indicate that the poster envisioned the Heaven's Gate message as also gibberish.[60] The most serious response might have been from a Univer-sity of San Francisco astronomer, who countered with both a religious and scientific retort: "Are you saying that you are an alien? You know what, I think you are making a faise [*sic*] claim in your article. I believe God created mankind and it is only God who created the earth, for that matter, the entire universe since the beginning of time. I'm an astrono-mer who knows stuff about aliens. If you are an alien, prove it to me."[61] The *Star Trek* newsgroup readers tended more toward the snarky than engaging. "[T]hat was about dumbest thing I've seen yet," one reader posted.[62] Another offered, " . . . and your point with posting this on a Star Trek board (or ANY other board for that matter) is . . . ? (oooooh, I can't wait to hear the answer to THIS question—biting my tongue as it is firmly planted in my cheek as I read this posting . . .)."[63] Only one poster seemed to take the statement seriously, noting that "I am very receptive to the idea of other species from other planets" and that *Star Trek* fans would be more accepting of such a fact, but the writer ended this apparently positive response by turning it on its head, saying that he was "forced by my next life-level admiral of the Xqizx dimension to write this . . . "[64] Yet generally readers of the newsgroup simply ignored the postings, with four of the newsgroup posts garnering no responses, and fewer than a dozen people responding to all of them combined.[65] These types of responses—and lack thereof—surely discouraged the members of Heaven's Gate. The group's anthology frames the failed UseNet experiment thusly, "It was clear to us that their [i.e., the statements] being introduced to the public at that time was premature."[66] The group posted several more times to UseNet in August and September 1996, with similar results.[67] One former member later told Balch and Taylor that the experience of the UsetNet postings and other attempts to communicate with outsiders using the Internet indicated that "we just were not able to interface with the public . . . it was time to leave."[68]

The UseNet postings included for the first time a URL, or uniform resource locator, an address that computer users might use to find the group's website. While ubiquitous today, at the time the World Wide Web was hardly a widely used system, and the group's creation of a website was novel. Analyzing a series of different polls and studies, Princeton sociologists Paul DiMaggio, Eszter Hargittai, and their colleagues explain that the Internet and its usage "began its rapid ascent only in the early 1990s, when graphical interfaces became widely available and commercial interests were allowed to participate."[69] They found that twenty-five million Americans—about 3 percent—used the Internet in 1995, with only about twenty thousand websites existing in that year. By 1999, Internet usage had increased to eighty-three million, and ten million web pages by 2000.[70] Clearly Heaven's Gate was on the leading edge of technological innovation, at least when it came to Internet communication and creating a web presence. The URL they first provided pointed to a web address they soon abandoned—http://www.indirect.com/www/lillo—but the group soon began hosting a website on an Internet domain of its own, the now-famous heavensgate.com, in 1996. This website represented one of the group's final attempts to reach out to the broader world with its message. The group's first website is lost and was never saved by any known website archive, so one cannot know what it contained. The first archived copy of the movement's web page dates only to December 22, 1996, when the movement had purchased the heavensgate.com domain and hosted a site on it.

The Heaven's Gate website in 1996 served as a clearinghouse for several sets of documents that the group had produced in the previous years: the "Our Position Against Suicide" statement, transcripts of two 1996 videotapes of Applewhite's teaching, a revised version of the E.T. Statement that members had posted to UseNet in 1995, and the movement's new anthology that they published in 1996. The majority of the content derived from the anthology, and in fact the group posted electronic files for their entire book online, free for download and with a broad copyright statement allowing free redistribution. While their use of an Internet website garnered wide media attention after the suicides, it was a quite late development within the movement and used merely as another means of posting information, one more form of media that they adopted alongside posters, newspaper advertisements, satellite television, videotapes, and books.[71] Despite some claims to the contrary, nothing about Heaven's Gate resembled what one might imagine as an "Internet religion."[72]

The movement's anthology represented a far vaster effort by the group's members in its final full year of existence, and provided the eponymous name that this twenty-year-old movement adopted in its final year of existence and now into perpetuity. Applewhite had used the capitalized term "Heaven's Gate" a year before in 1995 to refer to the idea of entrance into the next level, but the anthology represented the first time he or others used it to refer to the group itself.[73] That being said, the choice to use the name "Heaven's Gate" to refer to the group appears to be an intentional one, with ex-member Neoody explaining that Applewhite explained it to him and others, and meant it as a reference to himself and the Class as the only way ("gate") into the Next Level ("heaven").[74] It also represented the movement members' attempts to leave some record of the Next Level's teachings for posterity after they had left the Earth, and in this regard the publication of the anthology must be recognized as one of the initial actions that culminated in the suicides. Earlier in 1996, Nrrody and Glnody began compiling the movement's teachings and with the aid of Jwnody and others produced an anthology of the most crucial documents that the group had created over the years. Eventually titled, *How and When "Heaven's Gate" (The Door to the Physical Kingdom Level Above Human) May Be Entered: An Anthology of Our Materials*, the original edition includes material only until April 1996, indicating a late spring or early summer publication, before the movement filmed its two 1996 videos.[75] The group made some slight reorganizations and revisions and gave the second and final edition to ex-members Mrcody and Srfody at the time of the suicides, asking them to arrange for its publication and distribution.[76] Most of the materials included in the anthology originated from Applewhite, with the transcripts of the 1991–92 *Beyond Human* satellite series compromising the bulk of the book, but also including twenty-three statements written by members of the group as well as introductions by Jwnody and Applewhite. (Glnody wrote an introduction as well, but the second edition moved this to the section including statements by other members; Jwnody's introduction remained in the frontmatter.)[77] Jwnody positioned the anthology as a last legacy of the group, implying an awareness that the end of their earthly time was near, but also avoiding any specific statement as to how and when their mission would end. She wrote,

> And so this [book] brings us before the public once again, with our "farewell legacy." At the time of this writing, we do not yet know the extent of this seventh, and we suspect final, public involvement. This book, an anthology of our materials, begins "phase one." Nothing is predetermined. The response of the world to the Next Level will be monitored very carefully. What happens next remains in the balance.[78]

Since the records and digital logfiles no longer exist, it is impossible to know how many people downloaded the book from the heavensgate.com website. Mrcody and Srfody indicated that the book subsequently sold so poorly that the publishing and distribution company sold back to them the remaining copies as discounted remainders. One individual, Dvvody, joined the movement based on encountering the book and other material on the group's website and corresponding with members and Applewhite via email. (Dvvody's husband also considered joining, but did not for somewhat unclear reasons.)[79] Yet again, the effort of producing a three-hundred-fifty-page book and website seemed to have little net effect, with only one person joining and one other expressing interest. At this point, however, members looked solely to the Next Level and had broadly given up on attempting to reach other members of the human species.

Along with the book, the group produced two videos, both of which featured a serious-looking Applewhite presenting his teachings directly to the camera. Effectively videotaped lectures, the group provided the tapes free of charge or for nominal shipping fees. They also provided transcripts in English and German for these two tapes, both posted online on their website. The titles of the two tapes, *Last Chance to Evacuate Earth Before It's Recycled* and *Planet About To Be Recycled—Your Only Chance To Survive—Leave With Us*, convey the sense of apocalyptic urgency that members of Heaven's Gate had begun to feel. Years of rejection from outsiders and failed attempts to seek public awareness had resulted in the group's members beginning to believe that their mission was coming to a close and the Earth's inhabitants faced their final hours. In the words of Applewhite in the first minutes of the first tape, "Now, today we have quite a different urgency. It's urgent to me, and it's urgent to the students that sit before me. Our reason for speaking to you is because we feel to [sic] warn you of what is just around the corner. I'll try to just put it as briefly as I can and as clearly as I can. This planet is about to be recycled, refurbished, started over."[80]

Throughout the videotapes Applewhite explained the basics of Heaven's Gate's cosmology, indicating the nature of the Next Level—called by its synonym the Evolutionary Level Above Human in the videos—and his place in that cosmology. He focused on the Luciferians and their success in controlling human society, and by contrast the truth (with a capital "T" in the transcript) of what he and Nettles offered. Applewhite emphasized the need to overcome human practices and behaviors, and he called for potential candidates to join the Next Level to show curiosity and dig deeper into the materials that he and his co-religionists left behind. The majority of what he discussed followed in the same vein as the decades of material he and others in the movement had already produced, and there was no new theological material in the videos per se.

Yet Applewhite highlighted two issues on which he had not hitherto focused, namely his opposition to the category of "religion" and the nature of the individuals who possessed deposits or souls but were not part of his Class. As regards religion, Applewhite made a special distinction between the teachings of Heaven's Gate and those of religions and spiritual groups, insisting that the teachings of Heaven's Gate center on a physical reality and are spiritual only in the sense that they related to the mind or spirit. He did admit that Islam offered some value, since its members valued modesty, a strong connection with God, and would die for their faith. Yet he cautioned that Islam was ultimately no better than any other religion, and that "if the extent of your religious background was *Star Trek*—that in itself could be the best background you could have," hardly a ringing endorsement![81] Like his various other statements on religion, as well as those by Jwnody and other members—discussed previously in chapter 3—Applewhite here engaged partially in rhetorical positioning of his movement vis-à-vis other competing religious groups, but he also had recognized that religious leaders and movements had by and large rejected the teachings he offered, and he had come to see them as not open-minded seekers of Truth, but corrupted demagogues controlled by maleficent space aliens. "I hate the lower forces who have taken the very Truths that were initially the Truths, and have reduced them to 'religion,' and they made the religions more attractive and more human," he exhorted in the first of the videos.[82] "There is not a religion on the face of the globe that is of God, as it is today. All of those ideologies that are called religions use corrupted records and corrupted interpretations," he said in the second.[83] Religions, for Applewhite and fellow members of Heaven's Gate, had fallen away from their true nature as revelations of the Next Level and become mere tools for demonic space aliens to control humanity. Instead of teaching how to overcome the human level and earthly existence, they mired humans in terrestrial living in a broken world.

On one level, Applewhite's discourse about the corruption of all other existing religions merely follows a trope of other founders of new religious groups. The Prophet Muhammad similarly claimed that the earlier monotheistic religions of Judaism and Christianity had become corrupted, and that the revelations he offered served only to correct these corruptions.[84] Just over a millennium later the Bahá'í prophets and leaders made similar claims about Islam.[85] In the United States, the nineteenth-century prophet Joseph Smith, Jr. declared that Christianity had become corrupted after the end of the early apostolic era, and that his Church of Jesus Christ of Latter-day Saints (Mormons) came to renew and reestablish true religion.[86] One finds similar claims among numerous Protestant groups, Christian "primitivists" who believe that Christianity went astray after the first days of the early or primitive church and that only their preferred branches of Christianity recon- struct or renew the true religion.[87]

While in this regard Applewhite certainly falls in line with other prophets and reformers, his rejection of the very category of religion marks his work as somewhat different. Partially this reflects him and the adherents of Heaven's Gate as part of an anti-institutional, anti-rit- ual, individualistic religious current that has long categorized Ameri- can religion, but the widespread rejection that he and members of the movement experienced had clearly left its mark on Applewhite's view of religion. Somewhat defensively but quite reflexively, Applewhite explained that Heaven's Gate's message "would be easier to accept if it were more spiritual, if it were more complicated, if it had more ritual with it, or more trappings of religion." Yet, he continued, "in my Father's house, no incense is required, no flowing robes, no tinkling bells, no genuflecting, no sitting in the lotus position, no things of 'spirituality,' even though our Father's Kingdom requires cleansing of the spirit, the mind."[88] While a latent Protestant suspicion of ritual clearly exists in these words, the recognition that others did not consider his movement a true religion also explains why Applewhite so vehemently declared the world's religions and even the concept itself to be beyond repair.

The second concept that Applewhite highlighted involved the nature and fate of individuals who might be somewhat receptive to his teach- ings or perhaps followed an analogue path but were not members of the Class and did not intend to join them. As early as the first year of the formation of the movement that would become Heaven's Gate, Nettles and Applewhite had taught that there were "many ways up the moun- tain, but only one way off," to paraphrase from several of their mate- rials.[89] While they recognized the validity and value of other forms of spiritual seeking, they taught that only those who adopted their Human Individual Metamorphosis method, or the Process, would achieve the type of transformation that would allow entrance to the Next Level. Early on they also noted that those who did not join them were perhaps

unlucky or unfortunate, but could merely wait until the next representatives of the Next Level arrived a few thousand years hence and could
advance beyond human in a later incarnation.[90]

This sort of teaching fell by the wayside in the intervening years, and
Nettles and Applewhite seldom discussed the fate of those who did not
join their movement. In the final years of Heaven's Gate, Applewhite
at times seemed to imply that all those remaining on Earth were destined for recycling and destruction, hardly a pleasant prospect. Yet in
both the 1996 videos, Applewhite returned to his earlier teachings and
beliefs that he shared with Nettles, namely that advancement beyond
the human level existed as a possibility for some individuals not in
the Class, but only in the distant future. However, he made an important distinction in these videos. Such an opportunity existed only for
some humans, those with deposits or souls who had made some limited advancement in their earthly lives but were unable or unwilling to
make the final sacrifices to join the Next Level at this time. He explains
that this possibility exists primarily for those who trust and believe in
him and the Next Level but lack the strength to follow through. Such
individuals will be spared the spading over that deposit-less humans
will experience, and "will be kept in the keeping of the Kingdom Level
Above Human, and replanted at another time, and given another
chance."[91]

Why would Applewhite indicate that individuals might achieve
salvation and entrance into the Next Level—albeit far in the distant
future—without the need to join the Heaven's Gate movement? The
most likely possibility is that he suspected his movement would soon
be coming to an end, and that he left his message for posterity and
for the interim time between the departure of the Heaven's Gate elect
and the destruction of earthly human civilization. Another possibility, one upheld by former members Mrcody and Srfody, was that
these videos and other materials targeted the hundreds of former
members who had previously joined the Two over the years since
they founded the group, and that Applewhite hoped these former
members would find their way back to him and his teachings.[92] In
either case, these two final videos represented a sort of message in
a bottle that members of the movement hoped would help those left
behind after their exit.

Applewhite indicated one possible sort of person who might ben-
efit from this "message in a bottle": those who were part of the radical
fringe of society. He specifically called out members of what he called
religious cults and the right-wing militia and patriot movements as possessing the sort of worldview and outlook appropriate to the Next Level:
"even in patriot movements, or in militia movements, or in 'cults'; or in
this type of religious radical or another who know that this world is rotten, they are saying, 'I would rather die in service to my interpretation
of what God is than stay here.' Those young souls, those young spirits, those minds will be saved. They will be set aside—'put on ice,' so to
speak—and have a future, have another planting in the next civilization
for further nourishment."[93]

Members of right-wing militia movements, often associated with
racism, Neo-Nazism, radical conservative politics, and xenophobia
seem like odd bedfellows for the leader and member of a group that
was effectively pacifistic, lived communally as monastics, rejected any
sort of racism, and was rather apolitical. Yet this was not the first time
that Applewhite and other members of Heaven's Gate made reference
to such individuals, including the explicitly white supremacist Weavers
of Ruby Ridge. Why? And what clue might this give as to why members
of Heaven's Gate decided in 1997 that the time had come to depart the
Earth by their own hands? It is to this odd connection that we now turn.

Conspiracy Culture and the Art Bell Connection

Members of Heaven's Gate had long adopted a perspective that I call
"worldly dualism," meaning a dualistic way of looking at the world (and
distinct from, but parallel to, metaphysical dualism that envisions the
body and soul as distinct). Worldly dualism offers an important opportunity to understand why members of Heaven's Gate looked to adherents of a disparate array of alternative and radical worldviews—right-
wing militia members, gun enthusiasts, and members of other new
religions such as the Branch Davidians and Christian Identity—as at
least allied with them against government persecution and perhaps even
potential recruits for the Next Level at some point in the future. All of
these individuals upheld highly dualistic ways of envisioning the world
and all of them identified "mainstream society" including government,

media, and popular culture as the intrinsically negative other. But even more than this generally dualistic outlook, all of these other groups had by the 1990s become associated with ideas about government conspiracies, hidden knowledge, and secret agendas. Historian Michael Barkun has called this nexus "a culture of conspiracy," and specifically identified individuals within these groups as upholding varieties of "stigmatized knowledge."[94] This culture of conspiracy connects the various forces at work in the final years of Heaven's Gate, namely their appeal to radical groups, expectations of a government raid, and highly dualistic ways of thinking. It also provides a link to why the group members became enamored of a particular conspiracy theory that played a role in how the group ended, namely the beliefs about a spacecraft trailing the Hale-Bopp comet.

It is indisputable that the U.S. government has engaged in extensive covert activities that one might consider "conspiracies" such as various forms of espionage, weapons testing, and scientific research conducted under the veil of secrecy. Yet the culture of conspiracy to which Barkun refers and the type of conspiratorial thinking to which members of Heaven's Gate came to ascribe envisions a far vaster conspiracy of a shadow government pulling the strings behind the scenes, duping ordinary people and operating in concert with malevolent forces across the globe. Barkun explains that "the common thread of conspiracism [is] the belief that powerful, evil forces control human destinies."[95] Adherents of Heaven's Gate identified these forces as Luciferian in origin, meaning malevolent space aliens seeking to control Earth so as to harvest human souls, but other groups and individuals holding to conspiracist views might identify these forces as Illuminati, bankers, a New World Order, Jews, capitalist cabals, or any number of groups pulling the strings behind the scenes.

Barkun identifies a broad subculture of ufologically oriented conspiratorial thinking that had become prominent in the mid-1990s and shares the same perspective as members of Heaven's Gate. Adherents of such conspiracy theories accept a certain set of shared assumptions, namely that the federal government held or holds captured extraterrestrial technology and bodies, and that hostile extraterrestrials are involved in controlling the government. They also accept the veracity of major events associated with American ufology such as the Roswell

UFO crashes and the holding of extraterrestrials at a research base called "Area 51" in Nevada, a secret facility that the federal government only recently admitted it used for testing advanced spy planes and other high technology.

This ufological conspiracy material diffused into broader culture through television's *The X-Files*, a favorite of members of Heaven's Gate to which several members referred, and other science fiction television and films. But Barkun ascribes the rise of this type of conspiratorial thinking especially to Milton William Cooper's book *Behold a Pale Horse* (1991), which recounts what Barkun calls "a long-simmering Luciferian plot" to control human society.[96] Cooper, like members of Heaven's Gate, identified Luciferians as space aliens, and both those who follow Cooper as well as adherents of Heaven's Gate identified the Luciferians as engaged in a massive conspiracy to control governments, economies, and cultures. While Cooper disavowed any religious perspective and made no claims about what Heaven's Gate members called the Next Level, the two systems agreed on much, and particularly on the issue of the Luciferians, even to the extent that many who adopted Cooper's position looked to the Bible as evidence of Luciferian space alien influence and reread the story of the Fall precisely as did members of Heaven's Gate—as evidence of Luciferian work.[97] Barkun calls Cooper's work "not only among the most complex superconspiracy theories, it is also among the most influential, widely available in mainstream bookstores but also much read in both UFO and militia circles."[98] It has had broad influence, and Cooper's claims have percolated throughout ufological, radical political, and alternative religious countercultures.

Applewhite and members of Heaven's Gate clearly were not informed by Cooper, *Behold a Pale Horse*, and ufologists within Cooper's worldview, as the adherents of Heaven's Gate had developed and explained their beliefs in Luciferians in the previous decade and based on their own readings of the text.[99] Yet the spread of Cooper's views into a broadly diffuse world of alternative and radical "fringe" movements surely indicated to members of Heaven's Gate that these fellow travelers had at least an inkling of an idea as to the true nature of the world and the cosmos. Barkun shows that followers of ufologically oriented conspiracy theories had come to adopt many of the same positions as adherents of Heaven's Gate, including not only the long-standing claims of government cover-ups of UFO crashes but also beliefs in ancient astronauts, alien abductions, and the recovery of alien bodies by the U.S. government. Members of Heaven's Gate had cited and recommended books on many of these topics in its '88 *Update*, and by the mid-1990s they were able to witness the same ideas' broader diffusion into ufological and conspiratorial-oriented culture, even among anti-government activists, militia members, and white supremacist groups, none of whom shared the religious or social positions of Heaven's Gate.[100]

Members regarded these other radical and alternative groups as fellow travelers in at least some regards, as indicated by Stmody, who wrote in his contribution to the anthology, "those who hate this world and its corrupt systems, religions, morality, and laws are in a real sense our allies (although, of course, we may not agree with them on specific points). It seems that we have a common 'enemy'—the space-aliens with their 'alleged' conspiracies designed to prepare (program) the whole planet to accept a 'New World Order,' a 'New World Religion' that would destroy the ability of this world to function as a Next Level garden."[101] This statement, and another one Stmody wrote about many of the conspiracies being based on facts, shows the degree to which at least some members of Heaven's Gate explicitly invoked concepts drawn from a conspiratorial subculture—including concepts of a New World Order and that of conspiracy itself—and how these two worldviews had begun to connect.

Another member, Srrody, similarly invoked conspiracies in his Earth Exit statement, referring to both documented and suspected cases of government conspiracy, namely the well-documented Tuskegee syphilis experiments wherein government health workers intentionally misled and withheld treatments from poor African Americans so as to study the progression of their disease, as well as the alleged genetic experiments on urban African American babies in the 1990s.[102] While this generally white religious movement seldom focused on explicitly racial issues, in this case the way that government treated minorities reflected directly on how Srrody—who was white—believed it would respond to minority religions such as Heaven's Gate. Both cases revealed to Srrody the untrustworthiness of the U.S. government and the reality of a Luciferian takeover. Like the case of Stmody, Srrody's writing shows how conspiratorial thinking had entered the thought of Heaven's Gate.

Crucially, this connection between Heaven's Gate's religious world-view and the conspiratorial worldview that Barkun calls the realm of "stigmatized knowledge" appears to have become bidirectional by 1996. Believers in conspiratorial thinking tend to distrust what they call the mainstream media and at the time of the 1990s congregated on the Internet in the same sort of UseNet forums to which Heaven's Gate posted its messages, and also public access cable television, satellite television, mail-order videocassettes, and talk-radio shows.[103] There adherents of these worldviews could freely share their views, swap stories providing support and evidence of conspiracies, and present their views without being immediately rejected as paranoid or insane. Heaven's Gate had begun to utilize these media as early as 1991–92 with its satellite broadcast, and made forays into distributing videotapes as well. In those broadcasts Applewhite referenced other radical and alternative religious teachers using the same sort of media, indicating that members consumed as well as produced such alternative media materials.[104]

In 1996 one of the group's members, Tllody, "discovered an under-ground Internet radio show that talked about Government conspiracies, UFO's, misinformation and current events," in the words and recollection of Neoody.[105] Members became listeners, and soon adherents of the movement had plugged into an array of radio and Internet sources offering what Barkun would call stigmatized knowledge. According to the website links that the group later cited as "address[ing] related or connecting topics" to their own message, they indicated websites and other Internet sources associated with the New Age and channeling, alternative healing and science, ancient prophecies, Gnosticism, libertarianism, government conspiracies, and a plethora of UFO-conspiracy oriented websites. They also provided a link to an image gallery sponsored by NASA—America's governmental space exploration agency—indicating that not all government-linked organizations were entirely suspect.[106]

Yet it was two links that the members of Heaven's Gate provided as "related or connecting topics" that would provide the most crucial insight to how Heaven's Gate ended: Chuck Shramek's "Hale-Bopp Companion Page," and the web page for the Art Bell radio show, a late-night AM talk radio show that features discussion of conspiracies, paranormal, and the occult. It was to this radio show that Neoody likely referred in recalling Tllody's discovery, and it was this radio show that first brought to prominence the theory that a UFO trailed the recently discovered Hale-Bopp comet. This information, and the response it engendered from Applewhite and members of Heaven's Gate, signaled the beginning of the end of the terrestrial existence of Heaven's Gate.

Hale-Bopp Comet and the End of Heaven's Gate

From May 1996, when it first became visible, until December 1997, when one needed a telescope to glimpse it, Hale-Bopp comet captured the world's attention. Two amateur astronomers, Alan Hale and Thomas Bopp, independently discovered the comet on July 23, 1995, as it approached the orbit of Jupiter. An impressively large comet with a dust envelope as large as the sun itself, the comet was hailed as the "comet of the century," and expectations were high that it would put on a spectacular display.[107] Over the next two years the comet became increasingly visible. *Astronomy* magazine trumpeted the comet's display as a "long festival of Hale-Bopp" that would last over a year and culminate in late March 1997.[108] A bright comet observable even in light-polluted urban areas, the comet was particularly brilliant in the first months of 1997, reaching its closest point to Earth on March 22, 1997—the day the suicides began—and to the Sun shortly thereafter on April 1–2, 1997.[109]

Comets of course have a long history as objects of religious interpretation, with comets of antiquity and premodern times interpreted as portents by Jewish, Christian, and Islamic audiences.[110] Even into the modern age, historian Roland Numbers writes, "considerable evidence shows widespread concern with astronomical phenomena seen by the naked eyes: eclipses, meteors, and comets."[111] Comets in particular, Numbers indicates, served as omens or portents for both the common folk and the learned religious leaders during the dawn of the modern era. Folklorist Daniel Wojcik has argued that the value of comets as religious portents substantially declined in the twentieth century, especially after the advent of the nuclear age and with it the new symbols of human-mediated doom.[112]

Yet it was not solely the comet itself that attracted the notice or attention of members of Heaven's Gate. Rather, claims about a mysterious object, a "companion," following the comet that seemed to move

Figure 6.1. Hale-Bopp Comet, on March 14, 1997, as photographed from Earth. This brilliant comet was visible throughout much of the world, even in urban areas. Image © European Southern Observatory/E. Slawik.

unnaturally and even influence the movements of the comet became the focus of the group. While these claims would later be largely debunked, and the members of Heaven's Gate ultimately indicated that the nature of the mysterious object was in fact irrelevant, the intense interest in the companion and the comet among members of the fringe and conspiracy-oriented alternative media attracted the attention and interest of the group's adherents. Neoody remembers that "the comet's [purported] strange and irregular course of travel" interested Applewhite immediately. While Neoody did not comment on the companion, his coreligionist Anlody offered an extensive commentary indicating that while one could not know if the "controversial object" was in fact a "spaceship of the Next Level," the message of Heaven's Gate nevertheless called for preparation for exit from Earth. "We're not sure," Anlody admitted, but "[we] think there's a good possibility that Hale-Bopp is what we've been waiting for."[113] But what was this "controversial object" as Anlody called it?

On November 14, 1996, an amateur astronomer named Chuck Shramek had called the Art Bell AM radio show, *Coast to Coast*, claiming that he had photographed a mysterious "companion" following the comet. Bell's show had become an important and some would say central media form in the fringe and conspiratorial subculture, broadcast on three hundred and ninety stations and with more than nine million listeners each week at the time.[114] The show featured extended conversation about conspiracies, the occult, and ufology to which Bell invited listeners to respond by calling in to the program. Shramek called immediately after his observations of Hale-Bopp in order to report to Bell and his listeners what he believed he had found. He described the companion as a Saturn-like object, and immediately injected a sense of religious meaning to it: "[it was] so bright and strange I began to pray," Shramek later witnessed.[115] Shramek implied that the object may be an alien spacecraft, and Bell encouraged that interpretation. On the next radio broadcast of November 15, Bell featured another caller, Courtney Brown, who claimed to possess the power to engage in "remote viewing" and confirmed that the companion was an extraterrestrial spacecraft. Brown claimed that individuals involved in his Farsight Institute—Brown's New Age business that teaches individuals how to engage in the process of remote viewings—had determined that the companion was "larger than Earth, hollow and 'under intelligent control'—a kind of planetary spaceship hitching a ride on the comet," according to a *Washington Post* journalist who investigated the claims.[116] Later that month, on November 29, Brown and his assistant Prudence Calabrese again called Bell's program and claimed that they could provide an anonymously produced photograph that they indicated proved the existence of the spacecraft. Brown and Calabrese sent the image to Bell but requested the radio personality not distribute the photo until the anonymous photographers came forward and allowed it. No photographers ever revealed themselves, and Bell posted the photo on January 14, 1997 on his Internet web page. The photo shows a large glowing star-like object near the comet, which believers professed showed an alien spacecraft trailing Hale-Bopp comet. Members of Heaven's Gate would have seen this photograph on Bell's web page as well as the web page of Whitney Strieber, another Bell caller and a ufologist active in the alien conspiracy and ufological subcultures.

Both the Shramek photograph and the anonymous Brown/Calabrese photograph became immediately controversial. After examining the image, several astronomers judged that Shramek's Hale-Bopp companion was in fact a star with the rather unexciting name of SAO 141894, and the scientific consensus agreed with that interpretation.[117] A day after Bell posted the anonymous photograph from Brown and Calabrese, University of Hawaii astronomer David J. Tholen announced that the photograph appeared to be a doctored version of one that he had posted on the Internet in September 1995.[118] His analysis showed rather conclusively that the image Brown had claimed to show a companion was instead a digitally altered fraud. Bell and Strieber backtracked, but the idea they had spawned was still out there, now being copied and discussed on websites, UseNet newgroups, and elsewhere on the Internet and AM airwaves.

Courtney Brown and his Farsight Institute kept the issue alive well past January 1997 when the images were demonstrated to be false, though Brown himself eventually admitted the problems with the image. In February his Farsight Institute website still listed the results of four different professional remote viewers—that is, individuals who had graduated from the Institute's training program—and their viewings of the companion. Each viewer claimed to have seen an alien presence trailing Hale-Bopp. Invoking classic iconography from Western esotericism and Freemasonry, one viewer noted both a "big, hollow, expansive vortex of magnetic energy" as well as a "climate controlled space capsule . . . heavy, big, hollow, magnetic, and electric with energy . . . contain[ing] a pyramid, a central person, and an eye surrounded by energy."[119] Other professional viewers saw different physical objects, energy centers, and various spacecraft configurations.[120] Brown also posted thirty different viewing sessions from eleven of his students supporting and corroborating these visions.[121] Art Bell's website linked to these descriptions, and many like them, as well as various photographs claiming different "anomalous features" of the comet and a potential companion.[122] Chuck Shramek also continued to support his claims of a Hale-Bopp companion, and linked to his original image as well as others on his website, which also featured extended discussion of government cover-ups and ancient alien astronauts.[123]

Importantly, it was not the companion itself that indicated to Applewhite and members of Heaven's Gate that the time had come to exit Earth, but rather the unusual and remarkable nature of the entire Hale-Bopp episode: its marvelous discovery by amateur astronomers far further from Earth than one normally glimpses comets; the behavior of the comet itself, which seemed to spin and twirl as it approached; its brightness and nearly universal visibility across the entire Northern hemisphere and much of the Southern one as well; and of course the claims about the companion, whether they were true or not. The whole world seemed to be tuned in to Hale-Bopp and news about it, and this indicated to Applewhite and members of the group that the time had come to exit Earth.

Balch and Taylor indicate that Applewhite and Nettles had dated their initial meeting and religious work together to another comet, the Kohoutek comet of 1973.[124] The astrological interpretation of Applewhite's chart had first convinced him and Nettles to work together, and astrology had been an important practice of the Two earlier in their religious explorations. Looking to the skies for meaning therefore was hardly new for Heaven's Gate. The time had come, members believed, for their final exit from Earth. They updated their website with its now-famous statement.

RED ALERT: Hale-Bopp Brings Closure to Heaven's Gate. Whether Hale-Bopp has a "companion" or not is irrelevant from our perspective. However, its arrival is joyously very significant to us at "Heaven's Gate." The joy is that our Older Member in the Evolutionary Level Above Human (the "Kingdom of Heaven") has made it clear to us that Hale-Bopp's approach is the "marker" we've been waiting for— the time for the arrival of the spacecraft from the Level Above Human to take us home to "Their World"— in the literal Heavens. Our 22 years of classroom here on planet Earth is finally coming to conclusion— "graduation" from the Human Evolutionary Level. We are happily prepared to leave "this world" and go with Ti's crew.[125]

Over two decades previous, Nettles and Applewhite had taught that those who followed them could transform themselves into perfected extraterrestrial Next Level beings. Most would physically enter the Next Level spacecraft, but the two co-founders themselves would first lay down their human lives in a demonstration for the entire world to see. The Two had later rejected that physicalist interpretation of the demonstration and for a while taught that they too would enter heaven without first dying, but the death of Nettles had disproved that notion. Now, just over two decades later, Applewhite and the members of Heaven's Gate returned to the initial idea of departing the Earth outside of *human* bodies, but rather than biologically and chemically transforming themselves on Earth they looked to new Next Level bodies awaiting them on the spacecraft. In many ways, Heaven's Gate had come full circle.

Members of the movement prepared for the end of their time on Earth. It was patently clear to Applewhite and others that the federal government was not going to raid them, and that death by violent persecution was not going to happen. Suicide became the default option, making use of the instructions the group had studied three years earlier in Humphry's *Final Exit* and the drugs they had purchased for that contingency. In early 1997, members of the movement began to focus on preparations for the end, all the while keeping an eye on Hale-Bopp and its alleged mysterious companion. On Sunday, January 26, 1997, they purchased fifty patches to add to their uniforms, with each patch reading: "Earth Exit Monasteries." They also bought astronomy charts that same week, presumably to help them track the approach of Hale-Bopp. (The same week they also bought molasses, a chafing dish, laundry detergent, fertilizer, weedkiller, a table, and a chair, indicating that life went on at the same time they were preparing for the end.) They bought fabric for the uniforms and shrouds on February 20, and thirty-nine matching Nike shoes on March 1, 1997, all of which they used to complete their final uniforms.[126] Applewhite and other members of the group apparently were not satisfied with the first patches, as they had a second batch created, reading "Heaven's Gate Away Team." In addition to using the name "Heaven's Gate" for the group, these new patches also

Figure 6.2. On the left, one of the first batch of patches, subsequently rejected and replaced with one of the patches as shown on the right. Patch design © TELAH Foundation. Image © Benjamin E. Zeller.

included the previously invoked reference to the *Star Trek* concept of temporary visitors to a planet, an "Away Team." Members took account of their remaining funds and spent them on final forays into human earthly life, including a trip to Las Vegas to visit the Stratosphere, a world-famous casino that looks much like a flying saucer; visits to Wild Animal Park and Sea World amusement parks; dinner at several local restaurants; watching the Cannes-winning British film *Secrets & Lies*; and a final group meal of pizza.[127]

Importantly, in the week before the suicides, members recorded heartfelt Exit Videos explaining their reasons for exiting the human earthly world. Of the thirty-nine members of Heaven's Gate, all but four members created these videos, with Applewhite's the longest and the most focused on offering instruction. The videos served as opportunities for members to talk about what membership in the community of Heaven's Gate meant to them, why they had chosen to end their terrestrial lives, and how they hoped outsiders would perceive them. Most expected that they would be dismissed and ridiculed, but they pleaded for family and friends to understand that they had made their choices willingly and intentionally. Srrody spoke for many others when he said, facing directly into the camera, "People on the other side of the camera, you'll say 'you are deluded or you are brainwashed or whatever' . . . [but] from my perspective, this is a godsend."[128] Yrsody made a similar statement, trying to explain that she and others had chosen their actions deliberately and freely: "We are all choosing of our own free will to go to the Next Level with Ti and Do, and they are certainly not what the media is going to paint them out to be."[129] Nearly every one of the Exit Video statements included similar language.

In addition to the videos, copies of which were mailed to former members to distribute, two members—Glnody and Srrody—wrote "Earth Exit Statements." Each included summaries of the group's beliefs as well as a header, "Why I Want To Leave at This Time." Each answered that question by indicating that the Earth offered them nothing, and that they had put aside their human life and human needs in order to journey to their heavenly destination. In Glnody's words, "[i]t is my chance to go to God, to prove that I love His World [i.e., the Next Level]. How could I honestly say I love Him more than anything if I cling to this world at all costs and only leave here when I am forced to go when this vehicle ceases to function?"[130] Glnody's argument was devastatingly simple and in keeping with the trajectory and teaching of Nettles and Applewhite from the mid-1970s until then: the body was merely a vessel, and one had to move beyond it to advance to the true destination. Staying behind on Earth would represent the true eternal suicide.

Finally, the movement's members drafted a press release, dated March 22, indicating "Heaven's Gate 'Away Team' Returns to Level Above Human in Distant Space." The movement's final statement echoed its many other materials, though this one emphasized the adherents' identities as truly Next Level beings who had only temporarily occupied human bodies, a variant of the "walk-in" concept. In this regard, their suicides were not deaths at all, since the bodies had never truly been theirs and their souls never really belonged on Earth. The press release also indicated that Heaven's Gate remained open for just a while longer, and that "[d]uring a brief window of time, some may wish to follow us. If they do, it will not be easy. The requirement is to not only believe who the Representatives are, but, to do as they and we did. You must leave everything of your humanness behind. This includes the ultimate sacrifice and demonstration of faith—that is, the shedding of your human body."[131] Here, at the very end of the movement's terrestrial history, the willful termination of one's human existence, the suicide of the body, became the only possible avenue for eternal salvation.

Adherents mailed copies of these videos and computer files containing the statements and final updates for the web pages to several ex-members who had remained on good terms with the group, including Mrcody, Srfody, Neoody, Rkkody, Oscody, and several other individuals.[132] The letters were succinct and clear, asking these former members to post materials to the Internet and maintain it as long as they could. In the letter sent to Rkkody, they wrote, "[b]y now, having read the enclosed press release and the Earth Exit Statements by Students, you should be aware that we have exited our vehicles just as we entered them. . . . We are hoping that with your computer skills, you might choose to assist us in this capacity for whatever length of time feels right to you. We are particularly interested in having you upload the files on the third diskette entitled 'Earth Exit, final press release, and index page.'"[133] Mrcody and Srfody—whom Applewhite had charged to operate the group's TELAH Foundation and website—Rkkody, Neody, and other ex-members did this, creating a post-mortem Internet existence for Heaven's Gate that continues to exist. When the news of the suicides was delivered and the media descended onto Rancho Santa Fe, the Heaven's Gate web page with its complete copy of the movement's anthology and the final press release became the most important way that outsiders could understand who and what the group had been.

After receiving the package Neoody was the first to travel to Rancho Santa Fe to see for himself the bodily remains of his co-religionists, and it was he who reported the suicides to the legal authorities using a 911 telephone call. When the San Diego Sheriff's Department arrived, they found the thirty-nine bodies in careful order, each laid out on the appropriate bunk, dressed identically in black uniforms, with purple shrouds over their faces and upper bodies. The movement's members had taken the poison in waves, with each group cleaning and straightening up after the previous group's exit. If they had followed any particular ritual before or during the process of ending their terrestrial lives, we do not know. Nor do we know why they used shrouds, though certainly doing so is in keeping with established burial customs throughout the world. What we can say is that members left their earthly remains and their home in immaculate order. Members each had identification to aid investigators, and had left a checklist indicating how they had killed themselves. Adherents had taken out the trash and paid their last library fines. They signed out on the group's daily log sheet, what they called their "Comm Center Daily Log" that members had used since the 1980s to record who had what cars, keys, monies, and other equipment. In the column for "Estimated Time of Return," most members wrote simply "Never" or "Bye," though Glnody quoted Arnold Schwarzenegger's title character from the science fiction movie *The Terminator 2: Judgment Day*, writing, "Hasta La Vista, Baby." A few wrote question marks, and Dymody indicated "If instructed by Ti & Do," but the intent of members was clear: they had signed out of life on Earth, and would return only as Next Level beings in service to the Evolutionary Level Above Human.[134] They left no loose ends to mire them to Earth. Their time here was over.

The Rancho Santa Fe exits effectively marked the end of Heaven's Gate as a movement, though a few individual believers remain and maintain the group's intellectual property and web presence. Several former members, Rkkody (Chuck Humphrey), Jstody (Wayne Cooke), and Gbbody (Jimmy Simpson) all committed suicide over the coming year, joining their compatriots. But for all intents and purposes, "the Class Is Over!" in the words of a former member.[135] The suicides marked the conclusion of a religious movement that had begun almost exactly two decades earlier. Heaven's Gate has closed.

Afterword

Heaven's Gate as an American Religion

In 2012, the British synth-pop band Django Django released a song and music video they titled "Hail Bop," which drummer and producer David Maclean indicated in an interview with National Public Radio (NPR) meant "something that passes by once in a lifetime like a comet."[1] Despite the misspelled name, fans and listeners widely took the song as a commentary or contemplation on the Heaven's Gate suicides. Its lyrics invoke the religious sensibility of members of Heaven's Gate, the quest for heavenly salvation but the implication that it entails a separation from the Earth. "Always look at the white sky and you lose your head in the clouds // Wanna step onto them and float onto their ground," singer and guitarist Vincent Neff intones.[2] With the music video set in a computer-generated world that NPR's Robin Hilton called a "psychedelic landscape," but more accurately described as a futuristic saucer-shaped pod, the video concludes with the band members and the entire landscape twirling up into the atmosphere and spiraling into outer space. "I've been waiting here so long and now you've taken off again," Neff sings in his final line. Having been left behind by the departure of the saucer, the song's protagonist is left waiting, perhaps forever. "Before you know it's off again into deep space never to be seen again," Maclean explained of the song's meaning.[3]

Heaven's Gate's members ended their earthly lives to avoid this fate of being left behind, but one can also envision the history of the movement itself as Hale-Bopp-like in its brief intensity and sudden passing. Heaven's Gate itself has passed, off to deep space—or so its members believe—never to be seen again. Those of us still bound by our earthly lives are left to try to understand why and how the group began, developed, and ended as it did. Why does it matter that thirty-nine individuals chose to die in Rancho Santa Fe (plus four more soon after)? Or that several hundred joined and left over the previous decades? Why does the study of Heaven's Gate matter, given that the group was no more than a few hundred people at its peak, and not even four dozen at its demise? Why write a book about it, and why read it? The introduction indicated several reasons why Heaven's Gate is worth studying and understanding: that the movement reveals aspects of American religion and culture; that the movement blended foreign and familiar, exotic and ordinary in a particularly fascinating way; and that its story is worth telling, showing how members were not mere victims or zombies engaging in senseless self-violence.

Here I wish to return to these reasons, highlighting the first through noting the second and third. The story of Heaven's Gate is that of several hundred people who joined, stayed, left, or rejoined a highly intensive religious movement, all the while seeking otherworldly salvation. Even if one looks only to the end of the movement, one finds in the terminus of Heaven's Gate approximately forty individuals seeking meaning and transcendence in their lives, and ultimately deciding to transcend Earth itself and find solace and direction in the stars. In many ways, that impetus and that quest are not far removed from the religious or spiritual quests of many other Americans, some of whom are also "seekers," individuals looking for new and personally meaningful religious identities. Many of those seekers look outside of conventional churches, synagogues, and mosques, and toward groups such as Heaven's Gate, or materials produced by thinkers such as those who founded and led Heaven's Gate. A quick perusal of the spirituality and religion aisles at any local American bookstore shows the degree to which American seekers have sought out the same sort of material that interested members of Heaven's Gate: astrology, channeled wisdom from beyond, extraterrestrial life, ancient mysteries, and alternative bibles. At the time of this writing, the top non-fiction book in the "religion & spirituality" category of the Internet's largest bookstore website, Amazon.com, was Pam Grout's *E-Squared: Nine Do-It-Yourself Energy Experiments That Prove Your Thoughts Create Your Reality*, a text rooted in New Age religious teachings about an invisible cosmic energy field that enables humans to reach their fullest potential.[4] American religious consumers devour such materials. Heaven's Gate was in this way quite ordinary—even representative!—of American religious culture.

Heaven's Gate was American religion wrought small, a social barometer that revealed the religious climate at the turn of the twenty-first century. Having examined the group's history, development, worldview, beliefs, practices, and end with reference to that religious climate, this afterword very briefly lays out four ways that I see this to be true: its highly Protestant biblical grounding; its appeal to seekers of new and alternative religions; the place of science and techno-religious thinking in Heaven's Gate; and their interest in the end-times and apocalyptic thought. Together, these hint at powerful forces at work in American religious culture, forces that shaped the development of Heaven's Gate as well as a myriad of other religious movements, both old and new, well-respected and marginal.

Although at first glance seemingly bizarre, even alien, the beliefs, practices, and worldview of Heaven's Gate emerged from a highly Christian foundation, specifically American Protestantism. As shaped by waves of awakenings and revivals, and especially by the rise of the evangelical tradition in the nineteenth century, American Protestantism emphasizes the individual quest for salvation, the centrality of the Bible, salvation through otherworldly action, a primitivistic emphasis on restoring the "original" nature and meaning of Christianity, and a homespun hermeneutical model eschewing higher academic study of the Bible and emphasizing the common sense of relatively untrained people to ascertain the true meaning of the biblical text. Each of these elements appears in Heaven's Gate as well, as this book has laid out. Nettles and Applewhite long envisioned their religious work as discovering the true nature of the Bible through their idiosyncratic hermeneutic approach, and offering this rediscovered truth to the world where individuals could choose to accept it or not. Even at the end of the movement when Applewhite introduced a neo-Calvinist approach of predestination—itself a highly Protestant theological position—he left room for individuals to decide to accept their predestined state, a theological twist that nineteenth-century American evangelicals would recognize as a typically American synthesis of free-will Arminianism and predestinarian Calvinism.

One can posit several reasons why Protestant assumptions figured so heavily in Heaven's Gate. Nettles was raised Baptist, Applewhite was the son of a Presbyterian minister who himself briefly attended seminary. Yet even more importantly, Protestant models suffuse American religious culture, influencing how groups and individuals outside specific Protestant orbits have functioned in the American context. Jay P. Dolan's and Jonathan D. Sarna's research has shown how American Catholics and American Jews, respectively, have internalized Protestant categories and how this has influenced their religious practices and beliefs.[5]

Yet while influenced by Protestantism and revealing the broad diffusion of Protestant religious themes into American religious culture, Heaven's Gate clearly split from its biblical Protestant moorings and moved beyond into the realm of alternative religions. This itself is strikingly American, replicating a pattern stretching back to colonial times. Lacking a national religious establishment and with a long history of relative religious freedom—enshrined in legal form in Pennsylvania's Great Law (1682), Virginia Statute for Religious Freedom (1777), and of course the Bill of Rights (1789)—alternative religions have long thrived in American soils. Quakers, Shakers, Mormons, Millerites, Adventists, Jehovah's Witnesses, the Nation of Islam, Father Divine, Zen Beatniks, Hare Krishnas, Moonies, Neo-Kabbalists, Neo-Pagans, Satanists, New Agers, and innumerable gurus, mystics, and channelers have all made America their home. Of course such groups face difficulties and sometimes overt persecution, but their presence speaks to the persistence of this strand of American religiosity. While the individual players have changed, this element of alternative American religious culture continues to thrive.

Scholars have offered several reasons why groups like Heaven's Gate spring forth in America, ranging from the "supply-side" approach of William Sims Bainbridge, Rodney Stark, Roger Finke, and their co-authors that models American religion on an economic marketplace paradigm, to Jon Butler's or Catherine L. Albanese's intellectual- and cultural-history-based approaches that emphasize the spread of ideas through diffuse religious and social movements.[6] The structural, intellectual, and cultural arguments are all surely correct: America provides suitable and fruitful ground for the development of new religions and alternative forms of spiritual searching. These groups reflect not only their particular historical circumstances, but a strand of religious yearning that permeates American culture, a "democratization," in the words of historian Nathan O. Hatch, that enables individuals to create and lead their own religious movements, as well as join new ones.[7] Heaven's Gate reflects this strand of alternative American religiosity, continuing the tradition of these other groups of offering new religious options and opportunities that some individuals at least thought more fitting than other options.

Moving from social and cultural forces to specific elements of Heaven's Gate's religious worldview, one cannot help but notice the place of science and techno-religious thinking in Heaven's Gate and how this reflects a broader American preoccupation with science and technology in the late twentieth century. Of course this fascination is not new, and scholars have traced a pattern of interest in the scientific and technological innovations born of the "village enlightenment" back to the nineteenth century.[8] Yet the American postwar era—the decades after the development of the Atomic Bomb and the explosion of scientific and technological advances following it—witnessed science and technology becoming increasingly central. American popular culture fixated on new scientific developments such as nuclear science, Einstein's theories of relativity, and new medical discoveries. Technology became increasingly omnipresent in homes and leisure, invading kitchens, bedrooms, and living rooms through televisions and other new appliances. Americans looked to scientists for social and at times even moral leadership, and major technology companies such as DuPont promised "Better Things for Better Living . . . Through Chemistry," often shortened in the public mind to merely "better living through chemistry."[9]

Historian Paul Boyer has traced a profound connection between science-infused post-Bomb culture and American religious thought, both the obvious apocalyptic elements as well as more positive millennial dreams of utopian futures.[10] Religious movements as diverse as mainline Protestants, Catholics, Jews, Buddhists, and Evangelical Protestants have all responded to recent scientific and technological developments, often through either appealing to science as a support for existing theological positions, or attempting to redirect, control, or challenge scientific and technological advances or positions. Rabbinic or ecclesial statements on nuclear proliferation and environmental damage, the Evangelical-dominated Intelligent Design movement, Buddhist appeals to neuroscientific studies of meditation, and attempts from many quarters to harmonize the sometimes-bizarre discoveries of contemporary cosmology and physics with religious cosmologies all represent religious engagements with science and technology. I have elsewhere written of how new religious movements have been similarly engaged, using sometimes similar approaches.[11] Heaven's Gate tracks broader religious currents in this way as well.

For many observers, Heaven's Gate attracted the most interest because of the way it ended, and its leaders' and members' focus on the end-times and apocalypticism certainly captured widespread attention. Yet here too, Heaven's Gate represented a broader religious sentiment. American popular interest in millennialism has appeared in waves, with particular focus during times of perceived crisis such as throughout the Cold War and the "War on Terror."[12] Evangelical Protestant groups in particular often focus on interpreting the biblical book of Revelation with reference to current events. During the time of Heaven's Gate's emergence, Hal Lindsey's best-selling *The Late Great Planet Earth* heralded this form of Christian millennial thought with reference to the Cold War. Today, websites have replaced books as the main medium for dissemination of such ideas. Readers of websites such as "Rapture Ready," "Samaritan Sentinel," "Rapture Watch," and "Prophecy News Watch" keep Evangelicals apprised of global developments that might signal the end of times and the advent of Christ, with special interest in terrorism, politics, and economic problems.[13] Sandwiched between the end of the Cold War and the beginning of the War on Terror, mass interest in the possible religious relevance of the year 2000 and the possibility of a Y2K computer bug caused by deficient computer programming invoked similar millennial feelings. Heaven's Gate fits within this American apocalyptic trajectory.

Heaven's Gate in fact prefigured some of the later developments in millennial thought, especially in the way that they internalized and translated fears about government repression and control into a religious system. Decades later, concerns about such oppression and the emergence of a "new world order" have become so routine among millennially oriented Evangelical Protestants that one can barely speak of such fears as a form of stigmatized knowledge. Particularly after the emergence of the Tea Party, with its quasi-religious appeal to small government and rootedness of America within Christian values and morality, the sort of millennial suspicion Heaven's Gate directed at the federal government has become quite mainstream.[14] Their fears of global conspiracy meanwhile prefigured the left-wing Occupy movement and other anti-globalization groups that fear a global capitalist conspiracy undermining freedoms and the natural order.[15]

One could posit many other ways in which Heaven's Gate modeled, prefigured, or reflected developments in American religious culture and society more broadly. The manner in which members of Heaven's Gate incorporated elements drawn from popular culture—science fiction in their case—into a meaningful religious worldview reveals the breakdown between high and low culture, entertainment, and religion. Collectively, these and other manners in which Heaven's Gate was embedded within American culture demonstrate how and why this new religion is not the aberration that some might think. Heaven's Gate is a religious movement worth serious study. Members may have gone beyond what most Americans do, believe, and think about in their religious lives, but in many ways the adherents of this new religion were no different from other Americans. They engaged in spiritual quests, seeking a more meaningful and accessible relationship with what functioned for them as the divine. They looked to heavenly salvation, and asked what relationship bodily human existence could have to that otherworldly salvation. They delved into the Bible, and from it they created and lived within a religious worldview. They built homes and a meaningful social and physical world around that worldview. They formed a community and tried to live (and die) with meaning. In doing all this, they looked to the physical heavens in outer space and the beings and vehicles of that "Next Level." Like many Americans, they believed in UFOs, extraterrestrials, and superhuman intelligence. They merely fused those beliefs with their religious ones. Heaven's Gate was, in this sense, a UFO religion. But it was a particular kind. It was America's UFO religion.

Many of the materials I cite are located in a single anthology: Heaven's Gate, *How and When "Heaven's Gate" (The Door to the Physical Kingdom Level Above Human) May Be Entered: An Anthology of Our Materials* (Mills Spring, NC: Wildflower Press, 1997). The pagination within this book is complicated, with page numbers restarting within each chapter. "2:1" therefore refers to chapter 2, page 1; "A:3" refers to the afterword, page 3. Included in this anthology, the "'88 Update" has its own pagination as well, but I have followed its pagination within the chapter of the anthology encompassing this source. Of note, I also cite materials from the unpublished first draft of this book with a nearly identical title: Heaven's Gate, "How and When 'Heaven's Gate' (The Door to the Physical Kingdom Level Above Human) May Be Entered: An Anthology by Representatives from the Kingdom of Heaven," (1996), which has the same pattern of pagination.

NOTES TO THE INTRODUCTION

1. Alan Segal, *Rebecca's Children: Judaism and Christianity in the Roman World* (Cambridge: Harvard University Press, 1986), 2.
2. Jacob Neusner, *Judaism in the Matrix of Christianity* (Atlanta: Scholars Press, 1991); Bart D. Ehrman, *Jesus: Apocalyptic Prophet of the New Millennium* (New York: Oxford University Press, 2001); Daniel Boyarin, *Border Lines: The Partition of Judaeo-Christianity* (Philadelphia: University of Pennsylvania Press, 2004).
3. David G. Bromley and Anson D. Shupe, Jr., *Strange Gods: The Great American Cult Scare* (Boston: Beacon Press, 1981); Charles Y. Glock and Robert N. Bellah, eds., *The New Religious Consciousness* (Berkeley: University of California Press, 1976); Thomas Robbins and Dick Anthony, *In Gods We Trust: New Patterns of Religious Pluralism in America*, 2nd ed. (New Brunswick, NJ: Transaction Publishers, 1990).
4. Timothy Miller, ed. *America's Alternative Religions* (Albany: State University of New York Press, 1995); Harvey Cox, *Turning East: Why Americans Look to the*

Orient for Spirituallity—and What That Search Can Mean to the West (New York: Touchstone, 1977).

5. Pew Forum on Religion and Public Life, *"Nones" on the Rise: One in Five Religious Adults Have No Religious Affiliation* (Washington, DC: Pew Research Center, 2012).

6. Barry Bearak, "Death in a Cult: The Victims: Time of Puzzled Heartbreak Binds Relatives," *New York Times*, March 30 1997, A1.

7. For more on this debate, see Benjamin Zablocki and Thomas Robbins, eds., *Misunderstanding Cults: Searching for Objectivity in a Controversial Field* (Toronto: University of Toronto Press, 2001).

8. Lorne L. Dawson, "Raising Lazarus: A Methodological Critique of Stephen Kent's Revival of the Brainwashing Model," in *Misunderstanding Cults*, ed. Zablocki and Robbins; Benjamin Zablocki, "Toward a Demystified and Disinterested Scientific Theory of Brainwashing," in *Misunderstanding Cults*, ed. Zablocki and Robbins; Stuart A. Wright, "Reconceptualizing Cult Coercion and Withdrawal: A Comparative Analysis of Divorce and Apostasy," *Social Forces* 70, no. 1 (1991): 125–45.

9. There is evidence that a member was once confined, though it was because she believed she was under the influence of dangerous spiritual beings and requested that she be confined. She eventually decided to leave the group, and did so on good terms. The fact that the only documented case of such an imprisonment eventually led to the member's departure in fact further weakens the brainwashing charge! Robert W. Balch, email correspondence with author, October 16, 2013.

10. Rodney Stark and Roger Finke, *Acts of Faith: Explaining the Human Side of Religion* (Berkeley: University of California Press, 2000).

11. Max Weber, *The Theory of Social and Economic Organization*, trans. A. M. Henderson and Talcott Parsons, translation of Part I of *Wirtschaft und Gesellschaft*, 1922 ed. (New York: Free Press, 1947), 328.

12. Heaven's Gate, "Beyond Human—the Last Call, Session 12," in *How and When "Heaven's Gate" May Be Entered*, 4:158.

NOTES TO CHAPTER 1

1. Some sources erroneously indicate that Nettles was born in 1928. Her birth certificate indicates a birth date of August 27, 1927.

2. "Boisean Remembers Knowing Bonnie Lu, 'UFO Recruiter'," *Idaho Statesman*, November 2, 1975, 12D.

3. For more on Nettles's involvement in the Theosophical Society in America, see Catherine Wessinger, *How the Millennium Comes Violently: From Jonestown to Heaven's Gate* (New York: Seven Bridges Press, 2000), 232, n. 55.

4. Robert W. Balch, "Bo and Peep: A Case Study of the Origins of Messianic Leadership," in *Millennialism and Charisma*, ed. Roy Wallis (Belfast: The Queen's University, 1982), 28.

5. Barry Bearak, "Odyssey to Suicide—a Special Report; Eyes on Glory: Pied Pipers of Heaven's Gate," *New York Times*, April 28, 1997, A1; James S. Phelan, "Looking For: The Next World," *New York Times*, February 29, 1976, C62.

6. Frank Bruni, "Death in a Cult: The Personality; Leader Believed in Space Aliens and Apocalypse," *New York Times*, March 28, 1997, A1.

7. Robert S. Ellwood, Jr., "The Theosophical Society," in *Introduction to New and Alternative Religions in America, Vol. 3*, ed. Eugene V. Gallagher and W. Michael Ashcraft (Westport, CT: Greenwood Press, 2006), 48–53.

8. See Bruce F. Campbell, *Ancient Wisdom Revived: A History of the Theosophical Movement* (Berkeley: University of California Press, 1980).

9. Balch, "Bo and Peep," 34.

10. Jacques Steinberg, "Death in a Cult: The Leader; from Religious Childhood to Reins of a U.F.O. Cult," *New York Times*, March 29, 1997, A9.

11. Ibid.

12. At the time, Virginia's Union Theological Seminary (not to be confused with New York City's seminary of the same name) affiliated with the Presbyterian Church in the United States (PCUS), the southern branch of American Presbyterian. In 1983, the PCUS merged with the United Presbyterian Church of the United States of America (UPCUSA) to form the Presbyterian Church of the United States of American (PCUSA), the largest national Presbyterian denomination.

13. Hayden Hewes and Brad Steiger, *UFO Missionaries Extraordinary* (New York: Pocket Books, 1976), 27.

14. Steinberg, "Death in a Cult: The Leader," A9.

15. There is significant confusion over the nature of their separation. The 1968 divorce date seems most reliable. Applewhite's ex-wife indicated that they separated in 1964, though Balch, the first scholar to systematically study the movement, indicates they separated in 1965. Unfortunately it is not clear in which state and county the two resided during their separation and divorce, making the access of public records extremely difficult. Bearak, "Odyssey to Suicide," A1; James Brooke, "Death in a Cult: The Silence; for Ex-Wife of Leader, No Wish for the Limelight," *New York Times*, April 1, 1997, A18; Balch, "Bo and Peep," 30.

16. Bearak, "Odyssey to Suicide," A1.

17. Steinberg, "Death in a Cult: The Leader," A9.

18. Robert W. Balch, "Waiting for the Ships: Disillusionment and the Revitalization of Faith in Bo and Peep's UFO Cult," in *The Gods Have Landed: New Religions from Other Worlds*, ed. James R. Lewis (Albany: State University of New York Press, 1995), 143; Balch, "Bo and Peep," 33.

19. Evan Thomas, "Web of Death," *Newsweek*, April 7, 1997, 31.

20. Bearak, "Odyssey to Suicide," A1.

21. The letter to his friend is reproduced in Balch, "Bo and Peep," 30–31.

22. Perhaps the most obvious example of such a reductionist reading of Heaven's Gate is David Daniel, "The Beginning of the Journey," *Newsweek*, April 13, 1997, 36–37.

23. Robert Glenn Howard, "Rhetoric of the Rejected Body at 'Heaven's Gate,'" in *Gender and Apocalyptic Desire*, ed. Brenda E. Brasher and Lee Quinby (London: Equinox, 2006), 146–47.
24. Ibid., 149.
25. Susan Raine, "Reconceptualising the Human Body: Heaven's Gate and the Quest for Divine Transformation," *Religion* 35, no. 2 (2005): 99.
26. Robert W. Balch, email to author, September 14, 2013.
27. Raine, "Reconceptualising the Human Body," 101–8.
28. Mrcody and Srfody, oral history and interview, September 30–October 1, 2013.
29. Hayes Parker, as quoted in Bearak, "Odyssey to Suicide."
30. Balch, "Bo and Peep," 57.
31. Applewhite, quoted in Phelan, "Looking For: The Next World," 62.
32. Phelan, "Looking For: The Next World," 62.
33. Nettles and Applewhite, as quoted in Hewes and Steiger, *UFO Missionaries Extraordinary*, 82.
34. Phelan, "Looking For: The Next World," 62; Balch, "Bo and Peep," 35; Hewes and Steiger, *UFO Missionaries Extraordinary*, 25.
35. J. Gordon Melton, "New Thought and New Age," in *Approaches to the Study of the New Age*, ed. James R. Lewis and J. Gordon Melton (Albany: State University of New York Press, 1992), 18–19.
36. James R. Lewis, "Approaches to the Study of the New Age Movement," in *Approaches to the Study of the New Age*, ed. Lewis and Melton, 6–8.
37. James R. Lewis and Gordon Melton, eds., *Perspectives on the New Age* (Albany: State University of New York Press, 1992); Wouter J. Hanegraaff, *New Age Religion and Western Culture: Esotericism in the Mirror of Secular Thought* (Leiden: E.J. Brill, 1996).
38. Balch, "Bo and Peep," 36.
39. Ibid., 38.
40. Marshall Herff Applewhite and Bonnie Lu Nettles, "Bo and Peep Interview with Brad Steiger, January 7, 1976," in *UFO Missionaries Extraordinary*, ed. Hayden Hewes and Brad Steiger (New York: Pocket Books, 1976), 84.
41. Wade Clark Roof, *A Generation of Seekers: The Spiritual Journeys of the Baby Boom Generation* (San Francisco: Harper San Francisco, 1994), 70.
42. Ibid., 71.
43. Pew Forum on Religion and Public Life, *U.S. Religious Landscape Survey: Religious Affiliation: Diverse and Dynamic* (Washington, DC: Pew Research Center, 2008).
44. Balch, "Bo and Peep," 42.
45. Randall Herbert Balmer, *Mine Eyes Have Seen the Glory: A Journey into the Evangelical Subculture in America* (New York: Oxford University Press, 1989), 35.
46. Sales figures noted in William Martin, "Waiting for the End: The Growing Interest in Apocalyptic Prophecy," *Atlantic Monthly*, June 1982, 31.
47. Wessinger, *How the Millennium Comes Violently*, 16–17.

48. Bearak, "Odyssey to Suicide," A1.

49. Betty Penson, "During the Summer of 1974 UFO Couple Visited Boise Men," *Idaho Statesman*, Oct 26 1975, A1–2.

50. Bearak, "Odyssey to Suicide." See also Lynn Simross, "Invitation to an Unearthly Kingdom," *Los Angeles Times*, October 31, 1975.

51. Applewhite's own perspective and recounting of this incident is contained in Heaven's Gate, "'88 Update," in *How and When "Heaven's Gate" May Be Entered*, 3:5.

52. Ibid.

53. Human Individual Metamorphosis, "Statement #1: Human Individual Metamorphosis," held at American Religions Collection, ARC Mss 1, Department of Special Collections, University Libraries, University of California, Santa Barbara (1975). This source is identical to Heaven's Gate, "First Statement of Ti and Do," in *How and When "Heaven's Gate" May Be Entered*, 2:3–4.

54. The figure of forty-one comes from Simross, "Invitation to an Unearthly Kingdom," 5. The figure of eighty from Phelan, "Looking For: The Next World," 63. Balch mentions "about fifty." Robert W. Balch, "The Evolution of a New Age Cult: From Total Overcomers Anonymous to Death at Heaven's Gate," in *Sects, Cults, and Spiritual Communities: A Sociological Analysis*, ed. William W. Zellner and Marc Petrowsky (Westport, CT: Praeger Publishers, 1998), 1. See also Phyllis Gilbert, "I Was a Member of the UFO Cult," *Pageant*, March 1976, 47.

55. Again, the low figure is recounted in Simross, "Invitation to an Unearthly Kingdom," 6; the high figure originates in Phelan, "Looking For: The Next World," 63.

56. Balch, "The Evolution of a New Age Cult," 3–12.

57. Ibid., 15.

58. Ibid., 20.

59. Gilbert, "I Was a Member of the UFO Cult," 48.

60. Weber, *Theory of Social and Economic Organization*, 358–59.

61. Roy Wallis, "The Social Construction of Charisma," *Social Compass* 29, no. 1 (1982): 26.

62. Ibid., 35.

63. For more on the social construction of charisma, particularly as it relates to leadership of a NRM, see Wallis, "The Social Construction of Charisma," Timothy Miller, ed., *When Prophets Die: The Postcharismatic Fate of New Religious Movements* (Albany: State University of New York Press, 1991).

64. On the remaining three members who were still present for the Rancho Santa Fe suicides, see Balch, "The Evolution of a New Age Cult," 24.

65. "20 Missing in Oregon after Talking of a Higher Life," *New York Times*, 7 October 1975, 71.

66. United Press International, "Couple Asks for UFO Volunteers—Now 20 Missing," *Herald-News*, October 6, 1975, 1.

67. Applewhite reported that thirty-three joined, and Balch confirmed a number in that range. A contemporary newspaper account provides the lower estimate.

Balch, email to author, September 14, 2013. "20 Missing in Oregon after Talking of a Higher Life," 71.

68. "20 Missing in Oregon after Talking of a Higher Life," 71.
69. United Press International, "Couple Asks for UFO Volunteers—Now 20 Missing," 1.
70. United Press International, "It's the Second Coming . . . We Are All Going Home," *Herald-News*, October 7, 1975, 3.
71. Ibid.
72. Eve Muss, "'Grave Not Path to Heaven,' Disciples Told," *Oregon Journal*, October 10, 1975.
73. Muss, "'Grave Not Path to Heaven,' Disciples Told," 1.
74. Eve Muss, "No Disease Promised," *Oregon Journal*, October 9, 1975, n.p. This unnumbered newspaper clipping is held in the archives of the American Religions Collection, ARC Mss 1, Department of Special Collections, University Libraries, University of California, Santa Barbara. I have not been able to locate a copy of this article from other archival sources.
75. Muss, "'Grave Not Path to Heaven,' Disciples Told," 1.
76. Applewhite and Nettles, "Bo and Peep Interview with Brad Steiger, January 7, 1976," 98.
77. United Press International, "Couple Asks for UFO Volunteers—Now 20 Missing," 1; United Press International, "It's the Second Coming . . . We Are All Going Home," 3; Paul McGrath, "UFO 'Lost Sheep' Tell Cult Secrets," *Chicago Sun-Times*, October 16, 1975, 1.
78. "20 Missing in Oregon after Talking of a Higher Life," 71.
79. United Press International, "It's the Second Coming . . . We Are All Going Home," 3.
80. Tom Robinson, "I Found the Missing People from Waldport," *Northwest Magazine*, November 2, 1975, 14.
81. McGrath, "UFO 'Lost Sheep' Tell Cult Secrets," 1.
82. George Williamson, "'It Was a Sham': Why One Convert Left the UFO Cult," *San Francisco Chronicle*, October 13, 1975, 2.
83. Ibid.
84. Ibid.
85. Phelan, "Looking For: The Next World," 12.
86. Heaven's Gate, "'88 Update," 7.
87. McGrath, "UFO 'Lost Sheep' Tell Cult Secrets," 26.
88. Robert W. Balch, "'When the Light Goes out, Darkness Comes': A Study of Defection from a Totalistic Cult," in *Religious Movements: Genesis, Exodus, and Numbers*, ed. Rodney Stark (New York: Paragon House Publishers, 1985), 21.
89. Balch, "A Study of Defection," 21–22.
90. Heaven's Gate, "'88 Update," 7.
91. Balch, "A Study of Defection," 23.
92. Balch, "Waiting for the Ships," 154.
93. Balch, "A Study of Defection," 23.

NOTES TO CHAPTER 2

1. Robert W. Balch and David Taylor, "Salvation in a UFO," *Psychology Today* 10, no. 5 (1976): 60.
2. Robert W. Balch and David Taylor, "Seekers and Saucers: The Role of the Cultic Milieu in Joining a UFO Cult," *American Behavioral Scientist* 20, no. 6 (1977): 848.
3. Colin Campbell, "The Cult, Cultic Milieu and Secularization," in *A Sociological Yearbook of Religion in Britain* 5 (London: SCM Press, 1972), 122.
4. Scholars today are apt to divide Campbell's cultic milieu into the New Age movement, Western esoteric tradition, nature religion, and other various sub-traditions.
5. Douglas E. Kneeland, "500 Wait in Vain on Coast for 'the Two,' U.F.O. Cult Leaders," *New York Times*, October 10, 1975, 16.
6. Simross, "Invitation to an Unearthly Kingdom," G1.
7. Ibid., G4.
8. McGrath, "UFO 'Lost Sheep' Tell Cult Secrets," 1.
9. Robert Bellah et al., eds., *Habits of the Heart: Individualism and Commitment in American Life* (Berkeley: University of California Press, 1985), 221.
10. Robert Bellah, "Habits of the Heart: Implications for Religion," public address at St. Mark's Catholic Church, Isla Vista, California, 21 February 1986. Available online at: http://www.robertbellah.com/lectures_5.htm.
11. Pew Forum on Religion and Public Life, *U.S. Religious Landscape Survey*; Pew Forum, *"Nones" on the Rise*; Pew Forum, *Many Americans Mix Multiple Faiths: Eastern, New Age Beliefs Widespread* (Washington, DC: Pew Research Center, 2009).
12. Human Individual Metamorphosis, "Statement #3: The Only Significant Resurrection," held at American Religions Collection, ARC Mss 1, Department of Special Collections, University Libraries, University of California, Santa Barbara (1975).
13. Human Individual Metamorphosis, "Statement #1: Human Individual Metamorphosis."
14. Stewart M. Hoover, "The Cross at Willow Creek: Seeker Religion and the Contemporary Marketplace," in *Religion and Popular Culture in America*, ed. Bruce D. Forbes and Jeffrey H. Mahan (Berkeley: University of California Press, 2000), 139–53.
15. Human Individual Metamorphosis, "Statement #1."
16. Human Individual Metamorphosis, "Statement #2: Clarification: Human Kingdom— Visible and Invisible," held at American Religions Collection, ARC Mss 1, Department of Special Collections, University Libraries, University of California, Santa Barbara (1975).
17. Human Individual Metamorphosis, "Statement #3."
18. Wade Clark Roof, *Spiritual Marketplace: Baby Boomers and the Remaking of American Religion* (Princeton, NJ: Princeton University Press, 1999), 46.

19. Phelan, "Looking For: The Next World," 61.
20. Ibid., 63.
21. Pam Belluck, "Death in a Cult: Bewilderment Is All That's Left for Families," *New York Times*, March 30, 1997, A16.
22. Joanne Ditmer, "Durango Businessman Reported with UFO Group," *Denver Post*, October 23, 1975, 33.
23. Ibid.
24. Bearak, "Death in a Cult: The Victims," 1.
25. James David Hudnut-Beumler, *Looking for God in the Suburbs: The Religion of the American Dream and Its Critics, 1945–1965* (New Brunswick, NJ: Rutgers University Press, 1994).
26. Robert S. Ellwood, *The Fifties Spiritual Marketplace: American Religion in a Decade of Conflict* (New Brunswick, NJ: Rutgers University Press, 1997).
27. Eileen Barker, *The Making of a Moonie: Choice or Brainwashing?* (Oxford: Basil Blackwell, 1984), 146–48.
28. For example, consider the work of William Sims Bainbridge on The Family (né Children of God) and E. Burke Rochford on the International Society for Krishna Consciousness, both of which feature high rates of defection. William Sims Bainbridge, *The Endtime Family: Children of God* (Albany: State University of New York Press, 2002); E. Burke Rochford, Jr., "Hare Krishna in America: Growth, Decline, and Accommodation," in *America's Alternative Religions*, ed. Timothy Miller (Albany: State University of New York Press, 1995).
29. James T. Richardson, *Conversion Careers: In and Out of the New Religions* (Beverly Hills: Sage, 1978).
30. Applewhite (Do) and Nettles (Ti) were the exception.
31. Tddody, "Statement of a Crewmember," in *How and When "Heaven's Gate" May Be Entered*, A53.
32. Ibid., A54.
33. Ibid., A55.
34. Qstody, "My Ode to Ti and Do! What This Class Has Meant to Me," in *How and When "Heaven's Gate" May Be Entered*, A30.
35. Qstody, *Exit Video* (Rancho Santa Fe, CA, 1997).
36. Gldody, *Exit Video* (Rancho Santa Fe, CA, 1997).
37. Wknody, "A Matter of Life or Death? You Decide," in *How and When "Heaven's Gate" May Be Entered*, A19.
38. Yrsody, "The Way Things Are," in *How and When "Heaven's Gate" May Be Entered*, A25.
39. Deb Simpson, *Closing the Gate* (Murfreesboro, TN: privately published, 2012), 147–48; 162–63.
40. Ibid., 178.
41. Gbbody, letter to Deb Simpson, February 23, 1995, reproduced in *Closing the Gate*, 233.
42. Simpson, *Closing the Gate*, 198.

43. Frank Rich, "Heaven's Gate-Gate," *New York Times*, April 17, 1997, A23.
44. Thomas Robbins, Dick Anthony, and James McCarthy, "Legitimating Repression," in *The Brainwashing/Deprogramming Controversy: Sociological, Psychological, Legal, and Historical Perspectives*, ed. David G. Bromley and James T. Richardson, *Studies in Religion and Society* (New York: Edwin Mellon Press, 1983), 319.
45. Ibid., 319–27.
46. Sean McCloud, *Making the American Religious Fringe: Exotics, Subversives, and Journalists, 1955–1993* (Chapel Hill: University of North Carolina Press, 2004).
47. James T. Richardson, "Conversion and Brainwashing: Controversies and Contrasts," in *The Bloomsbury Companion to New Religious Movements*, ed. George D. Chryssides and Benjamin E. Zeller (London: Bloomsbury, 2014), 98.
48. Eileen Barker, "The Cage of Freedom and the Freedom of the Cage," in *On Freedom: A Centenary Anthology*, ed. Eileen Barker (London: London School of Economics and Political Science, 1997). See also Barker, *The Making of a Moonie: Choice or Brainwashing?*
49. Richardson, "Conversion and Brainwashing: Controversies and Contrasts," 99.
50. J. Gordon Melton, "Brainwashing and the Cults: The Rise and Fall of a Theory," in *CESNUR Digital Proceedings*, ed. Massimo Introvigne (1999), available online at http://www.cesnur.org/testi/melton.htm.
51. Janja Lalich, *Bounded Choice: True Believers and Charismatic Cults* (Berkeley: University of California Press, 2004), 17.
52. Ibid., 2.
53. Ibid., 18.
54. Human Individual Metamorphosis, "Statement #3."
55. Heaven's Gate, "Major and Lesser Offenses," in *How and When "Heaven's Gate" May Be Entered*, 2:9.
56. Lalich, *Bounded Choice*, 17.
57. To protect the privacy of these ex-members, I have used only their "ODY" names. In some cases these individuals have published under their birth names or other legal names. Neoody published a memoir under his legal name "Rio DiAngelo." Yet he prefers to be referred to as Neoody, and I do so throughout the book except when actually citing his memoir, Rio DiAngelo, *Beyond Human Mind: The Soul Evolution of Heaven's Gate* (Beverly Hills: privately published, 2007).
58. For more on these former members, see DiAngelo, *Beyond Human Mind*; Sawyer, "Sawyerhg's Blog," http://sawyerhg.wordpress.com; Crlody, "The Aftermath of Heaven's Gate," http://www.freewebs.com/crlody/; Crlody, "The Truth and Lies of Heaven's Gate," http://crlody.wordpress.com/2012/04/27/the-truth-and-lies-of-heavens-gate/. (Mrcody and Srfody do not have an active presence on the Internet, blogosphere, or print media, but do maintain the original Heaven's Gate website. Heaven's Gate, "Heaven's Gate—How and When It May Be Entered," http://www.heavensgate.com

NOTES TO CHAPTER 3

1. Thomas, "Web of Death," 27; Evan Thomas, "'The Next Level,'" *Newsweek*, April 7, 1997, 30; Gregory Beals, "Far from Home," *Newsweek*, April 7, 1997, 37.

2. Brad Stone, "Christ and Comets," *Newsweek*, April 7, 1997, 40.

3. Larry B. Stammer, John Dart, and James Rainey, "39 in Cult Left Recipes of Death: The Cult: Tract Offers Clues About Group's Theology, Motives," *Los Angeles Times*, March 28, 1997, A1.

4. Ninian Smart, *Worldviews: Crosscultural Explorations of Human Beliefs* (New York: Prentice Hall, 2000).

5. Gregory E. Peterson, "Religion as Orienting Worldview," *Zygon* 36, no. 1 (2001): 13.

6. Pierre Bourdieu, "Legitimation and Structured Interests in Weber's Sociology of Religion," in *Max Weber, Rationality, and Modernity*, ed. Scott Lash and Sam Whimster (London: Allen and Unwin, 1987), 126.

7. Hugh B. Urban, "The Devil at Heaven's Gate: Rethinking the Study of Religion in the Age of Cyber-Space," *Nova Religio: The Journal of Alternative and Emergent Religions* 3, no. 2 (2000): 270. This article, and several other ones cited (Chryssides, "Come on up, and I will show thee"; Zeller, "Scaling Heaven's Gate"), is also easily accessible in George D. Chryssides's anthology of the major essays most recently written on Heaven's Gate, George D. Chryssides, ed., *Heaven's Gate: Postmodernity and Popular Culture in a Suicide Group* (Farnham, UK: Ashgate, 2011).

8. Urban, "The Devil at Heaven's Gate," 269.

9. For an excellent example of Christian yoga, see Thomas Ryan, *Prayer of Heart and Body: Meditation and Yoga as Christian Spiritual Practice* (New York: Paulist Press, 1995).

10. Susan K. Roll, *Toward the Origins of Christmas* (Kampen, Netherlands: Kok Pharos, 1995); Mark Connelly, *Christmas: A Social History* (London: I.B. Taurus, 2001). For a consideration of more recent pastiche and innovations, see Penne E. Restad, *Christmas in America: A History* (New York: Oxford University Press, 1995).

11. See, for example, Françoise Dunand, *Isis: Mère Des Dieux* (Paris: Errance, 2000); Sabrina Higgins, "Divine Mothers: The Influence of Isis on the Virgin Mary in Egyptian Lactans-Iconography," *Journal of the Canadian Society for Coptic Studies* 3–4 (2012).

12. Urban, "The Devil at Heaven's Gate," 279–80.

13. George D. Chryssides, "'Come on up, and I Will Show Thee': Heaven's Gate as a Postmodern Group," in *Controversial New Religions*, ed. James R. Lewis and Jesper Aagaard Petersen Petersen (Oxford: Oxford University Press, 2005), 365. Also available in *Heaven's Gate: Postmodernity and Popular Culture in a Suicide Group*, ed. Chryssides.

14. Pew Forum on Religion and Public Life, *U.S. Religious Landscape Survey: Religious Affiliation: Diverse and Dynamic.*

15. Angela A. Aidala, "Social Change, Gender Roles, and New Religious Movements," *Sociological Analysis* 46, no. 3 (1985).
16. Glock and Bellah, *The New Religious Consciousness*.
17. Dick Anthony and Thomas Robbins, "Cultural Crisis and Contemporary Religion," in *In Gods We Trust*, ed. Thomas Robbins and Dick Anthony (New Brunswick, NJ: Transaction Publishers, 1981), 28.
18. Balch, email to author, September 14, 2013.
19. Balch, "The Evolution of a New Age Cult," 4.
20. Balch and Taylor, "Seekers and Saucers," 840.
21. Ibid., 852.
22. James R. Lewis, "Legitimating Suicide: Heaven's Gate and New Age Ideology," in *UFO Religions*, ed. Christopher Partridge (London: Routledge, 2003), 106.
23. Ibid.
24. Chryssides, "'Come on up, and I Will Show Thee,'" 359.
25. Ibid., 362.
26. Susan J. Palmer, *Aliens Adored: Raël's UFO Religion* (New Brunswick, NJ: Rutgers University Press, 2004).
27. Christopher Partridge, "The Eschatology of Heaven's Gate," in *Expecting the End: Millennialism in Social and Historical Context*, ed. Kenneth G. C. Newport and Crawford Gibbens (Waco, TX: Baylor University Press, 2006), 49.
28. Ibid., 65.
29. For more on hermeneutics, see Van A. Harvey, "Hermeneutics," in *Encyclopedia of Religion*, ed. Lindsay Jones (Detroit: Macmillan Reference USA, 2005). For the background and history of various approaches of biblical hermeneutics, see Stephen R. Haynes and Steven L. McKenzie, eds., *To Each Its Own Meaning: An Introduction to Biblical Criticisms and Their Application* (Louisville, KY: Westminster John Knox Press, 1993).
30. For more on the idea of extraterrestrial biblical hermeneutics, see my book chapter Benjamin E. Zeller, "Apocalyptic Thought in UFO Religions," in *End of Days: Understanding the Apocalypse from Antiquity to Modernity*, ed. Karolyn Kinane and Michael A. Ryan (Jefferson, NC: McFarland Press, 2009). My consideration of extraterrestrial biblical hermeneutics and Heaven's Gate was also laid out in Benjamin E. Zeller, "Extraterrestrial Biblical Hermeneutics and the Making of Heaven's Gate," *Nova Religio: The Journal of Alternative and Emergent Religions* 14, no. 2 (2010).
31. Chryssides, "Approaching Heaven's Gate," in *Heaven's Gate: Postmodernity and Popular Culture in a Suicide Group*, 2.
32. Arthur Versluis, *Magic and Mysticism: An Introduction to Western Esotericism* (London: Rowman & Littlefield, 2007), 1. See also Antoine Faivre, *Access to Western Esotericism* (Albany: State University of New York Press, 1994).
33. Brenda Denzler, *The Lure of the Edge: Scientific Passions, Religious Beliefs, and the Pursuit of UFOs* (Berkeley: University of California Press, 2001), 46.
34. Ibid., 122.

35. Pia Andersson, "Ancient Alien Brothers, Ancient Terrestrial Remains: Archeology or Religion?" in *Alien Worlds: Social and Religious Dimensions of Extraterrestrial Contact*, ed. Diana Tumminia (Syracuse, NY: Syracuse University Press, 2007).
36. Denzler, *Lure of the Edge*, 110.
37. Andersson, "Ancient Alien Brothers, Ancient Terrestrial Remains"; Anne Cross, "A Confederacy of Fact and Fiction: Science and the Sacred in UFO Research," in *Alien World*, ed. Tumminia.
38. See Richard Vitzthum, *Materialism: An Affirmative History and Definition* (New York: Prometheus Books, 1995).
39. Benjamin E. Zeller, *Prophets and Protons: New Religious Movements and Science in Late-Twentieth Century America* (New York: New York University Press, 2010).
40. Steven M. Tipton, *Getting Saved from the Sixties: The Transformation of Moral Meaning in American Culture* (Berkeley: University of California Press, 1982), 2–3.
41. John A. Saliba, "Religious Dimensions of UFO Phenomena," in *The Gods Have Landed: New Religions from Other Worlds*, ed. James R. Lewis (Albany: State University of New York Press, 1995), 54–55.
42. Christopher Partridge, ed., *UFO Religions* (London: Routledge, 2003); Zeller, *Prophets and Protons*; Carl Gustav Jung, *Ein Moderner Mythus* (Stuttgart: Rascher, 1958).
43. Heaven's Gate, "Planet About to Be Recycled—Your Only Chance to Survive—Leave with Us [Edited Transcript]," http://www.heavensgate.com/misc/vt100596.htm.
44. Human Individual Metamorphosis, "Statement #1," "Statement #2," "Statement #3."
45. Jnnody, "Incarnating and Discarnating," in *How and When "Heaven's Gate" May Be Entered*, A:89; Heaven's Gate, "'95 Statement by an E.T. Presently Incarnate," in *How and When "Heaven's Gate" May Be Entered*, 1:7; Lvvody, "Ingredients of a Deposit—Becoming a New Creature," in *How and When "Heaven's Gate" May Be Entered*, A:8; Jwnody, "Ti and Do as 'Smelling Salts,'" in *How and When "Heaven's Gate" May Be Entered*, A:2.
46. Notably, this website is not stored on the Wayback Machine (archive.org), the usual repository for such defunct websites.
47. Heaven's Gate, "Connecting Links," http://www.heavensgate.com/misc/link.htm. For Glnody's role on editing the website, see DiAngelo, *Beyond Human Mind*, 74.
48. Applewhite and Nettles, "Bo and Peep Interview with Brad Steiger, January 7, 1976," 137.
49. Jwnody, "Religions Are Humans' #1 Killers of Souls," A65.
50. The ellipses are from the original. Jwnody, "Religions Are Humans' #1 Killers of Souls," A:67.

51. Jwnody, "Religions Are Humans' #1 Killers of Souls," A:67.
52. Stmody, "Evolutionary 'Rights' for 'Victims,'" in *How and When "Heaven's Gate" May Be Entered*, A:75.
53. Stmody, "Evolutionary 'Rights' for 'Victims.'"
54. See Snnody, "Deposits," in *How and When "Heaven's Gate" May Be Entered*, A:80; Anlody, "Investments," in *How and When "Heaven's Gate" May Be Entered*, A:98.
55. Mikael Stenmark, "What Is Scientism?" *Religious Studies* 33(1997): 19.
56. Heaven's Gate, "'88 Update," 3:15.
57. Amy Harmon, "Escaping to Other Worlds," *Los Angeles Times*, April 2, 1997, A1.
58. Paul Kurtz, "Perspective on the Media: A Marriage Made in Heaven's Gate," *Los Angeles Times*, May 19, 1997, B5.
59. McCloud, *Making the American Religious Fringe*.
60. Benjamin E. Zeller, "Heaven's Gate, Science Fiction Religions, and Popular American Culture," in *Handbook on Hyper-Real Religions*, ed. Adam Possamai (Leiden: Brill, 2012); Carole M. Cusack, *Invented Religions: Imagination, Fiction and Faith* (Farnham, UK: Ashgate, 2010).
61. Zeller, "Heaven's Gate, Science Fiction Religions, and Popular American Culture."
62. Rkkody, interview with author, November 19, 1997.
63. Heaven's Gate, "'UFO Cult' Resurfaces with Final Offer [USA Today Advertisement]," in *How and When "Heaven's Gate" May Be Entered*, 6:7. See also an unused presentation written in 1993 and preserved in the group's 1997 anthology, which offers another example: Heaven's Gate, "Extraterrestrials Return with Final Warning," 5:4–5.
64. Heaven's Gate, "'UFO Cult' Resurfaces with Final Offer [USA Today Advertisement]", 6:7.
65. Leonard Nimoy, director, *Star Trek IV: The Voyage Home* (Paramount Pictures, 1986).
66. Heaven's Gate, "'UFO Cult' Resurfaces with Final Offer [USA Today Advertisement]," 6:7.
67. Heaven's Gate, "Crew from the Evolutionary Level above Human Offers—Last Chance to Advance Beyond Human," in *How and When "Heaven's Gate" May Be Entered*, 6:4; Heaven's Gate, "Exit Press Release: Heaven's Gate 'Away Team' Returns to Level above Human in Distant Space," http://www.heavensgate.com/pressrel.htm.
68. Crlody, "The Aftermath of Heaven's Gate."
69. Jwnody, "'Away Team' from Deep Space Surfaces before Departure."
70. Jwnody, "Overview of the Present Mission," in *How and When "Heaven's Gate" May Be Entered*, vii.
71. DiAngelo, *Beyond Human Mind*, 30.
72. Cusack, *Invented Religions*, 141.

NOTES TO CHAPTER 4

240　<<　NOTES TO CHAPTER 4

1. For more on the critique and reshaping of the field, see David D. Hall, ed., _Lived Religion in America: Toward a History of Practice_ (Princeton, NJ: Princeton University Press, 1997).

2. One notable example is Mary Farrell Bednarowski, _New Religions & the Theological Imagination in America_ (Bloomington: Indiana University Press, 1989).

3. Jim Rutenberg, "Mediatalk: AOL Sees a Different Side of Time Warner," _New York Times_, March 19, 2001, C11.

4. Drrody, _Exit Video_ (Rancho Santa Fe, CA, 1997), Video (VHS).

5. I received a photocopy of the marked pages of this Bible from Robert W. Balch. I am extremely grateful to him for sharing the text with me, and for his general willingness to share his thoughts and knowledge of the movement with myself and others.

6. Athalya Brenner and Jan W. van Henten, eds., _Bible Translation on the Threshold of the Twenty-First Century: Authority, Reception, Culture and Religion_ (New York: Sheffield Academic Press, 2002), 1–7.

7. Rosamond Rodman, "Heaven's Gate: Religious Otherworldiness American Style," in _The Bible and the American Myth: A Symposium on the Bible and Constructions of Meaning_, ed. Vincent K. Wimbush (Macon, GA: Mercer University Press, 1999).

8. For more on the scholarly treatment of Luke, see the summary included in Bart D. Ehrman, _The New Testament: A Historical Introduction to the Early Christian Writings_ (New York: Oxford University Press, 1997), 96–114.

9. Human Individual Metamorphosis, "Statement #1."

10. Ibid.

11. Heaven's Gate, "Bible Quotes Primarily from Previous Representatives to Earth from T.E.L.A.H.," http://www.heavensgate.com/b-2.htm.

12. Heaven's Gate, "Undercover 'Jesus' Surfaces before Departure."

13. On the 1975 debates, Balch, email to author, September 14, 2013. On the claims of Jesus aboard a UFO, "Bo and Peep Interview with Brad Steiger, January 7, 1976," in _UFO Missionaries Extraordinary_, ed. Hayden Hewes and Brad Steiger (New York: Pocket Books, 1976), 82–3.

14. Heaven's Gate, "Undercover 'Jesus' Surfaces before Departure."

15. Heaven's Gate, "He's Back, We're Back, Where Will You Stand? [Poster]."

16. Balch, email to author, September 14, 2013; Mrcody and Srfody, oral history and interview, September 30–October 1, 2013.

17. Heaven's Gate, "'88 Update."

18. Human Individual Metamorphosis, "Statement #1," "Statement #2," "Statement #3."

19. Human Individual Metamorphosis, "Statement #1."

20. Smmody, "T.E.L.A.H. – the Evolutionary Level above Human," in _How and When "Heaven's Gate" May Be Entered_, A:22.

21. Jwnody, "'Away Team' from Deep Space Surfaces before Departure."

22. Smmody, "T.E.L.A.H. – the Evolutionary Level above Human."
23. Mrcody and Srfody, oral history and interview.
24. The Hills reported experiencing their abduction account in 1961, but it was not reported publicly in the newspaper until 1965, and in book form until 1966. Strieber similarly reports a 1985 visitation in his 1987 book. Sylvia Fuller and John Levi Martin, "Women's Status in Eastern NRMs," *Review of Religious Research* 44, no. 4 (2003); Whitney Strieber, *Communion: A True Story* (New York: Beach Tree Books, 1987).
25. DiAngelo, *Beyond Human Mind*, 25.
26. David Keck, *Angels & Angelology in the Middle Ages* (New York: Oxford University Press, 1998), 1.
27. Jwnody, *Exit Video* (Rancho Santa Fe, CA, 1997).
28. Heaven's Gate, "'UFO Cult' Resurfaces with Final Offer [USA Today Advertisement]."
29. This is Clarke's Third Law, laid out in Arthur C. Clarke, *Profiles of the Future: An Enquiry into the Limits of the Possible* (New York: Holt, Rinehart, and Winston, 1984), 36.
30. Anlody, "Investments," in *How and When "Heaven's Gate" May Be Entered*, A:98.
31. Tim F. LaHaye and Jerry B. Jenkins, *Left Behind: A Novel of the Earth's Last Days*, ed. Left Behind (Wheaton, IL: Tyndale House Publishers, 1995).
32. Human Individual Metamorphosis, "Statement #1."
33. Human Individual Metamorphosis, "Statement #2," "Statement #3," 2.
34. Human Individual Metamorphosis, "What's Up?" (American Religions Collection, ARC Mss 1, Department of Special Collections, University Libraries, University of California, Santa Barbara, 1975).
35. For the earliest accounts of the Two's meetings, see "20 Missing in Oregon after Talking of a Higher Life"; Muss, "No Disease Promised"; Williamson, "'It Was a Sham'"; McGrath, "UFO 'Lost Sheep' Tell Cult Secrets." The *Oregon Journal* published an edited version of the transcript of the Waldport meeting, which also did not mention the demonstration: Muss, "'Grave Not Path to Heaven,' Disciples Told." (Photocopy of article available in American Religions Collection, ARC Mss 1, Department of Special Collections, University Libraries, University of California, Santa Barbara.) Nearly all the publications after October 18, 1975 mention the Two's belief in their impending demonstration, e.g., Austin Scott, "Music Teacher, Nurse Led Search for 'Higher Life,'" *Washington Post*, October 18, 1975; "Cults: Out of This World," *TIME*, October 20, 1975; James R. Gaines, "Cults: Bo-Peep's Flock," *Newsweek*, October 20, 1975; Simross, "Invitation to an Unearthly Kingdom." For the Two's discussion of the demonstration in their interviews, see Phelan, "Looking For: The Next World," 58; Hayden Hewes and Brad Steiger, *UFO Missionaries Extraordinary* (New York: Pocket Books, 1976), 70; Hewes and Steiger, "UFO Missionaries Extraordinary," 96–97.
36. See Williamson, "'It Was a Sham,'" 2; McGrath, "UFO 'Lost Sheep' Tell Cult Secrets," 26.

37. Hewes and Steiger, "UFO Missionaries Extraordinary," 96. For the New Testament's treatment of the three days preceding the resurrection, see Matthew 27:57–28:7, Mark 15:40–16:8, Luke 23:50–24:5, and John 19:38–20:18.
38. Phelan, "Looking For: The Next World," 58.
39. This episode is retold in Hewes and Steiger, *UFO Missionaries Extraordinary*, 18.
40. As cited in Hewes and Steiger, *UFO Missionaries Extraordinary*, 16.
41. Human Individual Metamorphosis, "What's Up?"
42. For the historical development of dispensationalism, including an institutional and cultural history of its spread through nineteenth-century evangelicalism, see George M. Marsden, *Fundamentalism and American Culture: The Shaping of Twentieth Century Evangelicalism, 1870–1925* (New York: Oxford University Press, 1980). For more on the twentieth century, see A.G. Mojtabai, *Blessed Assurance: At Home with the Bomb in Amarillo, Texas* (Boston: Houghton Mifflin, 1986).
43. Marsden, *Fundamentalism and American Culture*, 51.
44. See C. I. Scofield, *The Scofield Reference Bible* (New York: Oxford University Press, 1917), p. 1349, n. 1 (commenting on Rev. 19:19); p. 1269, n. 1 (on 1 Thess. 4:17); and p. 1228, n. 1 (on 1 Cor. 15:52).
45. Descriptions of the first through fifth dispensations appear in Applewhite and Nettles, "A Statement Prepared by the Two," 164–68. I cite the discussion of the sixth dispensation, Applewhite and Nettles, "A Statement Prepared by the Two," 168.
46. Applewhite and Nettles, "A Statement Prepared by the Two," 169.
47. Ibid., 159.
48. Ibid.
49. I refer to chapter 11 of the text, "The Ultimate Trip." Hal Lindsey, *The Late Great Planet Earth* (New York: Bantam Books, 1970). For comparison purposes, consider also the more recent dispensationalist fiction series *Left Behind*, the first of which was published shortly before the Heaven's Gate suicides in 1997, which not only assumes the concept of the rapture but also begins with a depiction of it. LaHaye and Jenkins, *Left Behind: A Novel of the Earth's Last Days*.
50. For a treatment of how Applewhite and Nettles might have encountered premillennial dispensationalism, see Benjamin E. Zeller, "Scaling Heaven's Gate: Individualism and Salvation in a New Religious Movement," *Nova Religio: The Journal of Alternative and Emergent Religions* 10, no. 2 (2006).
51. "Bo and Peep Interview with Brad Steiger, January 7, 1976," 82–83.
52. Muss, "'Grave Not Path to Heaven,' Disciples Told." n.p.
53. Applewhite and Nettles, "Bo and Peep Interview with Brad Steiger, January 7, 1976," 129.
54. In addition to the already cited statement in the Hewes and Steiger book, see the first statement's closing paragraph, "Those who can believe this process and *do* it will be 'lifted up' individually and 'saved' from death – literally." Human Individual Metamorphosis, "Statement #1."
55. The precise date of Nettles's death is in dispute since her survivors in the movement seemed to have filed a falsified death report. Balch was able to

access the death certificate, which listed a fraudulent first name and a date of passing of June 18. Former member Sawyer reports a date of passing of June 19. Regardless, she had been suffering from a recurrence of cancer for at least six months. Balch, email to author, March 12, 2013; Sawyer, "Heaven's Gate: Do Response to Ti Earlier Vehicle Exit," http://sawyerhg.wordpress.com/2009/09/.

56. Sawyer, "Heaven's Gate: Do Response to Ti Earlier Vehicle Exit."
57. Mrcody and Srfody, oral history and interview.
58. Heaven's Gate, "'88 Update," 3:12.
59. Applewhite and Nettles, "Bo and Peep Interview with Brad Steiger, January 7, 1976," 89.
60. Ibid., 149.
61. Muss, "No Disease Promised," n.p.
62. Sawyer, "Heaven's Gate: Do Response to Ti Earlier Vehicle Exit."
63. DiAngelo, *Beyond Human Mind*, 37.
64. Mrcody and Srfody, oral history and interview.
65. Heaven's Gate, "'88 Update," 3:8.
66. Diana G. Tumminia, *When Prophecy Never Fails: Myth and Reality in a Flying Saucer Group* (New York: Oxford University Press, 2005); Miller, *When Prophets Die*.
67. Mrcody and Srfody, oral history and interview.
68. Heaven's Gate, "Beyond Human—the Last Call, Session 2," 4:20.
69. Heaven's Gate, "Beyond Human—the Last Call, Session 4," 4:44.
70. Heaven's Gate, "Beyond Human—the Last Call, Session 3," 4:27.
71. Howard, "Rhetoric of the Rejected Body at 'Heaven's Gate'," 159–60.
72. Heaven's Gate, "Beyond Human—the Last Call, Session 3," 4:27.
73. Heaven's Gate, "Last Chance to Evacuate Earth before It's Recycled [Transcript of Videotape]," http://www.heavensgate.com/vt092996.htm.
74. Snnody, "Deposits," in *How and When "Heaven's Gate" May Be Entered*, A:80.
75. Jnnody, "Incarnating and Discarnating," A:89.
76. Heaven's Gate, "Beyond Human—the Last Call, Session 7," 4:83.
77. Partridge, "The Eschatology of Heaven's Gate; Zeller, "Scaling Heaven's Gate."
78. Heaven's Gate, "Beyond Human—the Last Call, Session 11," 4:121.
79. Zeller, "Scaling Heaven's Gate."
80. Balch, "Waiting for the Ships," 157. For more on the revolving door nature of Heaven's Gate, see their own material, especially the transcripts of their Last Call videocassette series, and Beyond Human, session 5, 4:52.
81. Mrcody and Srfody, oral history and interview.
82. Leon Festinger, Henry W. Riecken, and Stanley Schachter, *When Prophecy Fails* (Minneapolis: University of Minnesota Press, 1956), 27.
83. Festinger, Riecken, and Schachter, *When Prophecy Fails*, 27. For an examination of Festinger's main points as well as an analysis of his study, see Jon R. Stone, ed., *Expecting Armageddon: Essential Readings in Failed Prophecy* (New York:

Routledge, 2000). Consider especially the chapters by Stone, Zygmunt, and Melton.

84. David Chidester, *Salvation and Suicide: An Interpretation of Jim Jones, the Peoples Temple, and Jonestown* (Bloomington: Indiana University Press, 1991), 130.

85. Mrcody and Srfody, oral history and interview.

86. Balch, email to author, September 14, 2013.

87. DiAngelo, *Beyond Human Mind*, 47–48.

88. Heaven's Gate, "The Shedding of Our Borrowed Human Bodies May Be Required [Poster]," 6:11.

89. DiAngelo, *Beyond Human Mind*, 48.

90. Heaven's Gate, "The Shedding of Our Borrowed Human Bodies May Be Required [Poster]," 6:11.

NOTES TO CHAPTER 5

1. Benjamin E. Zeller, "Heaven's Gate: A Literature Review and Bibliographic Essay," *Alternative Spirituality and Religion Review* 1 (2009). Available at: http://www.academicpublishing.org/ASRR-1-1/02-HeavensGate.pdf.

2. Sarah M. Pike, *New Age and Neopagan Religions in America* (New York: Columbia University Press, 2004), 80; Jeffrey Kripal, *Esalen: America and the Religion of No Religion* (Chicago: University of Chicago Press, 2007).

3. Kay Alexander, "Roots of the New Age," in *Perspectives on the New Age*, ed. James R. Lewis and J. Gordon Melton (Albany: State University of New York Press, 1992), 42.

4. Hanegraaff, *New Age Religion and Western Culture*, 46.

5. J. Gordon Melton, Jerome Clark, and Aidan A. Kelly, eds., *New Age Encyclopedia: A Guide to the Beliefs, Concepts, Terms, People, and Organizations That Make up the New Global Movement toward Spiritual Development, Health and Healing, Higher Consciousness, and Related Subjects* (Detroit: Gale Research, 1990), xiii.

6. Pike, *New Age and Neopagan Religions in America*, 22.

7. Human Individual Metamorphosis, "Statement #1."

8. Human Individual Metamorphosis, "Statement #2."

9. Ibid.

10. Mrcody and Srfody, oral history and interview.

11. Pew Forum on Religion and Public Life, *Many Americans Mix Multiple Faiths: Eastern, New Age Beliefs Widespread.*

12. Scott Lowe, "Transcendental Meditation, Vedic Science and Science," *Nova Religio: The Journal of Alternative and Emergent Religions* 14, no. 4 (2011).

13. Thomas W. Segady, "Globalization, Syncretism, and Identity: The Growth and Success of Self-Realization Fellowship," *Implicit religion* 12, no. 2 (2009); Catherine Wessinger, "Hinduism Arrives in America: The Vedanta Movement and the Self-Realization Fellowship," in *America's Alternative Religions* (Albany: State University of New York Press, 1995); Douglas Renfew Brooks, ed., *Meditation*

Revolution: A History and Theology of the Siddha Yoga Lineage (South Fallsburg, NY: Agama Press, 1997).

14. Hall, *Lived Religion in America.*

15. Laurie F. Maffly-Kipp, Leigh Eric Schmidt, and Mark R. Valeri, eds., *Practicing Protestants: Histories of the Christian Life in America, 1630–1965* (Baltimore: Johns Hopkins University Press, 2006), 16.

16. Pierre Bourdieu, *Outline of a Theory of Practice* (Cambridge, UK: Cambridge University Press, 1977).

17. Pierre Bourdieu, "Genesis and Structure of the Religious Field," *Comparative Social Research* 13 (1991). Previously published as "Genèse et structure du champ religieux," *Revue française de sociologie* 12.2: 295–334.

18. Terry Rey, *Bourdieu on Religion: Imposing Faith and Legitimacy* (London: Equinox Publishing, 2008), 129.

19. Thomas A. Tweed, *Crossing and Dwelling: A Theory of Religion* (Cambridge, MA: Harvard University Press, 2006), 54.

20. Ibid., 68–69.

21. Ibid., 82.

22. DiAngelo, *Beyond Human Mind*, 29.

23. Balch, "Waiting for the Ships," 157.

24. DiAngelo, *Beyond Human Mind*, 30.

25. Tweed, *Crossing and Dwelling*, 103.

26. Carey Goldberg, "Death in a Cult: The Compound: Heaven's Gate Fit in with New Mexico's Offbeat Style," *New York Times*, March 31, 1997, A12.

27. Tweed, *Crossing and Dwelling*, 83.

28. DiAngelo, *Beyond Human Mind*, 56.

29. Goldberg, "Death in a Cult: The Compound," A12.

30. This is a paraphrase of several members, who recounted the experience to Mrcody and Srfody, who had left the movement by that time. Mrcody and Srfody, oral history and interview.

31. Tweed, *Crossing and Dwelling*, 99.

32. Kurt A. Bruder, "Monastic Blessings: Deconstructing and Reconstructing the Self," *Symbolic Interaction* 21, no. 1 (1998).

33. Lars Ivar Hansen, "Saami Society through Time," *American Anthropologist* 97, no. 1 (1995): 132–33.

34. Robinson, "I Found the Missing People from Waldport"; Balch and Taylor, "Seekers and Saucers."

35. Applewhite indicated that this event occurred some time between late 1976 and 1978, yet former members Mrcdy and Srfody pinpointed it to late 1977, based on their recollection of having left Wyoming because of the increasing cold immediately preceding the renaming. Mrcody and Srfody also provided the details of the renaming itself. Heaven's Gate, "'88 Update," 3:9; Mrcody and Srfody, oral history and interview.

36. Heaven's Gate, "Beyond Human—the Last Call, Session 4," 4:41.

37. Anlody, *Exit Video* (Rancho Santa Fe, CA, 1997).
38. Mrcody and Srfody, oral history and interview.
39. DiAngelo, *Beyond Human Mind*, 21–22.
40. Balch, email to author, September 14, 2013.
41. Brnody, "Up the Chain," in *How and When "Heaven's Gate" May Be Entered*, A60.
42. See for example Rkkody; DiAngelo, *Beyond Human Mind*.
43. DiAngelo, *Beyond Human Mind*, 95.
44. Drrody, "Exit Video." Emphasis added.
45. Nrrody, "The Truth Is . . . " in *How and When "Heaven's Gate" May Be Entered*, A15; Nrrody, *Exit Video* (Rancho Santa Fe, CA, 1997).
46. DiAngelo, *Beyond Human Mind*, 21.
47. Ibid., 22.
48. Mrcody and Srfody, oral history and interview; Sawyer, email to author, July 25, 2013.
49. Marc Augé, *Non-Places: Introduction to an Anthropology of Supermodernity*, trans. John Howe (London: Verso, 2009), 8.
50. Tweed, *Crossing and Dwelling*, 123.
51. Heaven's Gate, "'88 Update," 3:3.
52. Balch and Taylor, "Salvation in a UFO," 61; Balch, "A Study of Defection," 31.
53. Phelan, "Looking For: The Next World," 12.
54. Balch and Taylor, "Seekers and Saucers," 842–43.
55. Human Individual Metamorphosis, "Statement #3," 1.
56. Phelan, "Looking For: The Next World," 59.
57. Muss, "'Grave Not Path to Heaven,' Disciples Told," n.p. This source is held in the American Religions Collection, ARC Mss 1, Department of Special Collections, University Libraries, University of California, Santa Barbara. It is a newspaper clipping and does not include the original page number.
58. McGrath, "UFO 'Lost Sheep' Tell Cult Secrets," 1.
59. Williamson, "'It Was a Sham': Why One Convert Left the UFO Cult," 2.
60. Human Individual Metamorphosis, "Statement #3," 1.
61. Human Individual Metamorphosis, "Prospective Candidate Letter," http://www.rkkody.com/rkk/rkkomat.htm [Defunct].
62. United Press International, "Couple Asks for UFO Volunteers—Now 20 Missing," 1; United Press International, "It's the Second Coming . . . We Are All Going Home," 3; McGrath, "UFO 'Lost Sheep' Tell Cult Secrets," 26.
63. Williamson, "'It Was a Sham': Why One Convert Left the UFO Cult," 2.
64. Mrcody and Srfody, oral history and interview.
65. McGrath, "UFO 'Lost Sheep' Tell Cult Secrets," 26.
66. Pat Reed, "Two Women UFO Disciples Reveal Identity; Say They Are Not Cult," *Houston Chronicle*, November 26, 1975, 9.
67. Since the early days of Heaven's Gate were characterized by organizational confusion and a lack of centralized leadership, in all likelihood several different monetary practices developed simultaneously. After Nettles and Applewhite

gathered the group into a single community and instituted greater leadership, they also centralized the shared purse system.

68. Heaven's Gate, "The 17 Steps," 2:8.
69. Heaven's Gate, "Major and Lesser Offenses," 2:9.
70. Ibid.
71. Mrcody and Srfody, "Oral History and Interview with Author, September 30-October 1, 2013."
72. Williamson, "'It Was a Sham': Why One Convert Left the UFO Cult," 2.
73. Human Individual Metamorphosis, "Prospective Candidate Letter."
74. Heaven's Gate, *Class Meeting with Ti and Do, 15 July 1982* (1982), Audio Tape.
75. Heaven's Gate, "The 17 Steps," 2:8.
76. Gilbert, "I Was a Member of the UFO Cult," 48.
77. Smmody, "T.E.L.A.H. – the Evolutionary Level above Human," A22.
78. DiAngelo, *Beyond Human Mind*, 47.
79. Heaven's Gate, "Beyond Human—the Last Call, Session 5," 4:60.
80. Heaven's Gate, "Beyond Human—the Last Call, Session 10," 4:114.
81. David Grumett, "Dynamics of Christian Dietary Abstinence," in *The Way of Food: Religion, Food, and Eating in North America*, ed. Benjamin E. Zeller et al. (New York: Columbia University Press, 2014), 5.
82. Heaven's Gate, "'88 Update," 3:10.
83. Mrcody and Srfody, oral history and interview.
84. Balch, email to author, September 14, 2013.
85. B. Drummond Ayres, Jr., "Cult's Self-Denial Left Room for Pizza and Trip to Las Vegas," *New York Times*, April 4, 1997 1997, A, 16.
86. Human Individual Metamorphosis, "Prospective Candidate Letter."
87. Heaven's Gate, "Anonymous Sexaholics Celibate Church Introduction and Ways," http://www.rkkody.com/rkk/rkkomat.htm#intro [Defunct].
88. Ibid.
89. McGrath, "UFO 'Lost Sheep' Tell Cult Secrets," 26.
90. Mrcody and Srfody, oral history and interview.
91. DiAngelo, *Beyond Human Mind*, 45.
92. Ibid., 46.
93. Human Individual Metamorphosis, "Statement #3."
94. Marshall Herff Applewhite, "Do's Intro: Purpose—Belief," in *How and When "Heaven's Gate" May Be Entered*, iii.
95. Bruce Ellis Benson and Norman Wirzba, eds., *Phenomenology of Prayer* (Bronx, NY: Fordham University Press, 2005), 1.
96. Mrcody and Srfody, oral history and interview; Sawyer, email to author, July 28, 2013.
97. Brnody, "Up the Chain," A61.
98. Ibid.
99. Ibid., A62.
100. Ibid., A64.

101. Heaven's Gate, "Preparing for Service."
102. Ibid.
103. Ibid.
104. Ibid. Ellipses in the original.
105. Catherine L. Albanese, *A Republic of Mind and Spirit: A Cultural History of American Metaphysical Religion* (New Haven, CT: Yale University Press, 2007), 7.
106. Heaven's Gate, "Preparing for Service."
107. Albanese, *A Republic of Mind and Spirit*, 7.
108. I have elsewhere analyzed this prayer from the perspective of how it invokes technological, scientific, and physical language in service of religious goals. Zeller, *Prophets and Protons*, 138–41.
109. Heaven's Gate, "Preparing for Service."
110. Hanegraaff, *New Age Religion and Western Culture*, 56.
111. Catherine Bender, "Practicing Religions," in *The Cambridge Companion to Religious Studies*, ed. Robert A. Orsi (Cambridge: Cambridge University Press, 2011), 294.
112. R. Marie Griffith, *Born Again Bodies: Flesh and Spirit in American Christianity* (Berkeley: University of California Press, 2004), 255.
113. Stephen J. Stein, *The Shaker Experience in America: A History of the United Society of Believers* (New Haven, CT: Yale University Press, 1992).
114. Jeremy Rapport, "'Join Us! Come, Eat!'": Vegetarianism in the Formative Period of the Seventh-Day Adventists and the Unity School of Christianity," in *The Way of Food: Religion, Food, and Eating in North America*, ed. Benjamin E. Zeller et al. (New York: Columbia University Press, 2014); Kate Holbrook, "Good to Eat: Culinary Priorities among Mormons and the Nation of Islam," in *The Way of Food: Religion, Food, and Eating in North America*, ed. Benjamin E. Zeller et al. (New York: Columbia University Press, 2014).

NOTES TO CHAPTER 6

1. Robert W. Balch and David Taylor, "Making Sense of the Heaven's Gate Suicides," in *Cults, Religion, and Violence*, ed. David G. Bromley and J. Gordon Melton (Cambridge: Cambridge University Press, 2002), 224.
2. Heaven's Gate, "Our Position against Suicide," http://web.archive.org/web/19961222130009/http://www.heavensgate.com/.
3. Balch and Taylor, "Making Sense of the Heaven's Gate Suicides," 209–10.
4. Ibid., 223–26.
5. Catherine Wessinger, *How the Millennium Comes Violently: From Jonestown to Heaven's Gate* (New York: Seven Bridges Press, 2000), 229.
6. Ibid.
7. Ibid., 230.
8. Ibid., 244.
9. Lewis, "Legitimating Suicide: Heaven's Gate and New Age Ideology," 113.

10. Several former members continue to be active in disseminating the materials produced by the Class before its demise. These include Mrcody, Srfody, Rkkody (d. 1998), Jstody (d. 1997), Oscody (d. 2000), Crrlody, and Sawyer.
11. Wessinger, *How the Millennium Comes Violently*, 230.
12. Robert Jay Lifton, *Destroying the World to Save It: Aum Shinrikyō, Apocalyptic Violence, and the New Global Terrorism*, 1st ed. (New York: Henry Holt and Co., 1999), 325.
13. Ibid., 321.
14. Lalich, *Bounded Choice*, 98.
15. Ibid., 106.
16. Rodney Stark and William Sims Bainbridge, *A Theory of Religion* (New York: Peter Lang, 1987); Stark and Finke, *Acts of Faith*.
17. DiAngelo, *Beyond Human Mind*, 48.
18. Sawyer, email to author, July 25, 2013.
19. Sawyer estimates that thirty-six members remained. One of Balch's informants indicates it was closer to forty-eight. Sawyer, email to author, July 25, 2013; Balch, email to author, October 16, 2013.
20. Thirty-nine individuals died in Rancho Santa Fe. Several former members committed suicide after the main deaths in March 1997. The four confirmed ex-members are Rkkody (Chuck Humphrey, d. 1998), Jstody (Wayne Cooke, d. 1997), Gbbody (Jimmy Simpson, d. 1997), Oscody (Wayne Parker, d. 2000).
21. The best example of this language is found in the Heaven's Gate "Exit Press Release."
22. Heaven's Gate, "Heaven's Last Mission," in "How and When 'Heaven's Gate' (The Door to the Physical Kingdom Level above Human) May Be Entered: An Anthology by Representatives from the Kingdom of Heaven," first unpublished draft (1996), 1:2.
23. Balch and Taylor, "Making Sense of the Heaven's Gate Suicides," 220.
24. Heaven's Gate, *How and When "Heaven's Gate" May Be Entered*, 6:1–2.
25. Ibid., 6:3–11.
26. Sawyer, email to author, July 28, 2013.
27. DiAngelo, *Beyond Human Mind*, 43.
28. Ibid., 46.
29. Sawyer, email to author, July 25, 2013.
30. Marshall Herff Applewhite, *Do's Exit Video* (Rancho Sante Fe: Heaven's Gate, 1997).
31. Heaven's Gate, "Our Position against Suicide."
32. Ibid. For the earlier quote, see Hewes and Steiger, *UFO Missionaries Extraordinary*, 89.
33. Heaven's Gate, "Our Position against Suicide."
34. Balch and Taylor, "Making Sense of the Heaven's Gate Suicides," 221.
35. Heaven's Gate, "Our Position against Suicide."

36. Jeffrey Kaplan, *Radical Religion in America: Millenarian Movements from the Far Right to the Children of Noah* (Syracuse, NY: Syracuse University Press, 1997).
37. For more on the Branch Davidians, see James D. Tabor and Eugene V. Gallagher, *Why Waco?* (Berkeley: University of California Press, 1995); Stuart A Wright, *Armageddon in Waco: Critical Perspectives on the Branch Davidian Conflict* (Chicago: University of Chicago Press, 1995).
38. This account is found in Book VII, verse 400, of Flavius Josephus, *The Jewish War*, trans. H. St. J. Thackeray, vol. 3 (Cambridge, MA: Harvard University Press, 1997), 419.
39. For more on Jonestown, see Chidester, *Salvation and Suicide*; Rebecca Moore, *Understanding Jonestown and the Peoples Temple* (New York: Praeger, 2009).
40. DiAngelo, *Beyond Human Mind*, 49.
41. Derek Humphry, *Final Exit: The Practicalities of Self-Deliverance and Assisted Suicide for the Dying* (New York: Dell, 1991), 110–13.
42. For more on the possible use of weaponry, see Balch and Taylor, "Making Sense of the Heaven's Gate Suicides," 222.
43. DiAngelo, *Beyond Human Mind*, 55.
44. Heaven's Gate, "'95 Statement by an E.T. Presently Incarnate," 1:9; Stmody, "Evolutionary 'Rights' for 'Victims,'" A:76.
45. Neoody reports that Alxody and Vrnody were first to have the procedure done, in winter 1995 when the group was living in Phoenix. Sawyer indicates that Srrody underwent the procedure a year earlier in California, and that he himself was supposed to be the second volunteer but complications from Srrody's procedure led to the cancelation of his operation. DiAngelo, *Beyond Human Mind*, 57–58; Sawyer, "Two Witnesses Ti Do Father Jesus Part 12 Castration Suicide Born Again UFO Luciferians," http://sawyerhg.wordpress.com/2011/03/04/two-witnesses-ti-do-father-jesus-part-12-castration-suicide-born-again-ufo-luciferians/.
46. Todd S. Purdum, "Death in a Cult: The Inquiry; Last 2 Names of Cult Members Are Listed as Investigators Try to Find Their Families," *New York Times*, 1 April 1997, A18.
47. DiAngelo, *Beyond Human Mind*, 58.
48. Balch, email to author, October 16, 2013.
49. Heaven's Gate, *How and When "Heaven's Gate" May Be Entered*, 1:1–2.
50. Heaven's Gate, "Undercover Jesus Surfaces (Www.Indirect.Com/Www/Lillo)," (UseNet Post, 13 October 1995, Message-ID: <44a1do$69@news1.channel1.com>, 1995).
51. Ibid.
52. The group included an "edited/updated" version of this posting in their anthology that omits this description, but here I refer to the original UseNet posting.
53. Heaven's Gate, *How and When "Heaven's Gate" May Be Entered*, 1:2.
54. Balch, email to author, October 16, 2013.
55. Heaven's Gate, *How and When "Heaven's Gate" May Be Entered*, 1:2.

56. Heaven's Gate, "E.T. Speaks: Ufo's / Space Aliens / Reboot Civilization" (UseNet Post, 13 October 1995, Message-ID: <45m7sm$o9q@ddi2.digital.net>, 1995).
57. Ibid.
58. Several scholars have remarked upon the parallels between Q and various forms of the divine. For the most extended of such considerations, see Ross Shepard Kraemer, William Cassidy, and Susan L. Schwartz, *Religions of Star Trek* (Boulder, CO: Westview Press, 2001), 49–56.
59. P.H., "Re: E.T. Speaks: Ufo's / Space Aliens / Reboot Civilization," (UseNet Post, 17 October 1995, Message-ID: <45toqn$nou@status.gen.nz>, 1995).
60. D.F., "Re: E.T. Speaks: Ufo's / Space Aliens / Reboot Civilization," (UseNet Post, 19 October 1995, Message-ID: <466doi$2qs@portal.gmu.edu>, 1995).
61. C.C., "Re: E.T. Speaks: Ufo's / Space Aliens / Reboot Civilization," (UseNet Post, 18 October 1995, Message-ID: <4626qt$bvv@noc.usfca.edu>, 1995).
62. T.B., "Re: E.T. Speaks: Ufo's / Space Aliens / Reboot Civilization," (UseNet Post, 18 October 1995, Message-ID: <30854839.5625@freeway.net>, 1995).
63. Ellipses in original. R.S., "Re: E.T. Speaks: Ufo's / Space Aliens / Reboot Civilization" (UseNet Post, 16 October 1995, Message-ID: <DGJyoI.15qK@pen.k12.va.us>, 1995).
64. Ellipses in original. J.K., "Re: E.T. Speaks: Ufo's / Space Aliens / Reboot Civilization," (UseNet Post, 26 October 1995, Message-ID: <46okgl$buc@uwm.edu>, 1995).
65. UseNet archives are available through several sources. Interested readers should consult an Internet search engine to find the current archives.
66. Heaven's Gate, *How and When "Heaven's Gate" May Be Entered*, 1:2.
67. These posts were most easily accessible from the archives of Rkkody's website, Rkkody, "Newsgroup Postings," http://www.rkkody.com/rkk/rkkpost.htm [Defunct].
68. Ellipses added by author. Quoted in Balch and Taylor, "Making Sense of the Heaven's Gate Suicides," 221.
69. Paul DiMaggio et al., "Social Implications of the Internet," *Annual Review of Sociology* 27(2001): 307.
70. Ibid., 308.
71. See, for example, Thomas, "Web of Death."
72. Urban takes the strongest position in this regard, though he admittedly is interested not in Heaven's Gate itself but the condition of religion in late modernity. Urban, "The Devil at Heaven's Gate," 269.
73. "Heaven's Last Mission," 1:2.
74. Neoody, email to author, October 5, 2013.
75. On the authorship of the anthology, see DiAngelo, *Beyond Human Mind*, 58.
76. Mrcody and Srfody, oral history and interview.
77. Heaven's Gate, "How and When 'Heaven's Gate' (The Door to the Physical Kingdom Level Above Human) May Be Entered: An Anthology by Representatives from the Kingdom of Heaven."
78. Jwnody, "Overview of the Present Mission," ix.

79. Neoody reports that Dvvody's husband did not join because of health problems, but he himself told Balch and Taylor that he simply did not accept them or their message. Dvvody does not provide any clear indication. DiAngelo, *Beyond Human Mind*, 101; Balch, email to author, October 16, 2013; Dvvody, *Exit Video* (Rancho Santa Fe, CA, 1997).

80. Heaven's Gate, "Last Chance to Evacuate Earth before It's Recycled [Transcript of Videotape]."

81. Heaven's Gate, "Planet About to Be Recycled—Your Only Chance to Survive—Leave with Us [Edited Transcript]."

82. Heaven's Gate, "Last Chance to Evacuate Earth before It's Recycled [Transcript of Videotape]."

83. Heaven's Gate, "Planet About to Be Recycled—Your Only Chance to Survive—Leave with Us [Edited Transcript]."

84. Michael Cook, *Muhammad* (New York: Oxford University Press, 1983), 31–41.

85. Margit Warburg, *Baha'i*, Studies in Contemporary Religions (Salt Lake City, UT: Signature Books, 2003), 9–10.

86. Jan Shipps, *Mormonism: The Story of a New Religious Tradition* (Urbana: University of Illinois Press, 1985), 69–71.

87. Nathan O. Hatch, *The Democratization of American Christianity* (New Haven, CT: Yale University Press, 1989), 167–70.

88. Heaven's Gate, "Planet About to Be Recycled—Your Only Chance to Survive—Leave with Us [Edited Transcript]."

89. The most succinct version of this perspective is the statement that the Two provided for *UFO Missionaries Extraordinary*. Applewhite and Nettles, "A Statement Prepared by the Two," 167–68.

90. Hewes and Steiger, *UFO Missionaries Extraordinary*, 98.

91. Heaven's Gate, "Last Chance to Evacuate Earth before It's Recycled [Transcript of Videotape]."

92. Mrcody and Srfody, oral history and interview.

93. Heaven's Gate, "Last Chance to Evacuate Earth before It's Recycled [Transcript of Videotape]."

94. Michael Barkun, *A Culture of Conspiracy: Apocalyptic Visions in Contemporary America* (Berkeley: University of California Press, 2003).

95. Ibid., 2.

96. Ibid., 60.

97. Ibid., 123.

98. Ibid., 60.

99. See, for example, Heaven's Gate, "'88 Update."

100. Ibid., 3:17–18.

101. Stmody, "Evolutionary 'Rights' for 'Victims,'" A:76–A:77.

102. Srrody, "Earth Exit Statement: Why We Must Leave at This Time," http://www.heavensgate.com/exitsrr.htm.

103. Barkun, *A Culture of Conspiracy*, 20.

104. Heaven's Gate, "Beyond Human—the Last Call, Session 12," 4:159–60.

105. DiAngelo, *Beyond Human Mind*, 102.

106. Heaven's Gate, "Connecting Links."

107. David J. Eicher, "Here Comes Hale-Bopp," *Astronomy* 24, no. 2 (1996): 68.

108. Ibid.

109. *Scientific American*, "The Trail of Hale-Bopp," http://www.scientificamerican. com/article.cfm?id=the-trail-of-hale-bopp.

110. Wayne Horowitz, "Halley's Comet and Judean Revolts Revisited," *Catholic Biblical Quarterly* 58, no. 3 (1996); William E. Phipps, "The Magi and Halley's Comet," *Theology Today* 43, no. 1 (1986); E. S. Kennedy, "Comets in Islamic Astronomy and Astrology," *Journal of Near Eastern Studies* 16, no. 1 (1957).

111. Ronald L. Numbers, *Science and Christianity in Pulpit and Pew* (New York: Oxford University Press, 2007), 14.

112. Daniel Wojcik, "Embracing Doomsday: Faith, Fatalism, and Apocalyptic Beliefs in the Nuclear Age," *Western Folklore* 55, no. 4 (1996).

113. Anlody, "Investments," A:98.

114. Andrea Adelson, "After Midnight, a Radio Talk Show Is Growing Coast to Coast," *New York Times*, May 18, 1998, D7.

115. Ray LaFontaine, "Talk Radio's Comet Caper," *Washington Post*, February 23, 1997, C5.

116. Ibid.

117. Ibid.

118. David J. Tholen and Olivier Hainaut, "Fraudulent Use of a Ifa/Uh Picture," http://www.eso.org/~ohainaut/Hale_Bopp/hb_ufo_tholen.html.

119. Farsight Institute, "Farsight Professional 1: Hale-Bopp" http://web.archive.org/ web/19970228025402/http://www.farsight.org/et/prof/Hale_Bopp/p2.html.

120. Farsight Institute, "Professional Et Examples: Hale-Bopp," http://web.archive. org/web/19970228024034/http://www.farsight.org/et/prof/Hale_Bopp/.

121. Farsight Institute, "Student Project: Hale-Bopp," http://web.archive.org/ web/19970228025429/http://farsight.org/et/prof/Hale_Bopp/boppproject/.

122. Art Bell, "The Art Bell Web Page: Hale-Bopp Companion," http://web.archive. org/web/19961219235158/http://www.artbell.com/art/halebopp.html.

123. While no web archive exists of Shramek's web page in early 1997, one can compare the December 24, 1996 archive and May 8, 1999 archives to determine what materials did and did not change during that time period. Chuck Shramek, "The Great Comet of 1997," http://web.archive.org/web/19961224064739/http:// www.neosoft.com/~cshramek/.; Chuck Shramek, "The Chuck Shramek Home Page: Ufo's over Washington!" http://web.archive.org/web/19991014003523/ http://www.neosoft.com/%7Ecshramek/.

124. Balch and Taylor, "Making Sense of the Heaven's Gate Suicides," 223.

125. Heaven's Gate, "Heaven's Gate— How and When It May Be Entered."

126. The group's final financial ledgers are in the possession of Mrcody and Srfody of the TELAH Foundation, and I thank them for permission to examine them.

127. In addition to the actual ledgers, see also Ayres, "Cult's Self-Denial Left Room for Pizza and Trip to Las Vegas," 16.
128. Srrody, *Exit Video* (Rancho Santa Fe, CA, 1997).
129. Yrsody, *Exit Video* (Rancho Santa Fe, CA, 1997).
130. Glnody, "Earth Exit Statement: Why We Must Leave at This Time," http://www.heavensgate.com/exitgln.htm.
131. Heaven's Gate, "Exit Press Release."
132. Mrcody and Srfody, oral history and interview; Crlody, "The Aftermath of Heaven's Gate."
133. Crlody, "The Aftermath of Heaven's Gate."
134. The "Comm Center Daily Log" is in the possession of Mrcody and Srfody of the TELAH Foundation, and I thank them for permission to examine it.
135. Crlody, "The Truth and Lies of Heaven's Gate."

NOTES TO THE AFTERWORD
1. Robert Hilton, "First Watch: Django Django's 'Hail Bop,'" National Public Radio, http://www.npr.org/blogs/allsongs/2012/07/24/157232208/first-watch-django-djangos-hail-bop.
2. Django Django, "Django Django—Hail Bop (Official Video)," YouTube, https://www.youtube.com/watch?feature=player_embedded&v=JQGTORbJgB4.
3. Hilton, "First Watch: Django Django's 'Hail Bop.'"
4. Amazon.com, "E-Squared: Nine Do-It-Yourself Energy Experiments That Prove Your Thoughts Create Your Reality," http://www.amazon.com/E-Squared-Do-It-Yourself-Experiments-Thoughts-Reality/dp/1401938906/.
5. Jay P. Dolan, *The American Catholic Experience: A History from Colonial Times to the Present* (Notre Dame: University of Notre Dame Press, 1992); Jonathan D. Sarna, *American Judaism: A History* (New Haven, CT: Yale University Press, 2004).
6. Stark and Finke, *Acts of Faith*; Rodney Stark and William Sims Bainbridge, *The Future of Religion: Secularization, Revival, and Cult Formation* (Berkeley and Los Angeles: University of California Press, 1985); Jon Butler, *Awash in a Sea of Faith: Christianizing the American People* (Cambridge, MA: Harvard University Press, 1990); Albanese, *A Republic of Mind and Spirit*.
7. Hatch, *The Democratization of American Christianity*.
8. Craig James Hazen, *The Village Enlightenment in America: Popular Religion and Science in the Nineteenth Century* (Urbana: University of Illinois Press, 2000).
9. David J. Rhees, "Corporate Advertising, Public Relations and Popular Exhibits: The Case of Du Pont," *History & Technology* 10, no. 1/2 (1993).
10. Paul S. Boyer, *By the Bomb's Early Light: American Thought and Culture at the Dawn of the Atomic Age* (Chapel Hill: University of North Carolina Press, 1994).
11. Zeller, *Prophets and Protons*.

12. Thomas Robbins and Susan J. Palmer, *Millennium, Messiahs, and Mayhem: Contemporary Apocalyptic Movements* (New York: Routledge, 1997); Wessinger, *How the Millennium Comes Violently*.

13. Rapture Ready, "Rapture Ready," Rapture Ready, http://www.raptureready.com; Samaritan Sentinel, "Samaritan Sentinel," https://samaritansentinel.com/Home_Page.php; Rapture Watch, "Rapture Watch: A Global, End Times Prophecy Resource," Rapture Watch, http://www.rapturewatch.net; Prophecy News Watch, "Prophecy News Watch: Biblical Prophecy in the News," Prophecy News Watch, http://www.prophecynewswatch.com.

14. Christopher S. Parker, *Change They Can't Believe In: The Tea Party and Reactionary Politics in America* (Princeton, NJ: Princeton University Press, 2013).

15. Manuel Castells, *Networks of Outrage and Hope: Social Movements in the Internet Age* (Cambridge, UK: Polity Press, 2012).

BIBLIOGRAPHY

"20 Missing in Oregon after Talking of a Higher Life." *New York Times*, October 7, 1975, 71.

Adelson, Andrea. "After Midnight, a Radio Talk Show Is Growing Coast to Coast." *New York Times*, May 18, 1998, 7.

Aidala, Angela A. "Social Change, Gender Roles, and New Religious Movements." *Sociological Analysis* 46, no. 3 (1985): 287–314.

Albanese, Catherine L. *A Republic of Mind and Spirit: A Cultural History of American Metaphysical Religion.* New Haven, CT: Yale University Press, 2007.

Alexander, Kay. "Roots of the New Age." In *Perspectives on the New Age*, edited by James R. Lewis and J. Gordon Melton, 30–47. Albany: State University of New York Press, 1992.

Amazon.com. "E-Squared: Nine Do-It-Yourself Energy Experiments That Prove Your Thoughts Create Your Reality." http://www.amazon.com/E-Squared-Do-It-Yourself-Experiments-Thoughts-Reality/dp/1401938906/.

Andersson, Pia. "Ancient Alien Brothers, Ancient Terrestrial Remains: Archeology or Religion?" In *Alien Worlds: Social and Religious Dimensions of Extraterrestrial Contact*, edited by Diana Tumminia, 264–74. Syracuse, NY: Syracuse University Press, 2007.

Anlody. "Exit Video." Rancho Santa Fe, CA, 1997.

———. "Investments." In *How and When "Heaven's Gate" (the Door to the Physical Kingdom Level above Human) May Be Entered: An Anthology of Our Materials*, edited by Heaven's Gate, A:98–100. Mill Spring, NC: Wild Flower Press, 1997.

Anthony, Dick, and Thomas Robbins. "Cultural Crisis and Contemporary Religion." In *In Gods We Trust*, edited by Thomas Robbins and Dick Anthony, 9–31. New Brunswick, NJ: Transaction Publishers, 1981.

Applewhite, Marshall Herff. *Do's Exit Video*. Rancho Sante Fe, CA: Heaven's Gate, 1997.

———. "Do's Intro: Purpose—Belief." In *How and When "Heaven's Gate" (the Door to the Physical Kingdom Level above Human) May Be Entered*, edited by Heaven's Gate, iii–vi. Mill Springs, NC: Wild Flower Press, 1997.

Applewhite, Marshall Herff, and Bonnie Lu Nettles. "Bo and Peep Interview with Brad Steiger, January 7, 1976." In *UFO Missionaries Extraordinary*, edited by Hayden Hewes and Brad Steiger, 81–154. New York: Pocket Books, 1976.

———. "A Statement Prepared by the Two." In *UFO Missionaries Extraordinary*, edited by Hayden Hewes and Brad Steiger, 157–73. New York: Pocket Books, 1976.

Augé, Marc. *Non-Places: Introduction to an Anthropology of Supermodernity*. Translated by John Howe. London: Verso, 2009.

Ayres, B. Drummond, Jr. "Cult's Self-Denial Left Room for Pizza and Trip to Las Vegas." *New York Times*, April 4, 1997, 16.

Bainbridge, William Sims. *The Endtime Family: Children of God*. Albany: State University of New York Press, 2002.

Balch, Robert W. "Bo and Peep: A Case Study of the Origins of Messianic Leadership." In *Millennialism and Charisma*, edited by Roy Wallis. Belfast: The Queen's University, 1982.

———. "'When the Light Goes Out, Darkness Comes': A Study of Defection from a Totalistic Cult." In *Religious Movements: Genesis, Exodus, and Numbers*, edited by Rodney Stark. New York: Paragon House, 1985.

———. "Waiting for the Ships: Disillusionment and the Revitalization of Faith in Bo and Peep's UFO Cult." In *The Gods Have Landed: New Religions from Other Worlds*, edited by James R. Lewis, 137–66. Albany: State University of New York Press, 1995.

———. "The Evolution of a New Age Cult: From Total Overcomers Anonymous to Death at Heaven's Gate." In *Sects, Cults, and Spiritual Communities: A Sociological Analysis*, edited by William W. Zellner and Marc Petrowsky. Westport: Praeger Publishers, 1998.

———. Email with author. October 16, 2013.

Balch, Robert W., and David Taylor. "Salvation in a UFO." *Psychology Today* 10, no. 5 (October 1976): 58–66, 106.

———. "Seekers and Saucers: The Role of the Cultic Milieu in Joining a UFO Cult." *American Behavioral Scientist* 20, no. 6 (1977): 839–60.

———. "Making Sense of the Heaven's Gate Suicides." In *Cults, Religion, and Violence*, edited by David G. Bromley and J. Gordon Melton, 209–228. Cambridge: Cambridge University Press, 2002.

Balmer, Randall Herbert. *Mine Eyes Have Seen the Glory: A Journey into the Evangelical Subculture in America*. New York: Oxford University Press, 1989.

Barker, Eileen. *The Making of a Moonie: Choice or Brainwashing?* Oxford: Basil Blackwell, 1984.

———. "The Cage of Freedom and the Freedom of the Cage." In *On Freedom: A Centenary Anthology*, edited by Eileen Barker. London: London School of Economics and Political Science, 1997.

Barkun, Michael. *A Culture of Conspiracy: Apocalyptic Visions in Contemporary America*. Berkeley: University of California Press, 2003.

Beals, Gregory. "Far from Home." *Newsweek*, April 7, 1997, 36–39.

Bearak, Barry. "Death in a Cult: The Victims: Time of Puzzled Heartbreak Binds Relatives." *New York Times*, March 30, 1997, A1.

———. "Odyssey to Suicide—a Special Report; Eyes on Glory: Pied Pipers of Heaven's Gate." *New York Times*, April 28, 1997, A1, B8–B10.

Bednarowski, Mary Farrell. *New Religions & the Theological Imagination in America*. Bloomington: Indiana University Press, 1989.

Bell, Art. "The Art Bell Web Page: Hale-Bopp Companion." http://web.archive.org/web/19961219235158/http://www.artbell.com/art/halebopp.html.

Bellah, Robert. "Habits of the Heart: Implications for Religion." Public Address at St. Mark's Catholic Church, Isla Vista, CA. February 21, 1986.

Bellah, Robert, Richard Madsen, William M. Sullivan, Ann Swidler, and Steven M. Tipton, eds. *Habits of the Heart: Individualism and Commitment in American Life*. Berkeley: University of California Press, 1985.

Belluck, Pam. "Death in a Cult: Bewilderment Is All That's Left for Families." *New York Times*, March 30, 1997, A16.

Bender, Catherine. "Practicing Religions." In *The Cambridge Companion to Religious Studies*, edited by Robert A. Orsi, 273–95. Cambridge: Cambridge University Press, 2011.

Benson, Bruce Ellis, and Norman Wirzba, eds. *Phenomenology of Prayer*. Bronx, NY: Fordham University Press, 2005.

"Boisean Remembers Knowing Bonnie Lu, 'UFO Recruiter.'" *Idaho Statesman*, November 2, 1975, 12D.

Bourdieu, Pierre. *Outline of a Theory of Practice*. Cambridge, UK: Cambridge University Press, 1977.

———. "Legitimation and Structured Interests in Weber's Sociology of Religion." Translated by Chris Turner. In *Max Weber, Rationality, and Modernity*, edited by Scott Lash and Sam Whimster, 119–36. London: Allen and Unwin, 1987.

———. "Genesis and Structure of the Religious Field." *Comparative Social Research* 13 (1991): 1–44.

Boyarin, Daniel. *Border Lines: The Partition of Judaeo-Christianity*. Philadelphia: University of Pennsylvania Press, 2004.

Boyer, Paul S. *By the Bomb's Early Light: American Thought and Culture at the Dawn of the Atomic Age*. Chapel Hill: University of North Carolina Press, 1994.

Brenner, Athalya, and Jan W. van Henten, eds. *Bible Translation on the Threshold of the Twenty-First Century: Authority, Reception, Culture and Religion*. New York: Sheffield Academic Press, 2002.

Brnody. "Up the Chain." In *How and When "Heaven's Gate" (the Door to the Physical Kingdom Level above Human) May Be Entered*, edited by Heaven's Gate, A:60–64. Mill Springs, NC: Wild Flower Press, 1997.

Bromley, David G., and Anson D. Shupe, Jr. *Strange Gods: The Great American Cult Scare*. Boston: Beacon Press, 1981.

Brooke, James. "Death in a Cult: The Silence; for Ex-Wife of Leader, No Wish for the Limelight." *New York Times*, April 1, 1997, A18.

Brooks, Douglas Renfew, ed. *Meditation Revolution: A History and Theology of the Siddha Yoga Lineage*. South Fallsburg, NY: Agama Press, 1997.

Bruder, Kurt A. "Monastic Blessings: Deconstructing and Reconstructing the Self." *Symbolic Interaction* 21, no. 1 (May 1998): 87–116.

Bruni, Frank. "Death in a Cult: The Personality; Leader Believed in Space Aliens and Apocalypse." *New York Times*, March 28, 1997, A1, A19.

Butler, Jon. *Awash in a Sea of Faith: Christianizing the American People*. Cambridge: Harvard University Press, 1990.

Campbell, Bruce F. *Ancient Wisdom Revived: A History of the Theosophical Movement*. Berkeley: University of California Press, 1980.

Campbell, Colin. "The Cult, Cultic Milieu and Secularization." In *A Sociological Yearbook of Religion in Britain 5*, 119–36. London: SCM Press, 1972.

Castells, Manuel. *Networks of Outrage and Hope: Social Movements in the Internet Age*. Cambridge, UK: Polity Press, 2012.

C.C. "Re: E.T. Speaks: Ufo's / Space Aliens / Reboot Civilization." UseNet Post, October 18, 1995, Message-ID: <4626qt$bvv@noc.usfca.edu>, 1995.

Chidester, David. *Salvation and Suicide: An Interpretation of Jim Jones, the Peoples Temple, and Jonestown*. Bloomington: Indiana University Press, 1991.

Chryssides, George D. "'Come on up, and I Will Show Thee': Heaven's Gate as a Postmodern Group." In *Controversial New Religions*, edited by James R. Lewis and Jesper Aagaard Petersen Petersen, 353–70. Oxford: Oxford University Press, 2005.

———. "Approaching Heaven's Gate." In *Heaven's Gate: Postmodernity and Popular Culture in a Suicide Group*, edited by George D. Chryssides, 1–16. Farnham, UK: Ashgate, 2011.

———. ed. *Heaven's Gate: Postmodernity and Popular Culture in a Suicide Group*. Farnham, UK: Ashgate, 2011.

Clarke, Arthur C. *Profiles of the Future: An Enquiry into the Limits of the Possible*. New York: Holt, Rinehart, and Winston, 1984.

Connelly, Mark. *Christmas: A Social History*. London: I.B. Taurus, 2001.

Cook, Michael. *Muhammad*. Past Masters. Oxford; New York: Oxford University Press, 1983.

Cox, Harvey. *Turning East: Why Americans Look to the Orient for Spirituallity—and What That Search Can Mean to the West*. New York: Touchstone, 1977.

Crlody. "The Aftermath of Heaven's Gate." http://www.freewebs.com/crlody/.

———. "The Truth and Lies of Heaven's Gate." http://crlody.wordpress.com/2012/04/27/the-truth-and-lies-of-heavens-gate/.

———. "The Worldly Aftermath of Heaven's Gate." http://crlody.wordpress.com/2011/07/28/the-worldy-aftermath-of-heavens-gate/.

Cross, Anne. "A Confederacy of Fact and Fiction: Science and the Sacred in UFO Research." In *Alien Worlds: Social and Religious Dimensions of Extraterrestrial Contact*, edited by Diana Tumminia, 249–63. Syracuse, NY: Syracuse University Press, 2007.

"Cults: Out of This World." *TIME*, October 20, 1975, 25–26.

Cusack, Carole M. *Invented Religions: Imagination, Fiction and Faith*. Farnham, UK: Ashgate, 2010.

Daniel, David. "The Beginning of the Journey." *Newsweek*, April 13, 1997.

Dawson, Lorne L. "Raising Lazarus: A Methodological Critique of Stephen Kent's Revival of the Brainwashing Model." In *Misunderstanding Cults: Searching for*

Objectivity in a Controversial Field, edited by Benjamin Zablocki and Thomas Robbins, 379–400. Toronto: University of Toronto Press, 2001.

Denzler, Brenda. *The Lure of the Edge: Scientific Passions, Religious Beliefs, and the Pursuit of UFOs*. Berkeley: University of California Press, 2001.

D.F. "Re: E.T. Speaks: Ufo's / Space Aliens / Reboot Civilization." UseNet Post, October 19, 1995, Message-ID: <466doi$2qs@portal.gmu.edu>, 1995.

DiAngelo, Rio. *Beyond Human Mind: The Soul Evolution of Heaven's Gate*. Beverly Hills: privately published, 2007.

DiMaggio, Paul, Eszter Hargittai, W. Russell Neuman, and John P. Robinson. "Social Implications of the Internet." *Annual Review of Sociology* 27 (2001): 307–36.

Ditmer, Joanne. "Durango Businessman Reported with UFO Group." *Denver Post*, October 23, 1975, 33.

Django Django. "Django Django—Hail Bop (Official Video)." YouTube, https://www.youtube.com/watch?feature=player_embedded&v=JQGTORbJgB4.

Dolan, Jay P. *The American Catholic Experience: A History from Colonial Times to the Present*. Notre Dame: University of Notre Dame Press, 1992.

Drrody. "Exit Video." Rancho Santa Fe, CA, 1997.

Dunand, Françoise. *Isis: Mère Des Dieux*. Paris: Errance, 2000.

Dvvody. "Exit Video." Rancho Santa Fe, CA, 1997.

Ehrman, Bart D. *The New Testament: A Historical Introduction to the Early Christian Writings*. New York: Oxford University Press, 1997.

———. *Jesus: Apocalyptic Prophet of the New Millennium*. New York: Oxford University Press, 2001.

Eicher, David J. "Here Comes Hale-Bopp." *Astronomy* 24, no. 2 (1996): 68.

Ellwood, Robert S., Jr. *The Fifties Spiritual Marketplace: American Religion in a Decade of Conflict*. New Brunswick, NJ: Rutgers University Press, 1997.

———. "The Theosophical Society." In *Introduction to New and Alternative Religions in America, Vol. 3*, edited by Eugene V. Gallagher and Michael W. Ashcraft, 48–66. Westport, CT: Greenwood Press, 2006.

Faivre, Antoine. *Access to Western Esotericism*. Albany: State University of New York Press, 1994.

Farsight Institute. "Farsight Professional 1: Hale-Bopp. " http://web.archive.org/web/19970228025402/http://www.farsight.org/et/prof/Hale_Bopp/p2.html.

———. "Professional Et Examples: Hale-Bopp." http://web.archive.org/web/19970228024034/http://www.farsight.org/et/prof/Hale_Bopp/.

———. "Student Project: Hale-Bopp." http://web.archive.org/web/19970228025429/http://farsight.org/et/prof/Hale_Bopp/boppproject/.

Festinger, Leon, Henry W. Riecken, and Stanley Schachter. *When Prophecy Fails*. Minneapolis: University of Minnesota Press, 1956.

Finke, Roger, and Rodney Stark. *The Churching of America, 1776–1990: Winners and Losers in Our Religious Economy*. New Brunswick, NJ: Rutgers University Press, 1992.

Fuller, Sylvia, and John Levi Martin. "Women's Status in Eastern NRMs." *Review of Religious Research* 44, no. 4 (2003): 354–69.

262   << BIBLIOGRAPHY

Gaines, James R. "Cults: Bo-Peep's Flock." *Newsweek*, October 20, 1975, 32.

Gbbody. "Jimmy's Letter to Deb, 23 February, 1995." In *Closing the Gate*, Deb Simpson, 229–36. Murfreesboro, TN: privately published, 1995.

Gilbert, Phyllis. "I Was a Member of the UFO Cult." *Pageant*, March 1976, 45–50.

Gldody. "Exit Video." Rancho Santa Fe, CA, 1997.

Glnody. "Earth Exit Statement: Why We Must Leave at This Time." http://www.heavensgate.com/exitgln.htm.

———. "Exit Video." Rancho Santa Fe, CA, 1997.

Glock, Charles Y., and Robert N. Bellah, eds. *The New Religious Consciousness*. Berkeley: University of California Press, 1976.

Goldberg, Carey. "Death in a Cult: The Compound: Heaven's Gate Fit in with New Mexico's Offbeat Style." *New York Times*, March 31, 1997, A12.

Griffith, R. Marie. *Born Again Bodies: Flesh and Spirit in American Christianity*. Berkeley: University of California Press, 2004.

Grumett, David. "Dynamics of Christian Dietary Abstinence." In *The Way of Food: Religion, Food, and Eating in North America*, edited by Benjamin E. Zeller, Marie W. Dallam, Reid L. Neilson, and Nora L. Rubel, 3–22. New York: Columbia University Press, 2014.

Hall, David D., ed. *Lived Religion in America: Toward a History of Practice*. Princeton, NJ: Princeton University Press, 1997.

Hanegraaff, Wouter J. *New Age Religion and Western Culture: Esotericism in the Mirror of Secular Thought*. Leiden: E.J. Brill, 1996.

Hansen, Lars Ivar. "Saami Society through Time." *American Anthropologist* 97, no. 1 (1995): 131–33.

Harmon, Amy. "Escaping to Other Worlds." *Los Angeles Times*, April 2, 1997, A1–A2.

Harvey, Van A. "Hermeneutics." In *Encyclopedia of Religion*, edited by Lindsay Jones, 3930–36. Detroit: Macmillan Reference USA, 2005.

Hatch, Nathan O. *The Democratization of American Christianity*. New Haven, CT: Yale University Press, 1989.

Haynes, Stephen R., and Steven L. McKenzie, eds. *To Each Its Own Meaning: An Introduction to Biblical Criticisms and Their Application*. Louisville, KY: Westminster John Knox Press, 1993.

Hazen, Craig James. *The Village Enlightenment in America: Popular Religion and Science in the Nineteenth Century*. Urbana: University of Illinois Press, 2000.

Heaven's Gate. "First Statement of Ti and Do." In *How and When "Heaven's Gate" (the Door to the Physical Kingdom Level above Human) May Be Entered*, edited by Heaven's Gate, 2:3–4. Mill Springs, NC: Wild Flower Press, 1997.

———. "The 17 Steps." In *How and When "Heaven's Gate" (the Door to the Physical Kingdom Level above Human) May Be Entered*, edited by Heaven's Gate, 2:8. Mill Springs, NC: Wild Flower Press, 1997.

———. "Major and Lesser Offenses." In *How and When "Heaven's Gate" (the Door to the Physical Kingdom Level above Human) May Be Entered*, edited by Heaven's Gate, 2:9. Mill Springs, NC: Wild Flower Press, 1997.

———. *Class Meeting with Ti and Do, July 15, 1982*. Heaven's Gate, 1982. Audio Tape.

———. "Preparing for Service." Self-published. 1985.

———. "'88 Update." In *How and When "Heaven's Gate" (the Door to the Physical Kingdom Level above Human) May Be Entered*, edited by Heaven's Gate, 3:2–19. Mill Springs, NC: Wild Flower Press, 1997.

———. "Anonymous Sexaholics Celibate Church Introduction and Ways." http://www.rkkody.com/rkk/rkkomat.htm#intro [Defunct].

———. "Beyond Human—the Last Call, Session 1." In *How and When "Heaven's Gate" (the Door to the Physical Kingdom Level above Human) May Be Entered*, edited by Heaven's Gate, 4:1–15. Mill Springs, NC: Wild Flower Press, 1997.

———. "Beyond Human—the Last Call, Session 2." In *How and When "Heaven's Gate" (the Door to the Physical Kingdom Level above Human) May Be Entered*, edited by Heaven's Gate, 4:16–26. Mill Springs, NC: Wild Flower Press, 1997.

———. "Beyond Human—the Last Call, Session 3." In *How and When "Heaven's Gate" (the Door to the Physical Kingdom Level above Human) May Be Entered*, edited by Heaven's Gate, 4:27–38. Mill Springs, NC: Wild Flower Press, 1997.

———. "Beyond Human—the Last Call, Session 4." In *How and When "Heaven's Gate" (the Door to the Physical Kingdom Level above Human) May Be Entered*, edited by Heaven's Gate, 4:39–49. Mill Springs, NC: Wild Flower Press, 1997.

———. "Beyond Human—the Last Call, Session 5." In *How and When "Heaven's Gate" (the Door to the Physical Kingdom Level above Human) May Be Entered*, edited by Heaven's Gate, 4:50–61. Mill Springs, NC: Wild Flower Press, 1997.

———. "Beyond Human—the Last Call, Session 6." In *How and When "Heaven's Gate" (the Door to the Physical Kingdom Level above Human) May Be Entered*, edited by Heaven's Gate, 4:62–73. Mill Springs, NC: Wild Flower Press, 1997.

———. "Beyond Human—the Last Call, Session 7." In *How and When "Heaven's Gate" (the Door to the Physical Kingdom Level above Human) May Be Entered*, edited by Heaven's Gate, 4:74–84. Mill Springs, NC: Wild Flower Press, 1997.

———. "Beyond Human—the Last Call, Session 8." In *How and When "Heaven's Gate" (the Door to the Physical Kingdom Level above Human) May Be Entered*, edited by Heaven's Gate, 4:85–96. Mill Springs, NC: Wild Flower Press, 1997.

———. "Beyond Human—the Last Call, Session 9." In *How and When "Heaven's Gate" (the Door to the Physical Kingdom Level above Human) May Be Entered*, edited by Heaven's Gate, 4:97–108. Mill Springs, NC: Wild Flower Press, 1997.

———. "Beyond Human—the Last Call, Session 10." In *How and When "Heaven's Gate" (the Door to the Physical Kingdom Level above Human) May Be Entered*, edited by Heaven's Gate, 4:109–20. Mill Springs, NC: Wild Flower Press, 1997.

———. "Beyond Human—the Last Call, Session 11." In *How and When "Heaven's Gate" (the Door to the Physical Kingdom Level above Human) May Be Entered*, edited by Heaven's Gate, 4:121–40. Mill Springs, NC: Wild Flower Press, 1997.

———. "Beyond Human—the Last Call, Session 12." In *How and When "Heaven's Gate" (the Door to the Physical Kingdom Level above Human) May Be Entered*, edited by Heaven's Gate, 4:141–62. Mill Springs, NC: Wild Flower Press, 1997.

————. "Extraterrestrials Return with Final Warning." In *How and When "Heaven's Gate" (the Door to the Physical Kingdom Level above Human) May Be Entered*, edited by Heaven's Gate, 5:4–6. Mill Springs, NC: Wild Flower Press, 1997.

————. "'UFO Cult' Resurfaces with Final Offer [USA Today Advertisement]." In *How and When "Heaven's Gate" (the Door to the Physical Kingdom Level above Human) May Be Entered*, edited by Heaven's Gate, 5:3. Mill Springs, NC: Wild Flower Press, 1997.

————. "Bible Quotes Primarily from Previous Representatives to Earth from T.E.L.A.H." http://www.heavensgate.com/b-2.htm.

————. "Connecting Links." http://www.heavensgate.com/misc/link.htm.

————. "Crew from the Evolutionary Level above Human Offers—Last Chance to Advance Beyond Human [Internet Statement]." In *How and When "Heaven's Gate" (the Door to the Physical Kingdom Level above Human) May Be Entered*, edited by Heaven's Gate, 6:4. Mill Springs, NC: Wild Flower Press, 1997.

————. "He's Back, We're Back, Where Will You Stand?" [Poster]. In *How and When "Heaven's Gate" (the Door to the Physical Kingdom Level above Human) May Be Entered*, edited by Heaven's Gate, 6:9. Mill Springs, NC: Wild Flower Press, 1997.

————. "The Shedding of Our Borrowed Human Bodies May Be Required" [Poster]. In *How and When "Heaven's Gate" (the Door to the Physical Kingdom Level above Human) May Be Entered*, edited by Heaven's Gate, 6:11. Mill Springs, NC: Wild Flower Press, 1997.

————. "'95 Statement by an E.T. Presently Incarnate." In *How and When "Heaven's Gate" (the Door to the Physical Kingdom Level above Human) May Be Entered*, edited by Heaven's Gate, 1:7–12. Mill Springs, NC: Wild Flower Press, 1997.

————. "E.T. Speaks: Ufo's / Space Aliens / Reboot Civilization." UseNet Post, October 13, 1995, Message-ID: <45m7sm$09q@ddi2.digital.net>, 1997.

————. "Undercover Jesus Surfaces (www.Indirect.Com/Www/Lillo)." UseNet Post, October 13, 1995, Message-ID: <44a1do$69@news1.channel1.com>, 1997.

————. "Undercover 'Jesus' Surfaces before Departure." In *How and When "Heaven's Gate" (the Door to the Physical Kingdom Level above Human) May Be Entered*, edited by Heaven's Gate, 1:3–6. Mill Springs, NC: Wild Flower Press, 1997.

————. "Exit Press Release: Heaven's Gate 'Away Team' Returns to Level above Human in Distant Space." http://www.heavensgate.com/pressrel.htm.

————. "Heaven's Gate—How and When It May Be Entered." http://www.heavensgate.com.

————. "Heaven's Last Mission." In *How and When "Heaven's Gate" (the Door to the Physical Kingdom Level above Human) May Be Entered: An Anthology by Representatives from the Kingdom of Heaven*, 1:2. New Mexico, 1996.

————. *How and When "Heaven's Gate" (the Door to the Physical Kingdom Level above Human) May Be Entered*. Mill Springs, NC: Wild Flower Press, 1997.

————. "Last Chance to Evacuate Earth before It's Recycled" [Transcript of Videotape]. http://www.heavensgate.com/vt092996.htm.

————. "Our Position against Suicide." http://web.archive.org/web/19961222130009/http://www.heavensgate.com/.

———. "Planet About to Be Recycled—Your Only Chance to Survive—Leave with Us" [Edited Transcript]. http://www.heavensgate.com/misc/vt100596.htm.

Hewes, Hayden, and Brad Steiger. *UFO Missionaries Extraordinary*. New York: Pocket Books, 1976.

Higgins, Sabrina. "Divine Mothers: The Influence of Isis on the Virgin Mary in Egyptian Lactans-Iconography." *Journal of the Canadian Society for Coptic Studies* 3–4 (2012): 71–91.

Hilton, Robert. "First Watch: Django Django's 'Hail Bop'." National Public Radio, http://www.npr.org/blogs/allsongs/2012/07/24/157232208/first-watch-django-djangos-hail-bop.

Hoffmann, Bill, and Cathy Burke. *Heaven's Gate: Cult Suicide in San Diego*. San Francisco: HarperCollins, 1997.

Holbrook, Kate. "Good to Eat: Culinary Priorities among Mormons and the Nation of Islam." In *The Way of Food: Religion, Food, and Eating in North America*, edited by Benjamin E. Zeller, Marie W. Dallam, Reid L. Neilson, and Nora L. Rubel, 195–213. New York: Columbia University Press, 2014.

Hoover, Stewart M. "The Cross at Willow Creek: Seeker Religion and the Contemporary Marketplace." In *Religion and Popular Culture in America*, edited by Bruce D. Forbes and Jeffrey H. Mahan, 139–54. Berkeley: University of California Press, 2000.

Horowitz, Wayne. "Halley's Comet and Judean Revolts Revisited." *Catholic Biblical Quarterly* 58, no. 3 (1996): 456–59.

Howard, Robert Glenn. "Rhetoric of the Rejected Body at 'Heaven's Gate'." In *Gender and Apocalyptic Desire*, edited by Brenda E. Brasher and Lee Quinby, 145–64. London: Equinox, 2006.

Hudnut-Beumler, James David. *Looking for God in the Suburbs: The Religion of the American Dream and Its Critics, 1945–1965*. New Brunswick, NJ: Rutgers University Press, 1994.

Human Individual Metamorphosis. "Prospective Candidate Letter." http://www.rkkody.com/rkk/rkkomat.htm [Defunct].

———. "Statement #1: Human Individual Metamorphosis." American Religions Collection, ARC Mss 1, Department of Special Collections, University Libraries, University of California, Santa Barbara, 1975.

———. "Statement #2: Clarification: Human Kingdom—Visible and Invisible." American Religions Collection, ARC Mss 1, Department of Special Collections, University Libraries, University of California, Santa Barbara, 1975.

———. "Statement #3: The Only Significant Resurrection." American Religions Collection, ARC Mss 1, Department of Special Collections, University Libraries, University of California, Santa Barbara, 1975.

———. "What's Up?": American Religions Collection, ARC Mss 1, Department of Special Collections, University Libraries, University of California, Santa Barbara, 1975.

Humphry, Derek. *Final Exit: The Practicalities of Self-Deliverance and Assisted Suicide for the Dying*. New York: Dell, 1991.

J.K. "Re: E.T. Speaks: Ufo's / Space Aliens / Reboot Civilization." UseNet Post, October 26, 1995, Message-ID: <46okgl$buc@uwm.edu>, 1995.

Jnnody. "Incarnating and Discarnating." In *How and When "Heaven's Gate" (the Door to the Physical Kingdom Level above Human) May Be Entered*, edited by Heaven's Gate, A:89–97. Mill Springs, NC: Wild Flower Press, 1996.

Josephus, Flavius. *The Jewish War*. Translated by H. St. J. Thackeray. Vol. 3. Cambridge: Harvard University Press, 1997.

Jung, Carl Gustav. *Ein Moderner Mythus*. Stuttgart: Rascher, 1958.

Jwnody. "'Away Team' from Deep Space Surfaces before Departure." In *How and When "Heaven's Gate" (the Door to the Physical Kingdom Level above Human) May Be Entered*, edited by Heaven's Gate, A:38–45. Mill Springs, NC: Wild Flower Press, 1997.

———. "Religions Are Humans' #1 Killers of Souls." In *How and When "Heaven's Gate" (the Door to the Physical Kingdom Level above Human) May Be Entered*, edited by Heaven's Gate, A:65–70. Mill Springs, NC: Wild Flower Press, 1997.

———. "Ti and Do as 'Smelling Salts.'" In *How and When "Heaven's Gate" (the Door to the Physical Kingdom Level above Human) May Be Entered*, edited by Heaven's Gate, A:2–3. Mill Springs, NC: Wild Flower Press, 1997.

———. *Exit Video*. Rancho Santa Fe, CA, 1997.

———. "Overview of the Present Mission." In *How and When "Heaven's Gate" (the Door to the Physical Kingdom Level above Human) May Be Entered*, edited by Heaven's Gate, vii–ix. Mill Springs, NC: Wild Flower Press, 1997.

Kaplan, Jeffrey. *Radical Religion in America: Millenarian Movements from the Far Right to the Children of Noah*. Syracuse, NY: Syracuse University Press, 1997.

Keck, David. *Angels & Angelology in the Middle Ages*. New York: Oxford University Press, 1998.

Kennedy, E. S. "Comets in Islamic Astronomy and Astrology." *Journal of Near Eastern Studies* 16, no. 1 (1957): 44–51.

Kneeland, Douglas E. "500 Wait in Vain on Coast for 'the Two,' U.F.O. Cult Leaders." *New York Times*, October 10, 1975, 16.

Kraemer, Ross Shepard, William Cassidy, and Susan L. Schwartz. *Religions of Star Trek*. Boulder, CO: Westview Press, 2001.

Kripal, Jeffrey. *Esalen: America and the Religion of No Religion*. Chicago: University of Chicago Press, 2007.

Kurtz, Paul. "Perspective on the Media: A Marriage Made in Heaven's Gate." *Los Angeles Times*, May 19, 1997, B5.

LaFontaine, Ray. "Talk Radio's Comet Caper." *Washington Post*, February 23, 1997, 5.

LaHaye, Tim F., and Jerry B. Jenkins. *Left Behind: A Novel of the Earth's Last Days*, edited by Left Behind. Wheaton, IL: Tyndale House Publishers, 1995.

Lalich, Janja. *Bounded Choice: True Believers and Charismatic Cults*. Berkeley: University of California Press, 2004.

Lewis, James R. "Approaches to the Study of the New Age Movement." In *Approaches to the Study of the New Age*, edited by James R. Lewis and J. Gordon Melton. Albany: State University of New York Press, 1992.

———. "Legitimating Suicide: Heaven's Gate and New Age Ideology." In *UFO Religions*, edited by Christopher Partridge, 104–27. London: Routledge, 2003.

Lewis, James R., and J. Gordon Melton, eds. *Perspectives on the New Age*. Albany: State University of New York Press, 1992.

Lifton, Robert Jay. *Destroying the World to Save It: Aum Shinrikyō, Apocalyptic Violence, and the New Global Terrorism*. New York: Henry Holt and Co., 1999.

Lindsey, Hal. *The Late Great Planet Earth*. New York: Bantam Books, 1970.

Lowe, Scott. "Transcendental Meditation, Vedic Science and Science." *Nova Religio: The Journal of Alternative and Emergent Religions* 14, no. 4 (May 2011): 54–76.

Lvvody. "Ingredients of a Deposit—Becoming a New Creature." In *How and When "Heaven's Gate" (the Door to the Physical Kingdom Level above Human) May Be Entered*, edited by Heaven's Gate, A:8–14. Mill Springs, NC: Wild Flower Press, 1997.

Maffly-Kipp, Laurie F., Leigh Eric Schmidt, and Mark R. Valeri, eds. *Practicing Protestants: Histories of the Christian Life in America, 1630–1965*. Baltimore: Johns Hopkins University Press, 2006.

Marsden, George M. *Fundamentalism and American Culture: The Shaping of Twentieth Century Evangelicalism, 1870–1925*. New York: Oxford University Press, 1980.

Martin, William. "Waiting for the End: The Growing Interest in Apocalyptic Prophecy." *Atlantic Monthly*, June 1982, 31–37.

McCloud, Sean. *Making the American Religious Fringe: Exotics, Subversives, and Journalists, 1955–1993*. Chapel Hill: University of North Carolina Press, 2004.

McGrath, Paul. "UFO 'Lost Sheep' Tell Cult Secrets." *Chicago Sun-Times*, October 16, 1975, 1, 26.

Melton, J. Gordon. "New Thought and New Age." In *Approaches to the Study of the New Age*, edited by James R. Lewis and J. Gordon Melton, 15–29. Albany: State University of New York Press, 1992.

———. "Brainwashing and the Cults: The Rise and Fall of a Theory." In *CESNUR Digital Proceedings*, edited by Massimo Introvigne, 1999.

Melton, J. Gordon, Jerome Clark, and Aidan A. Kelly, eds. *New Age Encyclopedia: A Guide to the Beliefs, Concepts, Terms, People, and Organizations That Make up the New Global Movement toward Spiritual Development, Health and Healing, Higher Consciousness, and Related Subjects*. Detroit: Gale Research, 1990.

Miller, Timothy, ed. *When Prophets Die: The Postcharismatic Fate of New Religious Movements*, edited by Harold Coward, SUNY Series in Religious Studies. Albany: State University of New York Press, 1991.

———. ed. *America's Alternative Religions*. Albany: State University of New York Press, 1995.

Mojtabai, A.G. *Blessed Assurance: At Home with the Bomb in Amarillo, Texas*. Boston: Houghton Mifflin, 1986.

Moore, Rebecca. *Understanding Jonestown and the Peoples Temple*. New York: Praeger, 2009.

Mrcody and Srfody. "Oral History and Interview with Author, 30 September–1 October, 2013." Phoenix, AZ, 2013.

Muss, Eve. "'Grave Not Path to Heaven,' Disciples Told." *Oregon Journal*, October 10, 1975.
———. "No Disease Promised." *Oregon Journal*, October 9, 1975, n.p.
Neusner, Jacob. *Judaism in the Matrix of Christianity*. Atlanta: Scholars Press, 1991.
Nimoy, Leonard. *Star Trek IV: The Voyage Home*. Paramount Pictures, 1986.
Nrrody. *Exit Video*. Rancho Santa Fe, CA, 1997.
———. "The Truth Is . . .". In *How and When "Heaven's Gate" (the Door to the Physical Kingdom Level above Human) May Be Entered*, edited by Heaven's Gate, A:15–17. Mill Springs, NC: Wild Flower Press, 1997.
Numbers, Ronald L. *Science and Christianity in Pulpit and Pew*. New York: Oxford University Press, 2007.
Palmer, Susan J. *Aliens Adored: Raël's UFO Religion*. New Brunswick, NJ: Rutgers University Press, 2004.
Parker, Christopher S. *Change They Can't Believe In: The Tea Party and Reactionary Politics in America*. Princeton, NJ: Princeton University Press, 2013.
Partridge, Christopher, ed. *UFO Religions*. London: Routledge, 2003.
———. "The Eschatology of Heaven's Gate." In *Expecting the End: Millennialism in Social and Historical Context*, edited by Kenneth G. C. Newport and Crawford Gibbens, 49–66. Waco, TX: Baylor University Press, 2006.
Penson, Betty. "During the Summer of 1974 UFO Couple Visited Boise Men." *Idaho Statesman*, October 26, 1975, 1–2.
Perkins, Rodney and Forrest Jackson. *Cosmic Suicide: The Tragedy and Transcendence of Heaven's Gate*. Dallas, TX: Pentaradial Press, 1997.
Peterson, Gregory E. "Religion as Orienting Worldview." *Zygon* 36, no. 1 (March 2001): 5–19.
Pew Forum on Religion and Public Life. *U.S. Religious Landscape Survey: Religious Affiliation: Diverse and Dynamic*. Washington, DC: Pew Research Center, 2008.
———. *Many Americans Mix Multiple Faiths: Eastern, New Age Beliefs Widespread*. Washington, DC: Pew Research Center, 2009.
———. *"Nones" on the Rise: One in Five Religious Adults Have No Religious Affiliation*. Washington, DC: Pew Research Center, 2012.
P.H. "Re: E.T. Speaks: Ufo's / Space Aliens / Reboot Civilization." UseNet Post, October 17, 1995, Message-ID: <45toqn$nou@status.gen.nz>, 1995.
Phelan, James S. "Looking For: The Next World." *New York Times*, February 29, 1976, 12–13, 58–64.
Phipps, William E. "The Magi and Halley's Comet." *Theology Today* 43, no. 1 (1986): 88–92.
Pike, Sarah M. *New Age and Neopagan Religions in America*. New York: Columbia University Press, 2004.
Prophecy News Watch. "Prophecy News Watch: Biblical Prophecy in the News." Prophecy News Watch, http://www.prophecynewswatch.com.
Purdum, Todd S. "Death in a Cult: The Inquiry; Last 2 Names of Cult Members Are Listed as Investigators Try to Find Their Families." *New York Times*, April 1, 1997, A18.

Qstody. *Exit Video*. Rancho Santa Fe, CA, 1997.

———. "My Ode to Ti and Do! What This Class Has Meant to Me." In *How and When "Heaven's Gate" (the Door to the Physical Kingdom Level above Human) May Be Entered*, edited by Heaven's Gate, A:30–31. Mill Springs, NC: Wild Flower Press, 1997.

Raine, Susan. "Reconceptualising the Human Body: Heaven's Gate and the Quest for Divine Transformation." *Religion* 35, no. 2 (April 2005): 98–117.

Rapport, Jeremy. "'Join Us! Come, Eat!': Vegetarianism in the Formative Period of the Seventh-Day Adventists and the Unity School of Christianity." In *The Way of Food: Religion, Food, and Eating in North America*, edited by Benjamin E. Zeller, Marie W. Dallam, Reid L. Neilson, and Nora L. Rubel, 23–41. New York: Columbia University Press, 2014.

Rapture Ready. "Rapture Ready." Rapture Ready, http://www.raptureready.com. Rapture Watch. "Rapture Watch: A Global, End Times Prophecy Resource." Rapture Watch, http://www.rapturewatch.net.

Reed, Pat. "Two Women UFO Disciples Reveal Identity; Say They Are Not Cult." *Houston Chronicle*, November 26, 1975, 9.

Restad, Penne E. *Christmas in America: A History*. New York: Oxford University Press, 1995.

Rey, Terry. *Bourdieu on Religion: Imposing Faith and Legitimacy*. Key Thinkers in the Study of Religion. London: Equinox Publishing, 2008.

Rhees, David J. "Corporate Advertising, Public Relations and Popular Exhibits: The Case of Du Pont." *History & Technology* 10, no. 1/2 (1993): 67–75.

Rich, Frank. "Heaven's Gate-Gate." *New York Times*, April 17, 1997, 23.

Richardson, James T. *Conversion Careers: In and out of the New Religions*. Beverly Hills: Sage, 1978.

———. "Conversion and Brainwashing: Controversies and Contrasts." In *The Bloomsbury Companion to New Religous Movements*, edited by George D. Chryssides and Benjamin E. Zeller. London: Bloomsbury, 2014, 89–101.

Rkkody. Email with author. November 19, 1997.

———. "Newsgroup Postings." http://www.rkkody.com/rkk/rkkpost.htm [Defunct].

Robbins, Thomas, and Dick Anthony. *In Gods We Trust: New Patterns of Religious Pluralism in America*. 2nd ed. New Brunswick, NJ: Transaction Publishers, 1990.

Robbins, Thomas, Dick Anthony, and James McCarthy. "Legitimating Repression." In *The Brainwashing/Deprogramming Controversy: Sociological, Psychological, Legal, and Historical Perspectives*, edited by David G. Bromley and James T. Richardson, 319–27. New York: Edwin Mellon Press, 1983.

Robbins, Thomas, and Susan J. Palmer. *Millennium, Messiahs, and Mayhem: Contemporary Apocalyptic Movements*. New York: Routledge, 1997.

Robinson, Tom. "I Found the Missing People from Waldport." *Northwest Magazine*, November 2, 1975, 10–15.

Rochford, E. Burke, Jr. "Hare Krishna in America: Growth, Decline, and Accommodation." In *America's Alternative Religions*, edited by Timothy Miller. Albany: State University of New York Press, 1995.

Rodman, Rosamond. "Heaven's Gate: Religious Otherworldiness American Style." In *The Bible and the American Myth: A Symposium on the Bible and Constructions of Meaning*, edited by Vincent K. Wimbush, 157–73. Macon, GA: Mercer University Press, 1999.

Roll, Susan K. *Toward the Origins of Christmas*. Kampen, Netherlands: Kok Pharos, 1995.

Roof, Wade Clark. *A Generation of Seekers: The Spiritual Journeys of the Baby Boom Generation*. San Francisco: Harper San Francisco, 1994.

———. *Spiritual Marketplace: Baby Boomers and the Remaking of American Religion*. Princeton, NJ: Princeton University Press, 1999.

R.S. "Re: E.T. Speaks: Ufo's / Space Aliens / Reboot Civilization." UseNet Post, October 16, 1995, Message-ID: <DGJyoI.15qK@pen.k12.va.us>, 1995.

Rutenberg, Jim. "Mediatalk: AOL Sees a Different Side of Time Warner." *New York Times*, March 19, 2001, 11.

Ryan, Thomas. *Prayer of Heart and Body: Meditation and Yoga as Christian Spiritual Practice*. New York: Paulist Press, 1995.

Saliba, John A. "Religious Dimensions of UFO Phenomena." In *The Gods Have Landed: New Religions from Other Worlds*, edited by James R. Lewis, 15–64. Albany: State University of New York Press, 1995.

Samaritan Sentinel. "Samaritan Sentinel." https://samaritansentinel.com/Home_Page.php.

Sarna, Jonathan D. *American Judaism: A History*. New Haven, CT: Yale University Press, 2004.

Sawyer. "Heaven's Gate: Do Response to Ti Earlier Vehicle Exit." http://sawyerhg.wordpress.com/2009/09/.

———. Email with author. July 25, 2013.

———. "Sawyerhg's Blog." http://sawyerhg.wordpress.com.

———. "Two Witnesses Ti Do Father Jesus Part 12 Castration Suicide Born Again UFO Luciferians." http://sawyerhg.wordpress.com/2011/03/04/two-witnesses-ti-do-father-jesus-part-12-castration-suicide-born-again-ufo-luciferians/.

Scientific American. "The Trail of Hale-Bopp." *Scientific American*, http://www.scientificamerican.com/article.cfm?id=the-trail-of-hale-bopp.

Scott, Austin. "Music Teacher, Nurse Led Search for 'Higher Life.'" *Washington Post*, October 18, 1975, A7.

Segady, Thomas W. "Globalization, Syncretism, and Identity: The Growth and Success of Self-Realization Fellowship." *Implicit Religion* 12, no. 2 (2009): 187–99.

Segal, Alan. *Rebecca's Children: Judaism and Christianity in the Roman World*. Cambridge: Harvard University Press, 1986.

Shipps, Jan. *Mormonism: The Story of a New Religious Tradition*. Urbana: University of Illinois Press, 1985.

Shramek, Chuck. "The Chuck Shramek Home Page: Ufo's over Washington!" http://web.archive.org/web/19991014003523/http://www.neosoft.com/%7Ecshramek/.

———. "The Great Comet of 1997." http://web.archive.org/web/19961224064739/http://www.neosoft.com/~cshramek/.

Simpson, Deb. *Closing the Gate*. Murfreesboro, TN: privately published, 2012.

Simross, Lynn. "Invitation to an Unearthly Kingdom." *Los Angeles Times*, October 31, 1975, G1, G4–G6.

Smart, Ninian. *Worldviews: Crosscultural Explorations of Human Beliefs*. New York: Prentice Hall, 2000.

Smmody. "T.E.L.A.H. – the Evolutionary Level above Human." In *How and When "Heaven's Gate" (the Door to the Physical Kingdom Level above Human) May Be Entered*, edited by Heaven's Gate, A:22–23. Mill Springs, NC: Wild Flower Press, 1997.

Snnody. "Deposits." In *How and When "Heaven's Gate" (the Door to the Physical Kingdom Level above Human) May Be Entered*, edited by Heaven's Gate, A:80–84. Mill Springs, NC: Wild Flower Press, 1997.

Srrody. "Earth Exit Statement: Why We Must Leave at This Time." http://www.heavensgate.com/exitsrr.htm.

———. *Exit Video*. Rancho Santa Fe, CA, 1997.

Stammer, Larry B., John Dart, and James Rainey. "39 in Cult Left Recipes of Death: The Cult: Tract Offers Clues About Group's Theology, Motives." *Los Angeles Times*, March 28, 1997, 1.

Stark, Rodney, and William Sims Bainbridge. *The Future of Religion: Secularization, Revival, and Cult Formation*. Berkeley and Los Angeles: University of California Press, 1985.

———. *A Theory of Religion*. New York: Peter Lang, 1987.

Stark, Rodney, and Roger Finke. *Acts of Faith: Explaining the Human Side of Religion*. Berkeley: University of California Press, 2000.

Stein, Stephen J. *The Shaker Experience in America: A History of the United Society of Believers*. New Haven, CT: Yale University Press, 1992.

Steinberg, Jacques. "Death in a Cult: The Leader; from Religious Childhood to Reins of a U.F.O. Cult." *New York Times*, March 29, 1997, A9.

Stenmark, Mikael. "What Is Scientism?" *Religious Studies* 33 (1997): 15–32.

Stmody. "Evolutionary 'Rights' for 'Victims.'" In *How and When "Heaven's Gate" (the Door to the Physical Kingdom Level above Human) May Be Entered*, edited by Heaven's Gate, A:71–79. Mill Springs, NC: Wild Flower Press, 1997.

Stone, Brad. "Christ and Comets." *Newsweek*, April 7, 1997, 40–43.

Stone, Jon R., ed. *Expecting Armageddon: Essential Readings in Failed Prophecy*. New York: Routledge, 2000.

Strieber, Whitney. *Communion: A True Story*. New York: Beach Tree Books, 1987.

Tabor, James D., and Eugene V. Gallagher. *Why Waco?* Berkeley: University of California Press, 1995.

T.B. "Re: E.T. Speaks: Ufo's / Space Aliens / Reboot Civilization." UseNet Post, October 18, 1995, Message-ID: <30854839.5625@freeway.net>, 1995.

Tddody. "Statement of a Crewmember." In *How and When "Heaven's Gate" (the Door to the Physical Kingdom Level above Human) May Be Entered*, edited by Heaven's Gate, A:53–55. Mill Springs, NC: Wild Flower Press, 1997.

Tholen, David J., and Olivier Hainaut. "Fraudulent Use of a Ifa/Uh Picture." http://www.eso.org/~ohainaut/Hale_Bopp/hb_ufo_tholen.html.

Thomas, Evan. "'The Next Level." *Newsweek*, April 7, 1997, 28–35.

———. "Web of Death." *Newsweek*, April 7, 1997, 24–35.

Tipton, Steven M. *Getting Saved from the Sixties: The Transformation of Moral Meaning in American Culture*. Berkeley: University of California Press, 1982.

Tumminia, Diana G. *When Prophecy Never Fails: Myth and Reality in a Flying Saucer Group*. New York: Oxford University Press, 2005.

Tweed, Thomas A. *Crossing and Dwelling: A Theory of Religion*. Cambridge: Harvard University Press, 2006.

United Press International. "Couple Asks for UFO Volunteers—Now 20 Missing." *Herald-News*, October 6, 1975, 1.

———. "It's the Second Coming . . . We Are All Going Home." *Herald-News*, October 7, 1975, 3.

Urban, Hugh B. "The Devil at Heaven's Gate: Rethinking the Study of Religion in the Age of Cyber-Space." *Nova Religio: The Journal of Alternative and Emergent Religions* 3, no. 2 (2000): 268–302.

Versluis, Arthur. *Magic and Mysticism: An Introduction to Western Esotericism*. London: Rowman & Littlefield, 2007.

Vitzthum, Richard. *Materialism: An Affirmative History and Definition*. New York: Prometheus Books, 1995.

Wallis, Roy. "The Social Construction of Charisma." *Social Compass* 29, no. 1 (1982): 25–39.

Warburg, Margit. *Baha'i*. Studies in Contemporary Religions. Salt Lake City, UT: Signature Books, 2003.

Weber, Max. *The Theory of Social and Economic Organization*. Translated by A. M. Henderson and Talcott Parsons. Translation of Part I of Wirtschaft und Gesellschaft, 1922 ed. New York: Free Press, 1947.

Wessinger, Catherine. "Hinduism Arrives in America: The Vedanta Movement and the Self-Realization Fellowship." In *America's Alternative Religions*, edited by Timothy Miller, 173–90. Albany: State University of New York Press, 1995.

———.*How the Millennium Comes Violently: From Jonestown to Heaven's Gate*. New York: Seven Bridges Press, 2000.

Williamson, George. "'It Was a Sham': Why One Convert Left the UFO Cult." *San Francisco Chronicle*, October 13, 1975, 2.

Wknody. "A Matter of Life or Death? You Decide." In *How and When "Heaven's Gate" (the Door to the Physical Kingdom Level above Human) May Be Entered*, edited by Heaven's Gate, A:18–21. Mill Springs, NC: Wild Flower Press, 1997.

Wojcik, Daniel. "Embracing Doomsday: Faith, Fatalism, and Apocalyptic Beliefs in the Nuclear Age." *Western Folklore* 55, no. 4 (1996): 297–330.

Wright, Stuart A. "Reconceptualizing Cult Coercion and Withdrawal: A Comparative Analysis of Divorce and Apostasy." *Social Forces* 70, no. 1 (1991): 125–45.

———. *Armageddon in Waco: Critical Perspectives on the Branch Davidian Conflict*. Chicago: University of Chicago Press, 1995.

Yrsody. *Exit Video*. Rancho Santa Fe, CA, 1997.

———. "The Way Things Are." In *How and When "Heaven's Gate" (the Door to the Physical Kingdom Level above Human) May Be Entered*, edited by Heaven's Gate, A:24–26. Mill Springs, NC: Wild Flower Press, 1997.

Zablocki, Benjamin. "Toward a Demystified and Disinterested Scientific Theory of Brainwashing." In *Misunderstanding Cults: Searching for Objectivity in a Controversial Field*, edited by Benjamin Zablocki and Thomas Robbins, 159–214. Toronto: University of Toronto Press, 2001.

Zablocki, Benjamin, and Thomas Robbins, eds. *Misunderstanding Cults: Searching for Objectivity in a Controversial Field*. Toronto: University of Toronto Press, 2001.

Zeller, Benjamin E. "Scaling Heaven's Gate: Individualism and Salvation in a New Religious Movement." *Nova Religio: The Journal of Alternative and Emergent Religions* 10, no. 2 (Fall 2006): 75–102.

———. "Apocalyptic Thought in UFO Religions." In *End of Days: Understanding the Apocalypse from Antiquity to Modernity*, edited by Karolyn Kinane and Michael A. Ryan. Jefferson, NC: McFarland Press, 2009.

———. "Heaven's Gate: A Literature Review and Bibliographic Essay." *Alternative Spirituality and Religion Review* 1 (2009): 49–57.

———. *Prophets and Protons: New Religious Movements and Science in Late-Twentieth Century America*. New York: New York University Press, 2010.

———. "Extraterrestrial Biblical Hermeneutics and the Making of Heaven's Gate." *Nova Religio: The Journal of Alternative and Emergent Religions* 14, no. 2 (2010): 34–60.

———. "Heaven's Gate, Science Fiction Religions, and Popular American Culture." In *Handbook on Hyper-Real Religions*, edited by Adam Possamai, 59–83. Leiden: Brill, 2012.

ABOUT THE AUTHOR

Benjamin E. Zeller is Assistant Professor of Religion at Lake Forest College, in the Chicago metro area. He researches religious currents that are new or alternative, including new religions, the religious engagement with science, and the quasi-religious relationship people have with food. He is author of *Prophets and Protons: New Religious Movements and Science in Late Twentieth-Century America* (New York University Press, 2010), and co-editor of *Religion, Food, and Eating in North America* (2014) and *The Bloomsbury Companion to New Religious Movements* (2014). He is co-general editor of *Nova Religio: The Journal of Alternative and Emergent Religions*.